Dr Helen Likierman is a Consu... ing with families and children (fr... where there are emotional, so..., behavioural or learning concerns. After obtaining her Psychology degree in Manchester she trained and worked as a teacher of young primary school children before moving on to clinical training. Her PhD from the Institute of Psychiatry in London was on preschoolers' friendships and peer relationships. She worked for many years in clinical research and as a psychologist in the National Health Service, including in the Child and Family Department at Charing Cross Hospital. In addition to her current consultant work, she is School Counsellor at a large co-educational school and is the mother of two teenage children.

Dr Valerie Muter is a Consultant Clinical Psychologist with a wide range of experience working with young children's learning, emotional and behaviour problems. Her PhD from the Institute of Child Health, University College London, examined the language and reading development of young children with brain damage and her work at Great Ormond Street Hospital for Children centres on assessing the needs of children with neurological problems. She also holds Honorary Research Fellowships at the Institute of Child Health and at the Centre for Reading and Language, University of York. She has carried out extensive research into children's early reading development and has a special interest in assessing and advising on children's learning problems, in particular dyslexia and related difficulties.

Dr Helen Likierman & Dr Valerie Muter

Prepare Your Child for School

How to make sure your child gets **off to a flying start**

Vermilion
LONDON

3 5 7 9 10 8 6 4 2

Text and illustrations on pages 295 and 299 © Dr Helen Likierman
and Dr Valerie Muter 2006
Illustrations on page 147 © Nicola Smee 2006

Dr Helen Likierman and Dr Valerie Muter have asserted their moral
right to be identified as the authors of this work in accordance
with the Copyright, Design and Patents Act 1988.

First published in the United Kingdom in 2006 by Vermilion,
an imprint of Ebury Publishing
Random House UK Ltd.
Random House
20 Vauxhall Bridge Road
London SW1V 2SA

Random House Australia (Pty) Limited
20 Alfred Street, Milsons Point, Sydney,
New South Wales 2061, Australia

Random House New Zealand Limited
18 Poland Road, Glenfield,
Auckland 10, New Zealand

Random House (Pty) Limited
Isle of Houghton, Corner Boundary Road & Carse O'Gowrie,
Houghton 2198, South Africa

Random House Publisher India Private Limited
301 World Trade Tower, Hotel Intercontinental Grand Complex,
Barakhamba Lane, New Delhi 110 001, India

Random House UK Limited Reg. No. 954009
www.randomhouse.co.uk
Papers used by Vermilion are natural, recyclable products
made from wood grown in sustainable forests.

A CIP catalogue record is available for this book from the British Library.

ISBN: 0091906776
ISBN 13: 9780091906771 (from Jan 2007)

Design and layout by seagulls.net

Printed and bound in Great Britain by
Mackays of Chatham plc, Chatham, Kent

Contents

Acknowledgements

Kind colleagues have given their time and expertise to comment on earlier drafts of our manuscript. Their suggestions have been invaluable. So our thanks go particularly to Dr Richard Lansdown, Dr Orlee Udwin, Professor Margaret Snowling, Dr Angela Morgan and Professor Brian Butterworth.

We are also grateful to colleagues who have guided our thinking over the years, in particular Professor Sir Michael Rutter, Dr Michael Berger, Dr Maria Callias (especially for developing with Helen the scenarios featured in Chapter 4), Professor Margaret Snowling, Professor Charles Hulme and Professor Faraneh Vargha-Khadem.

We would like to thank David Chamberlain and Nicola Smee for their original illustrations. And our very special thanks to Julian Hale, Helen's husband, for his editorial skills, his huge amount of administrative and secretarial time and his general support.

Our supportive and perceptive editor, Julia Kellaway, has helped us in every possible way and we are most grateful to her.

Finally, we want to express our warmest thanks to the hundreds of children (including Helen's two, Tammy and Felix) and to the many parents who've worked with us and who – knowingly or not – have helped to shape our ideas.

Preface

Starting school is a key event in all our lives. Over our many years of clinical practice, we've been struck by how little advice there is available to guide parents through the specific challenges and struggles of helping their children get ready for school. We have also noticed that many parents want to know how to recognise and deal with problems as and when they arise. Our thoughts prompted us to write this book for all such parents and carers. Our aim is to help smooth the way to the school gate and make the transition a happy one for all concerned. We've drawn on our own research work and that of many others, but in particular on our own clinical experience of working with children and families. We've both had experience of working with young children in pre-school settings and in their homes – as well as working with older children.

A recent five-year survey of parents and teachers in the USA carried out by Dr Dorothy and Professor Jerome Singer indicated that more than a third of American school children started school unprepared. David Bell, the head of the UK schools' watchdog, Ofsted, was reported as saying in 2003 that the behavioural and verbal skills of children starting school were at an all-time low, with many unable to settle and not ready to learn. Head teachers also told him that some children could not even speak properly, use a knife and fork, follow instructions or behave adequately.

David Bell told the BBC News that many parents were not preparing their children for school: 'Everyone wants children to start well at the age of five, but we know that some children are ill-prepared for starting school.' And this remains the case because, according to David Hart of the National Association of Head Teachers, many children are starting school without basic skills. In 2005 he commented, 'Teachers and support staff have to spend time sorting them out so they are ready to be educated.' Alan Wells, director of the government-funded Basic Skills Agency, highlighted the importance of talking to children. A survey of head teachers in Wales found that they believed as many as 50 per cent of children start school lacking the communication skills necessary to learn effectively. Wells went on to say, 'If you fall behind in the early years in your school career, research shows you'll be behind when you leave.'

We believe it is important to spend time easing the transition from home and pre-school to school. As the American psychologist, Professor Laura Berk, says: 'Research shows that school readiness is not something to wait for. It can be cultivated.' She adds that, 'Children acquire the knowledge, skills and attitudes for school success through the assistance of parents and teachers.' Actually you will have already become adept at teaching your child many skills, right from birth. This has been shown in a study by Professors Barbara Tizard and Martin Hughes. Pre-school children were found to learn many valuable skills informally at home with their mothers, including general knowledge, conversation and problem-solving skills. Our book is about helping you develop and hone these skills of yours, so that you and your child can thrive and move forward into the school years.

You will notice that your child is referred to as 'he' or 'she' in alternating chapters. The use of a particular gender in no way implies that the chapter is more relevant to one gender than the other.

We hope this book will provide some reassurance about your own capabilities. We also hope we will give you even more ideas about what needs to be done, and help ensure you don't miss out on any vital areas of your child's pre-school development.

Introduction

The school years are looming. As if you didn't have enough to do already! Your baby grows into a toddler and zooms off to play-group before you've even had time to enjoy those amazing ups and downs, panics and excitements that go under the name of 'child development'. It sometimes doesn't seem like development at all, more a headlong plunge into ever more frantic activity and troubleshooting. It's scary and it's exciting.

One of the scariest and most exciting changes is your child's entry into the world of school. This brings a big transition from the small world of the home, the playgroup or nursery to the wider, more structured environment of school. There will be new experiences and, above all, new challenges. Not just for your child, but for you as well.

Most of you reading this book will have a child in the age range of two to five. And your child will have learned a huge amount already. Normally-developing pre-schoolers can talk, socialise with others, play with toys and materials, and look after themselves in many basic ways. They have an awareness of their own thoughts and of the world around them. Nowadays, almost all will have had a variety of opportunities to expand their learning, such as attending nursery school, playgroup or kindergarten. Some will have older brothers and sisters they can learn from. Most children will have had additional opportunities to relate to other adults and children outside their immediate family, such as relatives, neighbours, religious communities and friends. But is this enough?

Sometimes it's really hard as a parent to know how best to tackle some of the challenges so that you can avoid the pitfalls. In the following chapters you will find out how to make sure your child starts school happy, able to make friends, free from worry or fear, able to cope with the demands of the day's routines and the work, and able to develop into a contented, flourishing individual.

It's not just your child's ability to learn to read and write and do sums that's important for success at school. There's also the little matter of sitting still long enough to take in what a teacher has to say. There are classmates to contend with too, not the siblings, cousins and neighbours your child already knows. These bring potential new friends, but there may also be less friendly peers. And there is authority. Don't expect teachers always to treat your child as you might treat your own flesh and blood. Nice though they generally are, teachers have a whole class to deal with, and they expect a level of compliance and fitting in. If they can detect enthusiasm and competence, marvellous! Teachers, too, are human; they are going to enjoy their new charges all the more once they see they are prepared for school.

Getting off to a good start at school is really important. If the experience is an unhappy or negative one, there are some well-known bad effects. For example, children with problems relating to other children and making friends are more at risk of developing psychological problems in later life such as depression or behavioural difficulties. Also, children who make poor initial progress in learning to read develop persistent (and difficult to erase) negative attitudes towards books and reading. On the other hand, those who make a good start in these areas will have positive experiences and are more likely to be successful later in childhood and in adulthood.

How to Use this Book

This book is research-based, practical and tried and tested. Just as important, it empathises with you as a parent. Use it as a reference book – a resource for you to use as it suits you and your child. It is designed to be as comprehensive as possible. This means it might look a bit daunting at first. You might think, 'How can I possibly do all those things for my child?' You may be feeling guilty already! But that's not the intention. You may find you need to concentrate only on some – perhaps just a few – of the issues raised and the suggestions made; the rest may be there simply to reassure you that all is progressing well.

You don't need to read the book from beginning to end. However, most readers may find it useful to do so, if only to get an overall grasp of what is on offer and an overview of the main challenges of preparing your child for school.

You may have specific concerns: 'What I need most is advice on behaviour. How on earth can I stop my child from doing those embarrassing, naughty things?' Or: 'My child's problem is his speech. He doesn't seem to say anything anyone understands and he's already three.' You'll find the answers in this book, but it's also important to help your child develop a wide range of skills – self-care, emotional, social, behavioural, pre-educational – because they are all prerequisites for developing well. Everything interacts. That is why you will find many places where you are referred to issues raised in other chapters. So you may want to dip in and out of the book as and when you feel the need, but do give some thought to the whole picture as well.

Each chapter covers a different aspect of your child's life. Although these skills develop simultaneously, they may progress at slightly different rates from child to child. The development of one skill may affect, mildly or strongly, one other or several other skills. For instance, children with educational difficulties may be seen by other children as being less able, and this can in turn affect their self-esteem, friendships and behaviour. Such children may become unhappy and withdrawn or act the 'class clown'. Conversely, children with behaviour or attention problems may fall behind in their class work because they are not listening or concentrating, or because they are being naughty. In this way their educational progress is affected by their behaviour. In turn, these difficulties may affect their emotional state and social relationships.

So, as they prepare for school, children have to juggle many different aspects of life and learning. Don't feel you are failing as a parent if your child doesn't reach a particular level in some skill before starting school. You know how hard it is for you yourself to develop good 'juggling skills'. The following chapters will give you lots of ideas to help you and your child move towards a happy and successful life in the school years and beyond.

You might consider keeping this book handy for a few years after your child starts school. Many of the ideas and principles covered, particularly in the chapters on social, emotional and behavioural skills, will be just as relevant for your eight-year-old as for your four-year-old.

Should You Prepare Your Child for School?

When children start school, teachers build on skills that have already (they hope!) been put in place during those important pre-school years. Of course, getting off to a good start depends on what the child brings into school on day one. Children are not simply a blank page to be written on, products 'created' by the school experience.

Does your child have all the skills in place to make this transition from home to school a happy and easy experience? Throughout this book, you will have the chance to answer that question. Your child needs to acquire and develop many skills. You possess many skills that can help your child develop *his* skills. Checklists and questionnaires on all the main topics will help you stop and think carefully about exactly what your child has already absorbed and what he might do with some active help and encouragement.

But, you may well ask, is it your job to prepare your child for school? Maybe you feel your efforts might be better directed towards choosing a school, then letting teachers take over and do their job. It's true that most schools are staffed with excellent and dedicated teachers. Their job is to try and help each and every child develop his full potential. They will aim to bring out the best in each child, educationally, socially and emotionally. That is certainly the ideal. However, this may not always be easy. Teachers, like all of us, are busy and pressed for time. Bringing out the best in each child in a class is a wonderfully challenging, creative and worthwhile task. That's why most teachers choose the profession. They want to make a positive contribution to how the children in their care develop. But a teacher conscious of the needs of a whole group (the class) and community (the school) may sometimes see your child in a way that you, the parent, find hard to understand.

For example, you may describe your child to a friend by saying, 'Oh, he's got such wonderful energy!' Or, 'He's so deep, always thinking about things.' But the teacher may say to her colleague, 'Oh, he's an absolute tearaway, disrupting all the others. I'm at my wits' end.' Or, 'He's so quiet I despair of ever getting through to him – just one reaction would make me happy!' It's not that teachers are objective while parents' views are distorted, but it's natural for loving parents to view their child through rosy spectacles. A teacher, on the other hand, might well regard her charges with a measure of worldly wisdom, not to mention – on occasional Friday afternoons – world-weary scepticism.

As psychologists, we don't claim to have unique and perfect insight into any one child either. But we do see, talk to, assess and work with a great many children and their families. Like teachers, psychologists gradually come to observe patterns within the emotional, physical and educational complexity that is child-rearing.

At school, teachers also have to consider the wider picture. However much they try to meet the needs of all their charges, there's no doubt that some children, when they start out, will be at a greater advantage than others. This means that others will be at more of a disadvantage. For instance, children who come across as less mature and less able to cope are likely to have a harder time settling in.

For all parents, the issue of time is important. Our aim here is to help you make best use of the huge amount of time you already spend with your child. In the long run you will have more enjoyable time together: less time dealing with problems; less time engaging with him over worries or difficult behaviour; and less time needing to involve professionals, should difficulties become too much for you.

The Skills Your Child Needs for School

The skills children need for school have been separated into three main, overlapping areas:

- Getting into shape or general competence (self-care, behaviour, social skills, emotions).
- Learning to learn (play, concentrating, language).
- Educational learning (reading, number work, writing).

Each of these general areas needs a range of approaches:

- Assessing the importance of the particular skills and how each is relevant to your child's progress at school.
- What you might reasonably expect from your child coming up to school age – this will give you an idea of what is regarded as 'normal development'.
- Assessing your child's level of skill, using observations, checklists and questionnaires.
- Developing your child's skills (for example, using practical, play-based activities).
- Identifying and dealing with common problems in pre-school development.

Below is a short checklist for you to complete. This covers the different skill areas mentioned above. Of course, you shouldn't expect your child to have mastered all these skills as yet. He is likely to be better at some than others. This questionnaire will give you a flavour of some of the specific skills that will be covered in the chapters to come.

Check through these skills to see how far you feel your child has come already. It will also help you form a view about how much further you might need to go in preparing your child for school.

Is Your Child Prepared for School?

Do you think your child is able to...	Yes	To some extent	No	Don't know
Self-care				
Manage by himself in the toilet?	☐	☐	☐	☐
Cope with undressing and dressing by himself?	☐	☐	☐	☐
Cope with mealtimes without adult help?	☐	☐	☐	☐
Say his name, address and age?	☐	☐	☐	☐
Behaviour				
Do mostly what he is told?	☐	☐	☐	☐
Contain (usually) frustration and temper?	☐	☐	☐	☐
Stop himself distracting/interfering with others?	☐	☐	☐	☐
Understand and keep to set rules or boundaries?	☐	☐	☐	☐
Social				
Engage readily in play with other children?	☐	☐	☐	☐
Take turns in play?	☐	☐	☐	☐
Agree to share most toys and materials?	☐	☐	☐	☐
Emotion				
Deal with new situations?	☐	☐	☐	☐
Deal with changes in routine?	☐	☐	☐	☐
Separate happily from parent or carer?	☐	☐	☐	☐
Control his emotions (such as not crying at slight problems)?	☐	☐	☐	☐
Attention/Concentration				
Listen to and follow teachers' or other adults' instructions?	☐	☐	☐	☐
Finish a given activity lasting five to ten minutes?	☐	☐	☐	☐

Stay in a designated area, such as a seat or mat at nursery or meal times, for 10 to 15 minutes? ☐ ☐ ☐ ☐

Spoken language

Speak clearly so that he is understandable to others? ☐ ☐ ☐ ☐

Understand three-or-four idea sentences (such as *put* the *cup on* the *chair*)? ☐ ☐ ☐ ☐

Produce grammatically complete sentences of five to six words? ☐ ☐ ☐ ☐

Repeat a sentence of about 10 words? ☐ ☐ ☐ ☐

Reading

Recognise some of the letters of the alphabet? ☐ ☐ ☐ ☐

Blend or join two or three sounds to make a word (such as c-a-t makes cat)? ☐ ☐ ☐ ☐

Break spoken words up into syllables (such as pen-cil)? ☐ ☐ ☐ ☐

Number

Understand relative size (such as bigger/smaller, most/least)? ☐ ☐ ☐ ☐

Recognise and label simple shapes (such as circles, squares)? ☐ ☐ ☐ ☐

Match objects (such as colours, simple shapes, pictures)? ☐ ☐ ☐ ☐

Count objects up to 10? ☐ ☐ ☐ ☐

Writing

Control a pencil adequately? ☐ ☐ ☐ ☐

Copy lines (vertical/horizontal, circles/crosses)? ☐ ☐ ☐ ☐

Form some letters and numbers recognisably? ☐ ☐ ☐ ☐

Write his first name? ☐ ☐ ☐ ☐

You may find that many of these skills are already in place, or that your child finds some skills easy, but others need more preparation in order to be ready for school. You may also discover that you were not so aware of the importance of some skills. Do come back and redo the questionnaire after you've read the following chapters.

1
Hot Issues

Before dealing with the particular skills needed for school, there are a number of important topics to consider. When you move on to the following chapters, keep these general points in mind. They should help to put things into perspective.

Hothousing

What is meant by this much-used term? Some people believe that providing their children with a very high level of enriching learning experiences will bring great returns; it will increase their IQ and give them advantages over other children. Doing the best for your child is one thing, but in reality some children find themselves caught up in more intense levels of activity than they can cope with or profit from. Furthermore, the stresses and strains of overloading a child may have consequences for the whole family.

There is no convincing evidence that hothousing increases children's IQ. The only exception is in cases where children have been unusually deprived of adequate stimulation, most importantly language stimulation. Such children do benefit from intensive learning programmes. For instance, in the HeadStart programme in the USA, these pre-schoolers showed significant increases in IQ levels as a result of intensive pre-school teaching (these benefits were not maintained unless the children continued to receive good stimulation into their school years). However, for children who benefit from normal parenting and good nursery school experiences, hothousing will not turn any child into a genius!

Some of the general concepts in the notion of hothousing are fine: structure, organised activities and systematic teaching. But children also need opportunities for free play and self-discovery and time to 'chill out'. This enables children to develop independence, self-motivation and the ability to occupy and amuse themselves. It gives them the opportunity to make choices, become more creative and get the idea that relaxing can be as important as work (but don't let them run away with that idea!)

Preparing your child for school is not about increasing her IQ or teaching her to read and write (although some four-year-olds will be able to read short books and write some words and simple sentences). Rather, it is about making sure your child starts school confidently, able to deal with the social, educational, practical and behavioural demands of the classroom and playground. This means preparing your child emotionally and socially as well as intellectually and educationally.

It is a perfectly good idea, and not at all harmful, for your child to attend different organised pre-school activities, such as 'baby gym', dance or music classes. But don't overdo it. Make sure what you choose doesn't put too much pressure on your child. Remember, you're not in a race or competition with other parents – honestly! We all have a deep urge to do the best for our children, to 'give them what we never had', to 'give them a head start in life' and so on. There's nothing wrong with that. But it's never quite clear what really is for the best or what the side-effects of our well-meaning efforts might be. Being ambitious for your child can be a fine impulse, but in exaggerated form – or forced on a persistently unwilling child – it may backfire badly.

The thing to remember is that different children have hugely different energy levels, interests and abilities. Have the confidence to do what you feel is right for you and your child, even if it's different from what your friends or neighbours are doing. Your child doesn't have to be brilliant or the best at an activity – do whatever it is as long as she enjoys it. Of course there may be moments you need to encourage your child to persist or practise. But watch with care not to let your parental overdrive take over so you end up pushing too hard.

The way you prepare your child for school is crucial. Skills can be taught in ways that do not put excessive demands on your child – or put a strain on your relationship with her. Your child should be left with lots of time to enjoy non-structured activities. Many of the skills described in this book can be developed as part of day-to-day family routines (especially many self-care, play, language and social skills). Other skills need more structured activities that might take place in short play sessions (especially the pre-reading, pre-writing and pre-number skills). These are the essential foundation skills that children need to have in place before they begin formal instruction.

The 'Good Enough' Parent

'Good enough' parenting is about having realistic expectations and setting appropriate goals. It was popularised by the paediatrician and psychoanalyst, D.W. Winnicott, in 1960. It gets away from the idea of being a super parent or a gifted parent, notions that are linked with hothousing and with pushing children to their limits. It is about relaxing and enjoying parenting – enjoying your child, enjoying yourself. You are going to make mistakes from time to time – say things you wish you hadn't, lose your temper, overcompensate. But don't despair or overly reproach yourself. The occasional mistake of this sort should not affect your child's development in any significant way.

Being a parent is part of your life – a very important part, but not the only part. Remember that you also need to make time for other relationships – with partners, your own parents and even friends.

Do what needs to be done (the basics) and leave time for the frills. Relax!

Biology and the Environment

There has been a long-standing debate about what carries more weight, 'nature' (our genes and biological background) or 'nurture' (the environment and learning). Laura Berk says, 'A major reason child development researchers are interested in the nature–nurture issue is that they want to improve environments so that the child can develop as far as possible.'

Research has clearly demonstrated that many skills to do with intelligence – how we think, learn and remember – have a strong basis in inheritance (more than 50 per cent). Similarly, personality characteristics such as temperament, attention and activity levels, and even sociability, have strong genetic influences. Much more about genetics is understood now than ever before.

But genes are not destiny. Parents can provide their children with experiences that help them compensate for inborn weaknesses. For instance, children with an inherently difficult temperament can be helped by consistent, calm and clear management. They can be taught to relate well to adults and peers, and to learn better self-control. They can practise becoming better at coping in difficult situations. Children, too, from families with high rates of dyslexia (which is strongly inherited) can be helped to avoid the worst of their reading problems by specialist teaching. In fact, there are numerous ways in which inherited difficulties can be offset by the child's environment, and you will read more about how to do this in the following chapters.

For children with clear difficulties, it's better to act sooner rather than later. This provides more opportunity for the child to learn new patterns or habits. There is also less ground to make up as the child will not be so far behind her peers in learning, and there is no history of failure to overcome.

Your child's pre-school years are perhaps the best time to take active steps to help her make the most of her genetic endowment.

Individual Differences

There is normal variation between children in when and how fast skills develop (the idea of 'between children' differences). For instance, the average age that children are able to walk independently is around 15 months. But clearly some children are walking as early as 12 months (or even before), while others are not on their feet until around 18 months. Equally, some children about to start school are not going to be as mature or as ready for formal learning as others.

In addition, within any one child, different skills may develop at different rates (the idea of 'within the child' differences). At any given point in time, each child will have an individual profile of strengths and weaknesses. For instance, some three-year-olds will have very advanced speech and language, but poorer motor development that makes them clumsy and unable to dress themselves easily. Any one child starting school may therefore be mature or skilled in some areas but not in others.

If you ask whether your child is *ready* for learning the skills covered in this book, the answer is 'Yes'. But for different skills you might have different starting points. Each of these skills is approached in a gradual, step-by-step way. You start at your child's level and build up from there. Learning will carry on in school; you don't have to have reached an end point by the time your child starts school. Your child will learn and develop at her own pace, and will pick up some skills faster than others.

Gender/Sex Differences

Boys and girls are not the same. The emphasis on ignoring or even attempting to eliminate gender differences is now widely seen as naïve.

● Girls develop language skills faster. They show quicker vocabulary growth initially, though boys seem to catch up from the age of two. But girls retain an advantage in terms of their reading; throughout the school years they obtain higher scores on reading tests. Is this biological or environmental? It looks as though both are important. Girls have a larger language region of the brain than boys (biological). But it has also been shown that mothers often talk more to their toddler girls than to their toddler boys (environmental) – so girls have more language practice early on.

● In school, boys are greater 'risk takers' and end up with more cuts and bruises, whilst girls tend to be more cautious. Girls in general try harder than boys to please and to avoid failure.

● Developmental problems are much more common among boys. Speech and language disorders, reading difficulties, attention and overactivity problems, emotional and social immaturity, and naughty and aggressive behaviour are seen in three to five times as many boys as girls.

But let's put these differences into perspective. Over the total population of girls and boys, there are more similarities than differences. Differences are small, and they are evident only when you compare group averages. And there are large individual differences even among girls and among boys. There's nothing wrong with the girl who likes to play football or the boy who enjoys cooking – on the contrary!

Television

Parents often ask whether television can have a detrimental effect on their child's behaviour or development. Some hate it with a passion. Many see it as a good source of education and recreation. Some would not know what to do without it as a readily available pacifier and baby-sitter. Researchers in the USA found that children of around three years of age watch television for approximately one-and-a-half hours each day. This increases substantially as children get older. These figures hold true of most developed countries.

To date, research has focused mostly on particular aspects of behaviour – especially whether watching violent television (or videos) relates to more violent and antisocial behaviour. Reviews of studies show that there is indeed such a link. It is tempting to think that watching violent television directly causes violent behaviour among children, but the findings are not that clear cut. Some studies have shown that children who are already prone to violence or difficult behaviour are more likely to choose to watch violent programmes.

Research into the effects of television on learning has shown that pre-schoolers who watch educational programmes achieve better academic results, read more books and place a higher value on education later on. In contrast, another study has shown that watching 'entertainment television' (such as cartoons) takes children away from other activities like reading or interacting with others. Furthermore, this was also shown to lead to poorer academic performance.

So what conclusions can we draw from these studies about children watching television?

- How much should they watch? A study was conducted in a small, remote Canadian town. Children were assessed before the introduction of television into their community, and then again two years later. During this time the children showed a decline in their reading ability and creative thinking and an increase in verbal and physical aggression during play. Bearing this in mind, we suggest allowing some television – but not too much. To be more precise, we recommend around an hour a day, partly because it seems pointless to ban it entirely and partly because there are recognisable advantages. With younger children, and with those who have no older brothers or sisters, you can more easily get away with less 'box watching'.

- What should they watch? Children should of course watch only child-appropriate programmes, of which most should be educationally based. We don't think there is any harm in them watching cartoons or other strictly 'entertainment' programmes as part of their relaxation time, but programmes with a violent content should be avoided.

- Does it matter how much television you (the parents) watch? It seems there is a relationship between children's and parents' viewing habits. If parents watch a lot, so will their children. You might consider spending some of your viewing time together with your child. This is a fantastic opportunity to, first, expand on and develop further some ideas from educational programmes you've enjoyed watching together.

Second, sharing television experiences allows you and your child to make judgements about what you have seen. For example, do you agree with a character's particular point of view or behaviour? What would you and your child have done differently? Which character do you like best – and why?

Now let's move on to the skills your child will need for school. Look back at the checklist on pages 8–9 to remind yourself of the areas you need to concentrate on most.

PART A

GETTING INTO SHAPE

2
Self-care

Many of the skills and issues important for preparing your child for school may seem basic, but they are crucial. If self-care skills are not in place, your child will find it much harder to achieve many of the other, more obviously school-related skills.

What is Self-care?

The term 'self-care' refers to your child's ability to care for his own basic day-to-day needs. It is an important part of becoming independent. Self-care covers the practical skills involved in the following:

- Knowing his name and where he lives
- Knowing how to look after himself in the toilet
- Knowing how to dress and undress himself
- Dealing with meal times, including feeding himself
- Learning routines, such as bedtime

For most children, these skills develop naturally and easily through regular routines established at home from an early age. A child's ability to fit in with regular routines and structured activities is also an important part of his development. This is because regularity allows children to know what is happening and to predict what will happen next. This will help them to feel secure and confident.

The long-term aim is to make your child aware of what he needs to do on a daily basis and get on with doing it. You are not trying to create an automaton, rigid in his approach to life, but a child who can order and structure his regular activities. *You* also need time to do other things – perhaps caring for other children, doing domestic tasks such as cooking or washing … and even making time for yourself to have a break.

Helping your child care for himself makes for a much easier life at home. For example, if you are trying to leave the house quickly and it's cold or wet outside, it's far easier if he can get his coat buttoned up by himself. It's tempting to do the hard bits yourself. Sometimes it can't be helped – you just haven't got time for any other solution. And that's fine. But, whenever possible, make time for your child to do these little tasks independently.

Self-care is especially important when the time comes for your child to go to school. Teachers will expect him to be 'clean and dry', able to cope at school meal times and to dress and undress for sporting activities. The less time teachers have to spend helping and teaching children basic care skills, the more time they have available to concentrate on social and educational issues. Another issue is that a child unprepared in self-care may be seen as 'babyish' by other children. This could then affect friendships.

What Can We Expect of Pre-schoolers?

The checklist below covers all the different areas of self-care. See how far your child has developed in each area. For each item put a tick in the column that most closely applies to your child.

Self-care Checklist

Is your child able to:	completely/ always	partly/ sometimes	not at all
Give his name?	☐	☐	☐
Give his address?	☐	☐	☐
Give his phone number?	☐	☐	☐
Give his age?	☐	☐	☐
Undress without help?	☐	☐	☐
Put on his clothes (socks/trousers/shirt)?	☐	☐	☐
Do up buttons and toggles?	☐	☐	☐
Fasten his shoes?	☐	☐	☐
Sit at a table to eat a meal?	☐	☐	☐
Use a spoon and fork	☐	☐	☐
Willingly try new foods?	☐	☐	☐
Recognise (and act upon) the need to go to the toilet?	☐	☐	☐
Deal with clothes in the toilet?	☐	☐	☐
Use toilet paper properly?	☐	☐	☐
Flush the toilet?	☐	☐	☐
Wash his hands after using the toilet?	☐	☐	☐
Go to bed without fuss?	☐	☐	☐
Sleep through the night without disturbing you?	☐	☐	☐

If you have ticked 'completely/always' for most items, your child is going to be well prepared for looking after himself at school.

If you have ticked mostly the 'partly/sometimes' column, it would be a good idea to work on these skills to make your child more reliable and consistent.

If you have ticked the 'not at all' column for any of the items, it will be worth spending quite a lot of time getting these important skills up and running.

Social Self-care

Your child will remain under your supervision, or in the charge of a carer, for most of the time during his pre-school and early school years. There should be only very few occasions when he needs to face the outside world on his own. Sometimes, however, the ability to give basic information to an unknown person is vitally important.

Can your child say – when asked by an appropriate person – who he is, where he lives and, if possible, his phone number (or maybe even email for today's sophisticated youngsters)? From an early age – as soon as your child is talking – you will have taught him his full name. (Be careful with nicknames as some children believe they are part of their name. Helen's son Felix thought he was 'Felix Belix' for quite a long time!) So practise when you can. But do keep emphasising to your child that it is good to tell his name only to family members, friends, teachers and policemen but not to strangers who approach him (unless he is told it is all right by a carer or teacher). You do have to be careful to teach your child to discriminate between people who are safe to talk to and people to be wary of from an early age.

At school, your child will need to be able to respond to his name, for the school register for example. But there will be other times when he needs to say his name, perhaps for safety reasons (such as a fire drill) or for greeting people. It will also be helpful for him to know where he lives – if he gets lost (hopefully most unlikely) or if you are unable, for some reason, to collect him from playgroup or school. When he meets up with other children outside school, he will need to know where he and that other child live. So it is important for friendships too.

Dressing

Children learn to undress themselves fairly early on. Most children can manage to do this, with the exception of tricky fastenings, by the age of four. They may indeed love to pull off their clothes and run around stark naked and have great fun. But there is a considerably greater art and many more skills involved in putting clothes on. Clothes can often have idiosyncratic and fiddly fastenings. Many manufacturers of children's clothes have understood this and made their clothes more child-friendly; but buttons and zips may still pose problems for small fingers. Sometimes, for speed or because a child seems to find it difficult, parents or carers effectively do everything for their child. Try not to do this too much; your child needs to practise in order to learn.

Some children do have genuine difficulty dressing as their fine motor control is poor. That is, their fingers don't seem to work together well to complete simple practical actions. Others may not understand quite how clothes relate to their bodies, for instance, that shirts go at the top and trousers at the bottom. They may continue for some time to have difficulty in telling back from front and one side from the other. (Remember, in dressing, the skill needed is 'matching' – he doesn't need to know the concepts 'left' and 'right', but he does need to see that the left sleeve fits – or matches – his left arm.) Difficulties with learning these skills may be an early sign of dyspraxia (*see Chapter 11*). But don't panic. If this is the case for your child, you should keep on teaching the skills of dressing. Don't get cross if he is slow. Break the actions into even smaller steps if you need to. Get your child to talk his way through the steps, doing this with him at first. Make self-care learning part of your daily routine.

For most of you reading this book, your main focus is to check that your child can cope with the dressing and undressing skills needed for school. Concentrate on coats and shoes first.

Then check out what your child's school does for PE and games, and whether the children are taken swimming. Use the following general teaching principles for your child:

- Skills are best taught as part of a normal routine – but made as much fun as possible.
- Start with undressing – pulling off socks, shoes or trousers if he is not already doing this.
- If removing something is difficult, help your child with the first part of the action, then let him continue to finish it off. Psychologists call this 'backward chaining' and it is useful for teaching many skills. You start by physically helping your child through the action, such as pulling the sock over the heel, then letting him do the rest – that is pull the sock completely off. You then gradually reduce your assistance (by moving your action 'backward') as he gets better at doing this.
- Next, go on to dressing, beginning with putting on tops, bottoms, dresses and socks, using backward chaining if you need to.
- Buttons and toggles are separate issues. You can teach with a special button and buttonhole on a separate piece of material (perhaps cut out from some of your old clothes). You may have to think about the size and stiffness of the buttons and holes, and the number of buttons you use. Buttonhole 'trainers' can cover different levels of difficulty.
- Give lots of practice!
- Reward for achievement (every time while he is learning). Give praise, of course, but also have some small reward or 'positive reinforcer' at hand if you need to do a lot of training for a child who has difficulties (*see opposite*).

Reward or Positive Reinforcement

This is the giving of something pleasurable to encourage particular behaviours. The use of reinforcement is an extremely important way of shaping a child's behaviour. Almost anything your child values or likes can be used as a reward: food treats, time to watch television, a special game with you, stickers, a small toy, etc.

Important points for making sure reinforcements are effective:

1. Always give spoken praise (such as 'well done', 'you did a great job') in addition to something tangible like food or a toy.
2. Give rewards immediately after the child has done what you want him to do.
3. Be consistent in your approach – don't forget to give the reward each time your child does what you ask.
4. Keep the size of the reward appropriate to the behaviour. Small changes in behaviour require small rewards – like a sticker for trying a mouthful of new food.
5. Breakthrough behaviours (like using the toilet independently for the first time) would justify something larger, like a toy.
6. Don't give the reward if it hasn't been earned. However, if your target looks to be too high for your child to manage, it is good to reward him for being 'almost there' at the start of a new reward plan (see Chapter 3). As your child progresses, you should reward him for complete (rather than partial) success in achieving the target.

Eating

The first issue is cutlery versus fingers. Children need to learn to use both a spoon and a fork appropriately. The more complex skills, such as being able to use a knife to cut meat, may come later. By the time your child is four, he should be using spoons and forks daily and drinking from a proper glass or cup on his own (not just from a trainer beaker). If he is always eating finger food, he may get lazy in his habits. It is worth persevering (gently) with implements, as he will also be learning co-ordination skills that have a wider application, such as when he comes to use a pencil for writing.

Cultural variations in the use of cutlery and fingers should be taken into account – it is more acceptable in some cultures than others to use fingers for certain foods. Do fix your own rules about the use of fingers or implements – but try to be consistent. If your child is using fingers inappropriately, say, 'Wipe your fingers and try to use a fork now.' Offer some incentive, if necessary, for example: 'You can have first choice of second helpings/pudding if you can show me how well you can use your fork today.'

Meal times are also important social events. Sharing food with others provides children with the opportunity to develop many skills, including:

- Learning to sit still and attend to what he is doing
- Listening and responding to others round the table
- Understanding social customs – including waiting his turn, offering food to others, waiting for others to finish before leaving the table
- Socialising with others – talking about the day's events is often an important accompaniment to the meal
- Learning about nutrition and different types of food

Developing Good Meal Time Behaviours

Good meal time behaviours are learnt best when they are part of a regular family routine. There should be the opportunity several times a week for your child to sit on a chair at a table together with one or more adults, so that he can learn all the skills discussed above. Eating off a tray in front of the television is not the same. Eating at a table gives your child the opportunity to copy adult eating behaviour and to join in adult conversation. Children for whom meals are part of a social activity may be more likely to try out a wider range of foods.

The following suggestions are helpful in establishing the skills that can be learned at meal times shared with adults:

- **Do** keep child portions suitably small – young children don't need adult-sized portions (better for your child to ask for more than end up having an argument with you over 'wasting food').
- **Don't** allow frequent snacking (especially of highly fatty, salty or sugary foods) and especially don't allow 'grazing' (this is a term used to describe children who wander around almost constantly nibbling and chewing food).
- **Do** make sure that your child is able to build up an appetite before each meal by ensuring he doesn't eat anything for a couple of hours before starting the meal.
- **Do** try to keep your child at the table until he has finished his meal – though don't expect him to stay at the table if it is a lengthy, adult-focused meal.
- **Do** teach children to pass food and offer to others.
- **Do** 'model' or demonstrate your enthusiasm for food for your child to copy. A recent study of school-age children showed that the more families ate meals together, the more knowledge they had of nutrition and the more they chose healthy foods to eat.

There is much written about what to eat and what not to eat. Here are a few reminders of what is most relevant for the school child – but bear in mind that at least some of these eating habits are best learned before, rather than after, the first day of school:

- **Do** encourage your child to eat a healthy breakfast before setting off for nursery (and school). This means a selection from fresh fruit juice, fresh fruit, low-sugar cereals (including muesli or porridge), wholemeal toast and milk.
- **Do** make sure that packed lunches contain healthy foods – salads, sandwiches, fresh or dried fruit, unsweetened juices (avoiding too many fizzy drinks, sweets and crisps).
- **Do** encourage your child to try a wide range of foods, but don't expect him to eat everything – even young children have food preferences.
- **Don't** tell your child he needs to eat a particular food 'because it's healthy'. Label the food as 'yummy' or 'fun'.
- **Don't** give your child different food from the food you eat yourself – otherwise he won't realise that 'real food' is what everyone eats. There are of course exceptions (for instance some very hot and spicy foods or the occasional 'special adult' food).

Eating Too Much

We know that overweight children are putting their health at risk, and obese children even more so. What is also important, however, is the psychological effect on children of being over-weight. On a practical level, they find it more difficult to run around and join in games, but their social life is affected in more general ways. 'Unfortunately,' says Laura Berk, 'physical attrac-tiveness is a powerful predictor of social acceptance in Western societies.' Obese youngsters are particularly likely to be victims. As several studies have demonstrated, obese children are rated by their peers as 'unlikeable, sloppy, ugly, stupid, self-doubting and deceitful'. This sounds pretty harsh, but it's not uncommon to see overweight children being mocked in the street or the playground. No wonder that studies have also shown that many obese children feel more depressed and show more behaviour problems than 'average'-weight children.

Your health visitor or GP will be able to advise you on whether your child's weight is right for his height. If he is becoming overweight from eating too much, follow the guidelines for healthy eating, above. You may need to be quite firm and controlling to begin with, until he's learned for himself to watch the amount and type of foods he's eating. Be aware, too, of the many government and other guidelines that stress the importance of coupling healthy eating with regular exercise.

However, do give your child some choices about what he eats. For example, let him choose between jacket potatoes and boiled potatoes or between an apple and a pear. Don't fall into the trap of allowing a choice between a sandwich and a chocolate bar, and between water/milk and a fizzy drink.

Eating Too Little or Too Restricted a Diet

As a parent, you will undoubtedly be very concerned if your child never seems to eat very much or will eat only a few foods. Does that mean, you may ask, my child will become anorexic (this applies to boys as well as girls)? Or will he fail to grow properly?

In most cases, neither of these consequences will happen. Anorexia is more likely to occur if there are other things going on in the child's life that might upset him. Or if food and eating become a battle and an issue of control – even if, from your point of view, your concern is for his well-being and your aim is to encourage him to eat a healthy diet. Only if his diet is very restricted will his growth be affected. However, you will need to seek professional advice if you are worried. There can be other effects of a restricted diet. For example, if your child's diet means he eats largely sweet foods, this may damage teeth as well as provide poor nutrition.

Eating Action Plan: There are things you can do to try and improve your child's diet. The following action plan is useful for helping children who eat too little or restrict their foods.

Fill in the chart below to see which foods your child will eat and in what amounts. This will give you an idea of whether or not there is a problem. It is useful to put in the time of day and place so you can look at your child's eating patterns. Don't forget to include snacks! It may be that your child is snacking a lot during the day, and therefore eating very little at meal times.

Foods my child will eat	Amount	Time of day/ place

Now ask yourself: is your child eating something from each of the main food categories each day?

- Protein (meat, fish, eggs, cheese, beans, nuts)
- Carbohydrates (especially unrefined or wholegrain bread, pasta, potatoes, rice and cereals)
- Vitamins and minerals (found in fresh fruit and vegetables)
- Fats (found in butter, oil, meat, milk and cheese)

Regard the foods you've listed in the chart as your baseline or starting point.

1 For the next few meals, only put on your child's plate those foods and the amounts from your baseline that you know he will eat. Encourage him to finish everything on the plate – and reward him for doing this. This reward could be access to a preferred food, like a couple of spoons of ice cream. Some children who eat a restricted diet do not value food as a reward, however, so choose something else if your child would prefer it.

2 You will need to make absolutely sure that your child avoids *any* snacks or fizzy drinks between meals. Stick to a three-meal-a-day plan with only water in between. Anything else will simply fill him up and take away his appetite for the meal.

3 Try to make the plate look attractive. Some children like the idea of food laid out as a picture, say of a face or as part of a story theme.

4 If your child is eating too little, start by increasing the amount of food on his plate by very small steps (equivalent to a couple of peas at a time).

5 If you are happy about the amount your child eats but are concerned about the restricted range (for example, if he is not eating foods from all four categories listed above), you need a

slightly different plan. Start in the same way as before, using points 1, 2 and 3 above. Now start to introduce a very small amount of one new food. Choose this carefully. With many children you can discuss beforehand what they might like to start with (it is best if they can suggest something themselves). For other children, you will have to decide. Make it close to a type of food your child will already eat, if possible. For instance, if he will eat only chips, suggest baked potato wedges; if he likes beef burgers, try a chicken burger. New foods, like vegetables, can be introduced on the top of a pizza (choose just a small part) as well as being hidden in a sauce.

6 Use 'modelling' to encourage eating. You can model some of the eating behaviour yourself. To make it more fun for your child – and to make a stronger point – have a favourite toy or television character 'model' for you. Better still, invite over a friend or a neighbour's child with a good appetite who will model enthusiastic eating.

7 When your child does eat even the tiniest mouthful of a new food, reward instantly. Don't expect progress to be too fast to start with. Try the same new food for a few days running (or a few times in the week), if you can, as this may be easier than trying yet another new food too soon. Aim to ensure he doesn't get bored with it but try it often enough so he gets used to it. You are aiming to get him accustomed to eating that new food – and then to increase its amount from a small taste to several mouthfuls. Once a food becomes something your child will eat, enter it onto the chart on page 38; look first at the example opposite.

Here is an example of a chart for a child who was being introduced to the new foods chicken, eggs and broccoli. Note that only one new food has been introduced on any one day, and a record is being kept of the dates on which the child tried these new foods.

Amount eaten
(number of mouthfuls)

	Chicken	Eggs	Broccoli
4	6/11		
3			
2	2/11	6/12	
1		4/12	9/12

New food tasted

Here our child ate two mouthfuls of chicken on 2 November and four mouthfuls on 6 November. Eggs were introduced in the following month. Our child ate one mouthful on 4 December and then ate two mouthfuls on 6 December. Broccoli was started on 9 December.

Overleaf there is the chart for you to fill in for your child.

Amount eaten
(number of mouthfuls)

10
9
8
7
6
5
4
3
2
1

New food tasted

8 Once your child gets into a regular eating routine and is used to trying new foods, meal times should be easier for you both. Your child is also more likely to enjoy food and be more adventurous.

9 Remember, don't get angry if your child refuses to try a new food – and don't get into a begging or pleading exchange. Stay calm and don't force feed! Try again another day, and make your food and your rewards as attractive and appealing as possible.

Toileting

For your child to be ready to deal with school toilets, he needs to be able to:

- Recognise the physical 'urge to go' in time to get to the toilet
- Act on this and take himself to the toilet
- Be able to undress and dress himself appropriately
- Use toilet paper
- Know how, and be able, to flush the toilet
- Know how to wash his hands after he has been to the toilet

In the early stages of school, teachers will still give children plenty of opportunity to go to the toilet at set times; they are also likely to continue to offer assistance as needed. But it does help for children to be as independent as possible in this area. In addition to dressing and undressing, discussed earlier, most of the rest of the toileting issues are about having routines.

First, make regular times to visit the toilet – before and after meals is usually best. Add to this a regular habit of using toilet paper, then dressing, then flushing, then washing hands with soap and water. If these routines are not fully established, use a reward chart (*see Chapter 3*) to get them up and running. In the beginning you may need to prompt each stage by saying, for instance, 'Now what are you going to do?' If your child replies correctly, say 'Great' (or some variation). Only if your child is unsure or wrong, prompt him further by saying, for instance, 'Now you are going to ... wash your hands.' If you can remind him enough by saying, 'You are going to w–' then just do that.

When he gets to the end of the full routine, give the fullest praise. Only if your child needs a full Toilet Action Plan *(see pages 41 and 43)* would you really want to give a small reward, such as a sticker or treat food. Toileting occurs so frequently in the day that you're better off keeping your special rewards for other things: if everything is rewarded (apart from verbal praise, which is always good), then you greatly reduce the power of the individual reward.

Some facts about Bedwetting and Soiling

Wetting

- Up to 20 per cent of five-year-olds wet the bed
- Fewer than 2 per cent of 12- to 14-year-olds wet the bed
- Until the age of five, boys and girls wet the bed equally often
- By age 11, boys outnumber girls in bedwetting by 2:1

Soiling

- 2–3 per cent of three- to five-year-olds soil regularly
- By age 10 to 12, 1 per cent or fewer soil regularly
- The ratio of boys to girls soiling is 3:1

Frequently-asked Questions
What should I do if my child has frequent 'accidents'?
Most pre-schoolers and many other children, especially in the early school years, have daytime accidents at least occasionally. Some children may have been completely, or almost completely, dry for two or three years then suddenly start to wet their pants,

say, every other day. This may start because they are worried about something, there has been a change in routine, there has been a mild infection, or sometimes for no apparent reason. The child could then go on wetting because the new pattern becomes a habit. Once you are sure there is no physical cause (do check with your GP that there is no infection), talk to your child about possible sources of worry (friends, starting school, other family members). If there are no obvious worries – and even if there are – then think about a Toilet Action Plan.

Toilet Action Plan 1: Wetting

- Minimise the number of times you talk to your child about being wet.
- Don't get cross and give only minimum reassurance. A kindly 'Okay, let's get changed' is enough; otherwise you risk giving him too much attention for his wetting behaviour.
- Help him to change clothes, as necessary, with as little physical touching as possible. Be careful not to be unkind, but again don't be 'rewarding' either.
- Then you need your sticker chart. Try, for example, a 'tree' on the wall or bathroom door (put up a cardboard or wooden strip if you don't want it to be permanent). Each dry day earns the child a leaf – and each full branch a 'lucky dip' present. If your child wets several times a day, you may need to break the day into parts (such as morning and afternoon), with a small reward (leaf) for each part. If your child is also wetting at night, you could link the two together on the same chart, perhaps with a leaf for day and a flower for night. (*See Chapter 3 for more ideas about rewards.*)

How can I get my child to use a 'strange' toilet?

The basic solution is to introduce your child very gradually to other toilets. You could take him to a friend's house, then reward him for just standing close to the toilet, for standing closer still, for touching the toilet, then for sitting on it with the lid down, then with the lid up ... then with pants down until he does a pee in the (non-home) toilet. Then you are almost home and dry! Lots of practice in lots of toilets should in most cases mean no problem at school.

My child likes to wear a nappy to make sure he doesn't soil himself – what should I do?

Some children have a very strong attachment to their nappy and refuse to give it up. One way of sorting this out, with your child's agreement, is gradually to cut tiny bits off each nappy, making the one he uses smaller and smaller, until it disappears entirely. By the time you have chipped one down to almost nothing, or so it won't hold together any more, you should have solved the problem. Rewards are again the key – both for using the toilet appropriately and for having less (or no) nappy.

My child is dry in the day and at night but regularly soils himself – what should I do?

If your child has a problem with soiling – in his pants or depositing in inappropriate places – you may need professional help.

Children learn first to control their bladder during the day, but soon after also learn to control their bowels. This normally occurs between the ages of two and three. A few children just don't seem to get the idea at all. Other children get off to a good start and then go backwards. They may start to soil for different reasons. For example, they may become frightened of being in pain (perhaps because they have a small cut or fissure); they may have become constipated (so the soiling is mainly overflow); or they may have stopped recognising the signals from their bowels that they need to get to the toilet, and as a result get there too late.

First of all, if your child is in pain, you may need to check with a doctor. Special children's laxatives can make life easier for him and for you. You may also want to look at his diet carefully to make sure he is getting enough fibre, and that he is drinking plenty of water. These measures will help to bulk out and soften his stools. Then you could embark on a Toilet Action Plan.

Toilet Action Plan 2: Soiling

- To start with, reward your child for just sitting on the toilet – say three times a day, after meals. And, of course, give a huge amount of praise for a successful outcome.
- Once sitting on and using the toilet is starting to work, you can reward your child for having clean pants each evening.
- This same plan of action is fine for depositing in strange places – reward your child for depositing in the loo. However, you may need to find out why he is doing this. Is it in defiance? Is it because he is upset about something else? You will need to be kind; if you get angry with your child (and soiling, especially in inappropriate places, arouses strong feelings) it will be harder to change the pattern. If your child is worried or upset, he will need to be helped through this too. You might find it hard simply to ignore the wrongly deposited poo. In a calm and uncritical manner, point out to your child that 'This is not the place for poo – let's put it into the loo.' Try to say no more than this as the attention in itself could become rewarding. Don't force him to clean it up, but have him accompany you to the toilet to see where it should go. Finish by reminding him that if he does his poo in the loo, he will get a sticker for his chart (keep rewarding him for sitting on the loo).

Some toileting habits would certainly cause difficulties at school. Try not to be – or seem to be – unduly worried yourself. Your worry will only make your child more anxious. Something can definitely be done, no matter what the toileting problem. Don't feel embarrassed about seeking professional help.

Sleeping and Bedtime Routines

In some households – perhaps where parents work awkward hours or where there are many people, especially other children, around – it's hard to keep to a regular routine. The idea of a routine may not fit in with the lifestyle you imagine for yourself. But, with children, routines make life so much easier, for you and for them. They know what has to be done and when to do it, and will do it automatically once the routine is established. Following a routine doesn't mean you are rigid, boring or obsessive. You may, however, need tighter constraints when you first set up a routine. Once it is going fine, you can afford to relax and permit exceptions. Routines can, for instance, be more structured during term time and more fluid during the holidays.

The most noticeable overall routine concerns the structure of daytime and night-time events. Without a bedtime routine you do not have a sleep routine. Without a sleep routine you do not have a wake-up routine. Without a clear morning routine you do not have clear meal-time routines ... and so on.

Think about your child's day and fill in the chart below. For each activity it is easiest to work backwards in order to consider the best times for the routines to start.

Activity	Time
Getting ready for school/nursery Time school/nursery starts Time you have to leave to get to school/nursery on time	

Activity	Time
Time needed to dress and have breakfast (leave at least one hour)	
Ideal waking up time is:	
Getting ready for bed	
Ideal wake-up time	
Time your child needs to spend sleeping	
Ideal lights-out time	
Time your child needs for bedtime routine (undressing, bath, reading)	
Ideal bedtime is:	

Once you have worked out your ideal times to go to bed, to have lights out, to get up and to leave the house, you have your 'routine scaffolding'. Next you need to get yourself, your child and your whole family geared up to working within or alongside this structure. It is going to be a lot harder if the lifestyle of other members of the family works against your planned structure. For example, if your family always eats late – at your pre-schooler's bedtime – perhaps you could *all* eat earlier on, say two nights a week (or at weekends) so your pre-schooler can eat with the rest of you. The other nights you can put your pre-schooler to bed first, with the rest of the family eating later.

You can make an Evening Reminder Chart for your child if you like. It could help a reluctant youngster think more about times and routines, especially on weekdays. You might want to use cut-out pictures or little drawings to accompany the words on your chart. The pictures next to the words will help him understand what you are talking about.

Evening Reminder Chart

Activity	Done on Time				
	Mon	Tues	Weds	Thurs	Fri
Snack time	☐	☐	☐	☐	☐
Reading time	☐	☐	☐	☐	☐
Supper time	☐	☐	☐	☐	☐
Up to bed time	☐	☐	☐	☐	☐
Story time	☐	☐	☐	☐	☐
Lights out (sleepy time)	☐	☐	☐	☐	☐

If all (or most) activities for one evening are ticked, you could reward your child with (say) five minutes of extra story time.

Frequently-asked Questions

How can I help my child who is frightened of being alone in his room and needs us to stay with him until he falls asleep?
Start by finding out what is frightening him, then take any necessary steps to allay reasonable fears. It is important to listen to and acknowledge his concerns, even if you feel he is just trying to keep your attention. However, *continual* reassurance on your part for non-reasonable fears will be counter-productive. You can end up reinforcing that it is okay to be constantly seeking reassurance from you, repeatedly asking questions such as 'Will someone be able to break in?', 'Is it safe in the dark?' or 'Will you stay near me?'

Talk to your child about setting up a Bedtime Action Plan. With this he should be rewarded for being on his own in his room for a little while. Tell him you will leave him (to try to sleep, to read or just to enjoy his bed), but you will come back to check him in two minutes (then five, then ten). Over a week or two, gradually increase the amount of time you are out of the room. It is important that you agree with him what you are doing, and that you try to stick to what you have agreed. If you find you are being called back before the agreed time, and that he becomes distressed if you do not instantly return, go back to a one- or two-minute check routine. In this case, stay near his room but move yourself further away and increase the time much more gradually. Make sure you tell him how great he has been to stay in his bed (or his room). Keep increasing your emphasis on praise for being in bed; the fact that he is managing on his own should become less important. One of your main aims is to get him to fall asleep without needing you to be there to help him. Perhaps a favourite toy could be used as his 'special companion'. Children who are nervous of the dark might also be reassured by having a night light, at least until they are more confident about being left alone.

My child wakes us up to accompany him to the toilet or to have a drink – how can I change this?

If your child wakes up in the night – and wakes you – part of your aim is to train him to move away from a nightly pattern of waking to sleeping through the whole night. The other part is to get him not to wake you even if he wakes himself. So, if your child wakes in the night to go to the toilet, encourage him to do this without waking you. Get him to tell you that he has done this in the morning and reward him for this achievement. If he does wake you to take him to the toilet, talk to him as little as possible and stay only as close as absolutely necessary. Do not get pulled in to cuddle him or tell a story to get him back to sleep. Instead, set up a structured reward plan for not waking you; for instance, use a reward chart so that your child earns a sticker for each night he does not come to visit you or demand your attention.

Some children develop strong habits of getting up (sometimes more than once) in the night on a regular basis to go to the
toilet. The solution is not to stop all drinks in the evening, as this
has been shown not to make a difference. Your child instead
needs to train himself to increase his bladder capacity by waiting
a little longer. With luck he may fall asleep again. If he does hold
on too long then wets the bed, don't be upset. Praise him for
trying to hold on longer. Keep on with this approach for enough
time to see if it works. Bear in mind that some children may not
manage to do this until they are a little older, so they will need
to keep on going to the toilet.

Ideally, children should drink only water at night after they've
cleaned their teeth (if they have to drink anything). However, some
children wake their parents in the night asking for drinks, often fruit
juice or milk. This can usually be successfully managed by gradually
diluting the juice or milk with water. You should then find that your
child's night-time requests for a drink decrease dramatically.

How can I get my child to sleep the whole night in his own bed without him coming to sleep with us?

If your child comes frequently to your bed, the approach is similar to dealing with the issues raised above. He will need to be
rewarded for being in his own bed. When he does come to your
room, take him back to his own room with as little fuss or discussion as possible. However, it is also important for you to consider
why he might be coming to your bed. Some children come
because there may be more deep-seated family issues. By being in
your bed he can ensure there are no fights, or help keep parents
apart from each other. It may just be so much cosier and cuddlier
– and a hard habit for your child (and you?) to break.

It helps to make your child's own space as enticing as possible, whether he shares with brothers or sisters or has a room to

himself. Some children are fine when there are others sharing the room but dislike being alone. For others, an annoying brother or sister may be the main problem. Once you have identified any possible reasons that make your child prefer your bed to his, see what you can do to deal with them. Then you should be successful.

And Finally ...

Once you have worked your way through all the self-care areas that need attention, go back and redo the Self-care Checklist on page 25. Maybe use a different-coloured pen so you can see more easily how far you and your child have come. Remember, self-care is not about pushing your child out into the big wide world before he's good and ready. But with a little luck and good management, you will free yourselves up to enjoy a bit more independence and give each other more time to enjoy whole new areas of activity and fun.

3
Behaviour

Preparing your child so that her behaviour is acceptable to you, to her peers, to her wider circle and indeed to herself links in many ways to all the other chapters. In this sense it is central. It is really hard to learn new skills – or change old habits – if you do not have a 'behaviour change framework' to help you. This chapter is all about changing or guiding behaviour, whether the behaviour in question is 'naughtiness' to be reduced or stopped, or introducing new skills that your child doesn't yet have in her repertoire.

Preparing your child's behaviour for school means that she should be ready to:

- Fit in with routines and get on with teachers and peers
- Cope with teacher expectations and requests
- Understand and respond appropriately to reprimands or guidance
- Respond to instructions so that she can listen, take in information and learn

Developing your child's self-esteem is the key to preparing her behaviour for school. The approach outlined in this book is all about your child gradually increasing – and achieving – successful compliance and being rewarded or 'reinforced' for her efforts. She should be pleased with her achievements. Children with behavioural difficulties are likely to have low self-esteem because others around them (teachers and peers as well as parents) tend to show their negative feelings about disliked behaviours. So the child misbehaving in school is more likely than her classmates to be told off or have peer relationship problems, which will lead to lower self-esteem. On the other hand, positive reactions to acceptable behaviour will boost a child's self-esteem.

Learning Compliance

The pre-school period is the best time to establish acceptable patterns of behaviour in your child – and parental ways of coping. This is much harder to do when your child becomes physically strong and large, adept at answering you back and finding your weak spots. Some young ones seem to manage that quite well too, it has to be said, but if you can avoid getting into a cycle of ineffective shouting at a defiant, 'rude' or 'naughty' child, that will be very much better.

The child's age makes a difference to the kinds of behaviours you might expect. Almost all children in the stage of the 'terrible twos' have temper tantrums. Once a child learns the word 'no', she needs to practise using it to make sure she has got the concept absolutely right. That is both reasonable and normal.

Once children get to around three, three-and-a-half or even four years old, however, adults stop talking and smiling about their toddler sweetly 'asserting herself' and change to using language such as 'being difficult', 'hard to manage' and eventually 'showing behaviour problems'. Maybe the child's actual behaviour hasn't changed so much, but you – and other adults around the child – have changed your expectations and tolerance levels. That is quite right because the pre-school child over three normally has the understanding, the language ability and the social knowledge to enable her to do as she is asked, in reasonable situations, without major fuss or rage. She needs to be able to stop doing something instantly (or reasonably quickly) when asked. This is essential – otherwise she could, without realising it, be placing herself or others in a position of danger.

Your child needs to be able to do what you ask of her in a range of other situations too. Her ability to do this is known as 'compliance'. Children who are frequently 'non-compliant' will be considered a problem by most adults.

Bear in mind that some children will be developing more slowly than others. This means their ability to understand – and therefore their level of behaviour – will be below their actual age level. Expectations of behaviour will also need to be different for such children.

In addition to compliance, many perceived problematic behaviours in pre-school children are to do with hostility and aggression. Aggression can be shown in different ways: levelled at objects only; at people by physical means; at people by non-physical means (such as shouting or name-calling); or by all these ways at different times (or sometimes simultaneously). It is well recognised that if aggressive behaviours are not quickly curbed, there will be lasting problems for your child. Antisocial behaviours are definitely not a plus for future progress at school. Children need to learn to control themselves and their behaviour.

Complete the following checklist to see how well your child is behaving.

How Well-behaved is Your Child?

For each question tick the behaviour that comes closest to describing your child.

Will your child usually stop what she is doing when you ask her to?

Fairly quickly and easily ☐

With a little persuasion ☐

Only with a big fuss and grumble ☐

Often has a temper tantrum and refuses ☐

Will your child respond to routine instructions such as 'Please wash your hands/come to the table/come and get undressed'?

Fairly quickly and easily ☐

With a little persuasion ☐

Only with a big fuss and grumble ☐

Often has a temper tantrum and refuses ☐

Will your child respond to other requests such as 'Let's read a book/go out/turn off the television'?

Fairly quickly and easily ☐

With a little persuasion ☐

Only with a big fuss and grumble ☐

Often has a temper tantrum and refuses ☐

Does your child damage/hit/kick/attempt to destroy objects?

Only quite exceptionally or not at all ☐

Now and again ☐

Regularly ☐

Does your child deliberately hit/kick/bite or in other ways attempt physically to hurt any other person?

Only exceptionally (when very young or provoked) or not at all ☐

Now and again ☐

Regularly ☐

If 'now and again' or 'regularly', what have the circumstances generally been?

Unprovoked ☐

Clearly and/or recently provoked ☐

Because angry about some previous event ☐

To whom have the aggressive acts been directed?

To you (parents or one parent) ☐

To brother or sister ☐

To other children (known? just met?) ☐

To other adults (what type of relationship?) ☐

Does your child use bad language (name-calling, swearing) directed at other people?

Only exceptionally (when very young or provoked) or not at all ☐

Now and again ☐

Regularly ☐

Does your child attempt to harm herself such as by biting herself or pulling out her hair?

Only exceptionally (when very young or provoked) or not at all ☐

Now and again ☐

Regularly ☐

Does your child deliberately do 'naughty' things like hiding others' possessions, taking sweets when asked not to, or throwing toys around when asked to clear up?

Only exceptionally (when very young or provoked) or not at all ☐

Now and again ☐

Regularly ☐

If you find that your child (either most of the time or frequently):

- Won't comply with routine tasks without difficulty;
- Won't readily respond to most other requests;
- Engages in deliberately 'naughty' (as opposed to occasional 'mischievous') behaviour; or
- Is physically or verbally aggressive towards objects and/or people

then clearly her behaviour is a real problem that has to be dealt with – now, before it gets worse, and certainly before she goes to school.

If the behaviours that concern you are largely provoked, then you could try to find ways of removing or lessening the provocation, even if you still have to deal with the behaviours themselves.

If your child is regularly hurting herself deliberately, you might want to consider whether she is in fact showing signs of emotional distress. Think what possible causes there might be and use Chapter 5 to help you.

What Do You Do When Your Child Misbehaves?

Consider what you did the last couple of times your child misbehaved and you had to take some action. Look at the questions opposite and tick any of the boxes that apply.

Did you...

Grin and bear it and say nothing? ☐

Make excuses for her – She's so tired/frustrated/sickly/ in the shadow of her brother/sister'? ☐

Punish her by depriving her of something? ☐

Send her to her room/out of your room? ☐

Tell her off firmly and leave it at that? ☐

End up having a shouting match about what she has done? ☐

Lose your cool completely and shout furiously or lash out? ☐

Other (List..) ☐

Now consider the following as well. How effective did you feel your strategies were – and are in general:

Effective overall? ☐

Sometimes effective, sometimes not? ☐

Often or regularly ineffective? ☐

Were there any adverse consequences to behavioural incidents such as:

She seemed to listen/be subdued but then did the same thing again soon after? ☐

She listened but then went and did some different naughty thing soon after? ☐

She shouted and was rude to you? ☐

Other? (List..) ☐

What do you think now about your child's behaviour and how it affects your family life? Do you feel your strategies are not effective or, if effective on one level, lead to further problems later? Do you find yourself so angered by your child's behaviour that you end up 'losing it' too? Don't feel too guilty if you find yourself in this position. Children can be incredibly annoying and seem to know just what buttons to push and when to push them. You would not be the first parent to end up behaving much like your pre-schooler yourself! But losing your cool is not a good way. To avoid the points of conflict, have a plan to deal with your child in all difficult situations.

Preparing an Action Plan

First let's consider two tasks you might find helpful before you start any structured action plan for improving your child's behaviour. The first is to look at your general approach to discipline and managing or parenting your child – your 'parental style'. The second is making observations of your child so you can get a better understanding of what the problems are (or if indeed there really are any).

1. Parenting Style

Parenting style refers to your overall attitude to, and your general practice of, parenting rather than particular behaviours. The occasional moment that you might lose your temper is not the point.

Psychologist Dr Diana Baumrind observed many pre-school-age children with their parents and went on to note four different child-rearing styles: authoritarian, permissive, uninvolved and authoritative. Understanding these parenting styles will be of enormous help to you in dealing with your child's behaviour.

The **authoritarian style** is characterised by strong insistence that the child behaves well, or achieves the parents' expected standards. The methods used involve strong control, more of a 'do as I say … because I told you to' approach. These parents move beyond the authoritative guidance (*see below*) and use criticism and punishment to achieve control rather than praise, explanations and discussion.

The **permissive style** is characterised by a laid-back approach, with no, or few, expectations of the child: what she does is fine, regardless of her real capability to make decisions. The parents are warm and caring but may not notice all the child's needs or attend sufficiently to them.

The **uninvolved style** is characterised by detachment of the parents from much of what the child is doing. The child has to 'bring herself up', 'make her own decisions' and 'do her own thing'.

The **authoritative style** is characterised by a balanced, caring and warm approach to the child. Standards expected for behaviour (that is, 'boundaries') are in place, but the demands made are reasonable and fair. This approach involves sensitivity and attention to the child's needs, acknowledgement of her efforts and discussions, explanations and negotiations to achieve goals. You, the parent, need to take control but your manner is more of a 'guider' than either a 'law enforcer' or, at the other extreme, an equal 'pal'.

Into which category do you think you would place yourself?

If you find yourself with no tools other than shouting to help you get your child to behave, then you could be moving towards an *authoritarian* rather than *authoritative* style. Or have you already decided that 'giving up' is the only possible route, which is all too likely to lead either to the *permissive* or to the *uninvolved* style. These two last styles of child rearing have, like the authoritarian, been shown to be ultimately less than helpful for the child.

Even for pre-schoolers, a number of research studies have shown that an authoritative approach – firm but fair, warm and attentive, both accepting and involved but sensitive to the child's needs – is best. The best results come when parents try to help their child develop self-control; try to explain and guide rather than force; try to encourage their child; and when there are disagreements, to arrive at a joint decision. It may sound like a counsel of perfection but it is important to aim towards it.

2. Observing Your Child's Behaviour

You might find it useful to make objective observations of your child's behaviour and record them on the chart below. This will take a little time – at least a week of daily observations should give you a good picture overall, and would take in good days and bad days and other chance daily changes. The longer the period of observation, the more representative it will be of how she generally behaves. If, once you get a reasonable idea of the pattern, you feel that things are all right, the best policy is to take no further action. In other words, you can keep on observing and recording for as long as you feel it would be helpful, even if you don't need to follow it up for the moment. If, however, things are not all right, then clearly you will need to take some action.

First decide on the behaviours that you want to keep track of and record these in the **Behaviour** column. They would typically be temper tantrums (define what this means in your child's case) or separately kicking, screaming, biting, hitting, pushing, throwing; non-compliance with your requests; or self-harming behaviour such as head-banging. These will be your 'target behaviours' that you want to change.

Next, when you observe your child doing any of your target behaviours, get your chart and fill in the **Date, Time** and **Place** column. As soon as you are able (and have got your perhaps shattered and bruised wits about you again) start to make your records. The longer you leave it before recording, the more likely you are to forget the details.

Think carefully about what happened before the behaviour incident. This is called the 'antecedent/s'. For example, you asked your child to come and sit down to eat a meal. She was playing

Date/Time/Place	Antecedents	Behaviour	Consequences

with her train and asked for a few minutes more. Half an hour later she still refused to come to the table … Write this down in the **Antecedents** column. Write down, too, any 'context' antecedents – things that happened, say, earlier that morning or even a previous day, that might be relevant. For example, an older brother wouldn't come to the table when asked. This information can be helpful for you in thinking about how to alter the 'environmental triggers' in order to change the behaviours.

Now for the consequences, that is, all that happened after the behaviour(s). Record in the **Consequences** column what you did or said … what your child subsequently did or said … what you did next. Sometimes, as a result of what you did, your child showed another (or more of the same) of your target behaviours. In this case you can record the sequence by putting an arrow back into the Behaviour column – and follow that up by recording what happened after that in the Consequences column. You should keep going until the whole behaviour incident stops. There isn't always a clear reason why a child stops having a tantrum. Sometimes children just seem to run out of steam and start smiling again. Sometimes someone else in the family may say or do something to make your child stop – for example, an older child may say, 'Come and play with me'. See if you can note any particular patterns because they will give you ideas on what else you could change.

Your chart could look something like this:

Date/ Time/ Place	Antecedents	Behaviour	Consequences
10 Oct., 11am, home/ living room	Mum asked to switch off TV and come to bath	→ Refused to turn off TV [non-compliance] →	→ Mum repeated request
		Said 'No, go away, you horrid mummy' [non-compliance and rude]	Mum and dad shouted, 'Stop being rude. Come now please.'
		Kicked brother [kick]	Both parents told her off again
		Started screaming [temper tantrum] for 15 mins	She wouldn't listen. Told her no more TV for a week
		Screamed more [temper tantrum] then stopped suddenly	Smiled sweetly and asked for a chocolate biscuit and a cuddle (gave both then no more problem)

Try to be honest with yourself. If you lose your cool, write it down. This is not an exercise in pointing the finger of blame at you or your partner. It's the first step along a path of change for your child and for you. But you need to see what is happening before you can ever hope to make a difference.

When you have made your observations for long enough to get a good idea of the pattern, ask yourself the following questions:

How often did you observe the target behaviours?

Several times a day? ☐

Once a day? ☐

Two or three times per week? ☐

About once a week? ☐

Not observed at all lately? ☐

Was getting your child back on track

Very easy? ☐

Fairly easy? ☐

Middling? ☐

Fairly difficult? ☐

Very difficult? ☐

The answers to these questions give you some idea of the extent of the problem currently – and how much of a problem it is to you.

Did you notice any particular patterns, such as problems at bedtime or only when a younger brother or sister is around? Are there more problems with behaviour for the parent left at home when the other parent is working away or comes home late? Or is the most difficult behaviour reserved for the times when a frequently absent parent returns? Think about whether your observations match up with any ideas or theories you might have had beforehand. If you have observed any patterns to the problems, you can consider whether there is anything you might do to change things.

Taking the example of problems arising only or mainly when brothers and sisters are around, try to find time alone with your child. This can be hard, but perhaps a relative or neighbour could help out or, if your other children are old enough, arrange for them to go to a friend. If a parent's work hours make a difference, sometimes a change is possible; this may become the solution to the child's behaviour problem because it makes the way you manage your family easier. Think, too, about the adults in the family. Are you a single parent and feeling insufficiently supported? Or are both parents in the home but have a problematic relationship? Both these situations are likely to make it harder for you to do the job of parenting as well as you might like, and in turn might affect the behaviour of your child. Solutions to improving your child's behaviour are likely to work better if you are feeling supported by a good network.

Look at the observation records you made of your child's behaviours and how you dealt with them. Did you find yourself quitting the scene in despair? Did you find yourself giving harsh punishments or commands on a frequent basis? Did you find yourself insisting that a child do something, regardless of what she was already involved in – without any consideration of whether it was reasonable of you to make demands on her at that moment, and whether you could have found a different way around the conflict?

After checking out these points, you may still feel that, actually, you generally do try very hard and see yourself as an 'authoritative' parent. That's good, but it's not always easy to be that kind of parent. Certain cultural backgrounds make it particularly difficult. Some cultures insist very strongly that 'children should be seen and not heard'; that a parent's or other adult's word is *always* right and *always* takes precedence; that you should not hand out praise too liberally or the child will become big-headed; that if you are not controlling and insistent, you will spoil the child; or that if you 'give her an inch she will take a mile'.

Check with yourself whether or not you really agree with any of these views. If you do, it would be quite hard for you – harder than it's going to be for others – to let yourself take a more easy-going approach. But remember, permissiveness is not what you should be aiming at either. It really is possible to find a middle way – at least most of the time. One further reason why it is important to try is that it will almost surely be easier for you and your child in her adolescence if you have found achievable ways of dealing with conflict (and potential conflict) in these early years.

But why is it better to adopt the authoritative approach rather than the others? Permissive parenting results in children who don't bother much with conventional politeness. They do their own thing, even if their choices involve large amounts of television or computer games rather than homework. As a result, their academic performance suffers as teenagers; they are more likely to defy authority and may become antisocial. Yet they may still rely for a long time on their parents to do things for them.

Authoritarian styles seem to create unhappy children. These children may react against overly severe authority, especially in adolescence. They, like their parents, are more likely to use force too. Compared with children of permissive or uninvolved parents, however, they tend to do better in school and are less antisocial.

Becoming an Authoritative Parent

Good 'nurturance' (parents' caring behaviours that are aimed at encouraging their children) and *moderate control* have been shown by Diana Baumrind to be the key parenting skills for becoming an authoritative parent. For you to develop good nurturance, you need to:

- Engage in affectionate and friendly interaction with your child.
- Be considerate of your child's wishes and needs.
- Be interested in your child's daily activities.
- Respect your child's point of view.

- Express pride in your child's accomplishments.
- Give support and encouragement to your child, especially during stressful times.

For you to develop 'moderate control' (discipline that is neither too heavy-handed nor too lax), you need to:

- Offer reasons and explanations for the requests/demands/ expectations you have of your child.
- Notice and acknowledge good behaviour.
- When misbehaviour occurs, try to look at both your and your child's view of the problem and reach a 'just' solution.
- Use 'consequence-oriented' discipline – expect your child to make up for her wrong-doing – where possible.
- Avoid harsh physical punishment, ridiculing or otherwise putting down your child, or attacking her sense of self-worth.
- Use 'positive reinforcers' including praise, reward and approval to gain compliance.

Developing Good Nurturance

As the first step to developing your nurturance skills, fill out the following questionnaire:

a) Do you play with (not just keep an eye on) your child?

Several times a day ☐

About once a day ☐

Occasionally ☐

Rarely ☐

b) Do you find you have to turn down your child's requests to do things or have things?

Rarely ☐

Sometimes ☐

Often ☐

c) Do you find yourself and your child touching each other affectionately?

Several times a day ☐

About once a day ☐

Occasionally ☐

Rarely ☐

d) If your child asks for something or asks to do something that you disapprove of or know to be unreasonable, how do you deal with this?

Agree it would be nice but explain why it can't be possible now … or ever ☐

Offer alternative possibilities and suggestions ☐

Suggest that if some things aren't done now, there might be a possibility later/in future or in modified form ☐

Tell your child it's not possible but give no explanation, alternative or expression of regret at turning down her request ☐

e) Do you know what your child likes doing best/what her favourite toys are?

Yes ☐

No ☐

Not sure ☐

If not sure, make a list and check afterwards with your child to see how accurate you were

f) Do you talk to your child about what she has done during the day/her play and activities?

Several times a day ☐

About once a day ☐

Occasionally ☐

Rarely ☐

g) When your child expresses her own opinions, do you usually

Say 'Stop being a know-all'? ☐

Say 'Children should be seen and not heard'? ☐

Say nothing (perhaps because you think a child's view isn't very worthwhile anyway)? ☐

Make a comment to show you have heard and are thinking about the view expressed? ☐

h) How often do you find yourself noticing that your child has achieved something and praise her for it or tell someone else in her hearing how well she has done?

Several times a day ☐

About once a day ☐

Occasionally ☐

Rarely ☐

For question (a), the highly nurturing parent will play regularly with their child, but it may be slightly different for working and non-working parents. If you are a working parent, do you make a big effort to play with your child when you are at home, and have you found ways to get round feeling tired or being pre-occupied with home or with work issues? Do you wait for your child to ask you to play with her or do you initiate play? The highly nurturing parent will initiate as well as wait to be asked.

For question (b), do you acknowledge your child's requests to do things or have things – or do you find the constant stream of requests/demands annoying? Do you not want to 'spoil' your child by 'giving in', or do you find you are too busy to think about most of her demands? The nurturing parent needs to keep listening to what the child is saying, to keep talking about what she wants and to anticipate her needs.

For (c), do you regularly kiss, cuddle, hug and affectionately touch your child? The nurturing parent will do this regularly – to boys as well as to girls. It is not 'babyish' or 'unmanly' to show affection.

For (d), how do you deal with your child's unreasonable requests? The nurturing parent listens, but rather than just turning the child down, offers explanations and alternatives – and possible compromises.

For question (e), how do you keep abreast of your child's interests and activities? This is easier of course with younger children, but it is a question to keep asking yourself – and checking with your child.

Do you talk to your child about what she has done during the day (f)? The nurturing parent does this on a regular basis.

For (g), how do you greet your child's expression of opinions? The nurturing parent needs to find ways – different ways – of making the child feel valued and not stupid. You do not have to *agree* with the views, but do acknowledge them as 'interesting', 'intelligent' or 'imaginative'. Or if the ideas are really poor, you could praise her for *thinking* about the issue and coming up with her idea or opinion. This will encourage self-confidence and the desire to try out, risk and explore ideas. You could even gently suggest some more 'appropriate' ideas.

For question (h), how often do you praise your child for achievements? The nurturing parent needs always to be on the lookout for the child's mini successes, achievements and milestones. Look out for opportunities to praise her – this will make her feel good. Telling someone else in her hearing is a great – and more subtle – way of praising, but do use both approaches. Be generous with your comments – once a year does not make your positive comments more valuable or somehow better because of their scarcity. You also want to avoid the risk of being seen as the parent who only seems to notice what your child has done wrong – who only ever tells her off. You might be concerned that if you do nothing but praise, you're doing your child a disservice, making her feel she can do no wrong or become big-headed. Of course these are valid points, and you do need to watch out. But with a pre-school child especially, you do need to make sure that *the balance is tipped in favour of praise*. You are trying to build up her feelings of self-worth. Holding back on praise just in case will not help here. It's not as if you are going to praise her for having a temper tantrum. But there's nothing wrong with praising for little, ordinary things like putting on her coat herself. Or you can find other ways of acknowledging and appreciating her efforts, such as a wink, a hand squeeze or a kiss. You can be more extravagant in your praise for the bigger things.

Developing Moderate Control

The second key parenting skill for becoming an authoritative parent is developing *moderate control*.

Don't feel bad if you have found it difficult to get your child to behave. By the word 'behave' you will probably think of your child's behaviour in terms of your own standards and expectations. It might help to check first that your expectations are not too high, that is, impossible for a child of her age and ability level to achieve. Think first what is possible for her to achieve. If you have no other children with whom to make comparisons, ask friends, neighbours and relatives. Try to get a wide range of views – what is normal can vary widely. Beware the neighbour or family member who might be less than accurate in what they tell you about their own children; they may want you to get a good impression and not let you feel their child is out of control or that there is something wrong.

Now, look back at the list of Baumrind's six pointers needed to exert moderate control (*see page 67*); these are put to you again below, this time in the form of questions for you to consider.

1. Do you offer reasons and explanations for the requests/ demands/expectations you have of your child rather than simply telling her to do this or that?

Most young children can or soon will (you hope) understand that your requests are not imposed just to make their lives a misery. Sometimes your child might *know* your wishes are for her own welfare – and not *care*; or she suspects the requests have been made for the sake of a small brother or sister – so especially not care! But whatever your child's ulterior motive or level of understanding, the simple solution is not to spend time discussing with her why she thinks you are cross. In the heat of the moment she will understand and behave better with just a clear but brief explanation plus 'reinforcement' of a better way to act.

However, if you never explain to a child why what she is doing is wrong or has a bad effect on others, this soon leads to her feeling hard done by and that people are being unfair to her. She never really gets to think about other people, just about what is happening to her. The more she feels unjustifiably picked on and ordered around by you, the more likely she is – especially in the future – to refuse to co-operate, to dig her heels in, and so get into a cycle of conflict with you. You just need to pick a quiet moment to discuss the broader issues of what is right and wrong and why parents get cross.

At the right moment, therefore, reasons and explanations are important. However, generally speaking, more is required than explanations alone to enable a child to behave differently.

2. Do you notice your child's good behaviour and acknowledge it in a positive way?

Do *notice* your child's good behaviours – and let her know you have noticed. You could comment warmly on some of the things she does during the day. Look out for instances of sitting quietly when waiting, say, in a shop; being a 'good companion' at a meal time; kindly offering a toy to her baby brother; not getting cross when her sister knocks over her toys – and so on. Verbal praise, in a tone of voice that shows you are pleased, will help a lot in making your child more likely to do these things that pleased you again. Try to catch yourself every day, more than just once, finding things about your child's behaviour that you can let her know you are pleased with.

But remember that any attention to a child in the form of positive or negative – or even neutral – comments can be rewarding. Try not to say too much when a child is doing wrong (even such remarks as, 'That behaviour makes me sad' can be reward-ing). Comment more when her behaviour is fine.

3. Do you manage to find just and fair solutions after mis-behaviour has occurred?

Try to look at both sides – yours and your child's – to reach a *just solution*. If you think of it, this is really a 'conflict resolution' scenario. You might – and probably will over the years – need to bring out all your personal strengths and skills in diplomacy, nego-tiating, peacemaking and compromising. If you wish ultimately for a resolution of a sticky situation that does not mean a break-down in communication or even a crisis in the whole relationship, you had better practise hard in your child's pre-school period.

Sometimes – say when your child has refused to put her coat and shoes on to go out, and you have to take her to a dentist's appointment – you just have to find a way to do what you need to do (with firm but kind insistence). Of course, it's better to try to anticipate and prevent such situations than have to deal with them as a crisis. However, if your child has, say, destroyed her brother's drawing or already poked and provoked her sister to tears, then it is too late to prevent. Should you just let this go by? Well, you cannot ignore what has happened. It is best to listen to both sides, preferably in such a way as to let each feel heard (and to try not to label either as 'to blame'), then move on. Sometimes it is really hard to unravel what has happened, and sometimes both children are a bit to blame – even if one is more so than the other. If the disagreement is between a parent and the child – say over property left out or destroyed, or food thrown and furniture ruined – you will need to keep your cool. The punishment cannot always fit the damage done (and some-times small children can inflict mighty large damage with a single careless gesture), but it does have to take into account the child's intentions, her limited ability to think consequentially, and of course her age.

The need for discussion and negotiation over solutions for 'misbehaviour' will increase over the years. If the processes and procedures are in place now, early on, it will be easier for you in the future.

4. Does the way you tackle misbehaviour help your child understand why what she did was wrong and also help her find positive ways of putting things right – that is, do you use 'consequence-oriented' discipline?

If your child has made a mess on the floor – deliberately – then it is a sensible move to expect her to help clean up. This should be only after she (and you) have calmed down. If there has been a big fuss, she should not be forced or coerced unpleasantly. But sometimes you might hold her hand firmly to 'help' her clean up at least a token portion of the mess. There are other things that can be 'put right' by a child; she can help to mend a broken toy or build up a knocked-down tower. Psychological hurts (name-calling, teasing) or physical hurts to others (kicking, knocking over) require a consequence-oriented discipline of a different kind. You should not bite back a child who has bitten, or call her names to see how she would like it. You want your child to get away from doing such things, not make her more skilled or amused by seeing what you can do. Your aim in this case – the ideal consequence – is to get her to apologise or to express regret.

5. Does the type of punishment you use help your child feel she has learned something positive from you about how to behave, or is she more likely just to feel bad about herself, and perhaps dislike and fear you too?

Avoid harsh punishments. Physical punishment such as hitting your child, however angry you are, is really counterproductive in the long run. However bad the behaviour, however mad you feel driven, think of yourself being the one with the tantrum and your child the mere provoker. If you can't keep your cool, how will she?

Kids can drive parents to the ultimate depths of fury. If you follow the suggestions in this chapter, not only should you feel better (because your child has not got the better of you), but your child will also be less likely to use violence. In the heat of the moment, think of your own anger-management techniques (look away, count to 10, take a couple of slow breaths). Think 'cool' – remember you are a thinking adult and that you *can* find other ways to get around your child's annoying behaviour.

Non-physical punishments, such as forcing your child to stay in her room for hours, or depriving her of meals or all toys for a week, would also be excessively harsh and give her much just cause for resentment later. The same goes for putting your child down – for example, telling her she is useless, worthless, a naughty child (rather than a good child who occasionally demonstrates some naughty or non-worthy-of-her behaviour). Telling her you wish she hadn't been born, that she is an ugly misfit and not nearly as worthy/clever/polite as her older sibling will certainly not improve her behaviour. Much worse, such messages are very damaging to her feelings of self-worth, to her relationship with you, to her attitude towards authority, to her future relationships with others, and perhaps even to the way she subsequently lives her life. Of course, any parent can lose their cool and say things they don't mean. If you do, now and again, this need not lead to lasting damage; it is important for you to apologise when you have been in the wrong and to find ways to make sure your child believes that you really love and want her and that you believe in her.

There are times when you have to say 'No'. When you have to stop your child from doing something she shouldn't, such as throwing food from the table, say 'No' firmly and clearly. Next, state equally clearly what you expect her to do, for instance: 'Please keep your food *on* the table (or in your bowl).' If she keeps on with the behaviour – throwing food repeatedly – then read on below (*Setting up a Reward Action Plan*) for tips on what you can do.

6. Do you make regular use of praise, reward and approval and other positively reinforcing approaches with your child?

Do make plenty of use of *positive reinforcement to gain compliance*. This is really the key to obtaining control without coercion, good behaviour without tears, and motivation without stress.

Positive reinforcement is *reward to show your approval for particular aspects of your child's behaviour*. It can be a concrete reward (for example a toy, special food, some stickers), time spent doing something enjoyable (such as playing a game with a parent or an outing) or social approval (such as a positive comment or a hug and a kiss). Giving children positive rewards does not mean you are *bribing* them. A bribe is a reward in advance for something you want them to do – or perhaps more typically not to do. For example, you take your child to a theme park because she has promised she will be 'good' for the whole of the next week. Positive reinforcement is a reward, justly earned, for a specific behaviour that has already taken place. Note that the reward comes *after*, or as a *consequence* of, behaving well.

Social approval should always be part of your reward, even when you also give something concrete. Most young children will respond to praise alone, but for many something 'extra' is required to make a difference to their behaviour. See the following section for ideas for setting up rewards schemes.

Setting up a Reward Action Plan

The effectiveness of a reward plan depends almost entirely on how it is set up and carried out. Of course, there could be some children who do not respond to positive reinforcement; some young children may not understand; some may not care about being rewarded with objects or food; and, extremely rarely, some may not respond to social praise. Usually, however, something can be found that is rewarding for your child. For example, one 14-year-old boy with an extremely low IQ would do almost anything for the pleasure of having a balloon blown up – then left to fly noisily around and fall to the ground. He learned lots of language signs (he couldn't use intelligible speech) on the strength of being rewarded with the balloons. It was a real pleasure to see this rather melancholy boy chuckle loudly and rub his hands together gleefully at the sight of the balloon. So, one just has to find the *right* trigger to excite interest in each individual child. Most, even young, children will be more than happy to assist with making a list of things they especially enjoy and that would make a good reward, but you might need to suggest some as well. Be aware that something chosen today may not be considered rewarding tomorrow. That's normal. You just need to have plenty of ideas and go with the flow.

With a pre-school child for whom a Positive Reinforcement Action Plan is required, the aspects of behaviour needing change should be clearly specified (such as reducing the frequency and intensity of temper tantrums, eating with cutlery, complying with requests) rather than using vague terms like 'being good' or 'not naughty'. Your clarity about the targets will also help your child understand exactly what is expected of her.

Below are some principles about using rewards and verbal reinforcement to help shape behaviour.

- The **size of the reward** must be geared to the effort and time put in by the child. If you give major presents after a couple of days, you will have nothing left for the child to feel it is worth making an effort for after a week or so. The plan will then quickly fail. If, on the other hand, you give too little or not often enough, the pre-school child can't readily grasp that something nice really will be coming. The best is to aim for something small most days or every couple of days, such as a toy car, bracelet or some item your child is collecting like cards or small models (in addition to regular praise, several times a day). Perhaps something on a larger scale can be earned after a week or 10 days of reasonably successful achievement on the target behaviours (such as an outing or a bigger toy).

- **Timing** is important. Reinforcement should be given *immediately*. That is, the reward must follow the behaviour immediately – whether this is praise or something more concrete like a sticker.

- You need to **be consistent** about giving rewards/positive reinforcement. When it is earned it is earned. Your child needs to know her efforts have been appreciated. But if you forget, say, to add up the units on any one day, then you will lose the power of your plan. Why should your child make an effort when, from her point of view, you do not? Sometimes circumstances can be difficult for you, of course, but you need to find a way round them so your child doesn't get the idea that what she has achieved (even if only on a small scale) is not important.

- The reinforcements/rewards need to **come as a direct consequence** of what your child has done. If she hasn't earned the reward or unit or part of the reward plan, then she shouldn't get it. If she has earned it, she should. When you are setting up a scheme, it is good to reward an 'almost there' to encourage her. For example, if your plan was to increase concentration and you started with a target of five minutes, and to begin with she is brilliant for four minutes, reward as if for five. You can then try to raise your target expectation back to five minutes – talk with your child to see if she thinks she could, next time, keep going for a whole five minutes until the buzzer sounds. (The advantages of timing tasks using a buzzer or kitchen timer rather than a clock to improve concentration are explained in Chapter 7.) If you discuss with her what would be fair, you are likely to get a better response than if you just say, 'No, you didn't meet your target.'

Encouragement and inducement to achieve are better tools than coercion and insistence. Another example might be if you are trying to get your child to stay in her own bed at night without waking you. If she stayed in her bed (or room) but called out and woke you, you should reward her for staying in her own room. You could, however, then amend the plan to give 'bonus points' for not calling out. In other words, you do not label your child's attempts to comply with the plan as 'failures' because they fall short, but find a way to boost further effort on her part whilst still feeling good about what she has already done.

Preparing a Reward Chart

Charts are a handy way of keeping a record and of showing your child (and you) what good progress she has made. Charts allow you to turn attention towards your child's successes and away from what she has failed to do or from how inadequate or naughty she is. Charts allow children more opportunities to feel good about themselves.

Charts can be done in lots of ways. With young children they need to be simple and clear to understand. You can use stickers, ticks, colouring in or marbles in cylindrical tubes, so one tick or sticker forms your basic 'unit' of reinforcement or reward. Make your choice of type of unit relevant to what you are targeting and what your child likes. Stickers on a bedpost might be good to reward a bed-wetter for dry nights or a poor sleeper for staying in bed. Another idea is to put drawings of people in a train carriage with, say, three units of reinforcement to one head (one unit to colour in the face, one unit to add a hat, and one unit for the shoulders), three heads to a train window, and as many windows as you fancy for your carriage. When each window is 'full', your child could earn something special like a very small toy, a food treat or a dip in a small trinkets lucky dip bag. For each carriage, your child could earn a slightly larger toy or an outing for a meal, a movie or a place of interest. Another creative idea is to use 'advent calendar' charts. For these, the child opens a little 'door' on part of a big picture and finds behind it a picture (perhaps promising a treat) or some small fun item. Remember to keep regular and meaningful verbal praise at the centre of your reward scheme.

Sample Reward Charts

This first chart shows how a child can earn a smiley face sticker for each of the three morning behaviours. She can also earn a special sticker (call it a special bumper sticker or whatever else takes your or her fancy) after being successful for all her three main targets on the same day (a 'full house').

When Sophie Gets Up in the Morning

	Mon	Tues	Weds	Thurs	Fri	Sat	Sun
Get up when mum asks		☺		☺	☺		
Eat breakfast (in 15 mins – without dawdling)		☺	☺	☺	☺		
Dress self ('happily')			☺	☺	☺		
'Full house' – GREAT				✸	✸		

The next example, for your child 'keeping her cool' (so with no temper tantrums), is good for when she has reached a more advanced stage, such as earning a full house most of the time. This is a good moment to move the goal posts and tell her that she now has to get a full house of stickers for three days in a row, after which she will earn a bigger and better sticker.

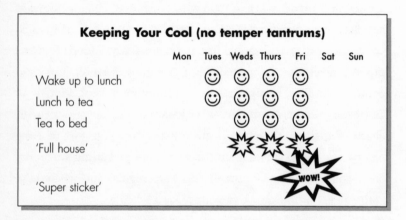

The third and last sample chart shows what you might do to encourage a child who is finding it hard to achieve a full house on a given day. Here you tell her that she will get a bumper sticker each time she gets three smiley faces, even if this takes a number of days. It doesn't matter how long it takes, though if each bumper sticker is linked to a treat such as a box of raisins, things should speed up.

What if things are not progressing quickly enough?

If your child doesn't make progress as quickly as you would like, you may think it is a case of all give on your side and all take on your child's. You may be tempted to give up or even to remove a star/smiley face/sticker as a punishment for some naughty behaviour. That would not be a wise move: if you abandon the programme or do anything to make your child abandon it, you have lost a powerful tool. You will be forced back to coercion or to permissiveness by giving up. *Please do not remove any stars/smiley faces/stickers.* Your child deserved them. Instead, think what has gone wrong. Were you giving a high enough value to target behaviours? Do you need to give, say, three stars or smiley faces for 'keeping cool' when provoked by a younger sibling. (Should you be doing a similar scheme with her sibling aimed at reducing the provocations?) Did you build in enough bonuses for other good behaviour, for consecutive days of good scores? Ask yourself:

- Are your charts sufficiently interesting and colourful and therefore rewarding for a pre-school child?
- Have you made the target behaviours clear enough and broken down into sufficiently small steps for your child to manage easily?
- Have you remembered to complete them every single day without fail?
- Have you (both parents preferably) had time to admire with your child her chart and her achievements?
- Have you checked with her that the rewards are indeed rewarding, or if she has any concerns about the plan?
- Have you (or some relative) been giving extra toys/goodies recently, so removing the incentive for your child to 'earn' things for herself?
- Could it be that you are sometimes still 'rewarding', and so reinforcing, the very behaviour you are trying to stop or

reduce? Letting your child get away with naughty behaviour, such as screaming, by, say, giving her a sweet to keep her quiet is bad news for you; your child's behaviour will take much longer to sort out if she learns (which she certainly and instantly will) that she only has to scream louder or insist more for you to give in at least some of the time. Giving in some of the time means that you are teaching her that persistence pays off. So do watch out for this too.

Check all the above and alter your plan as necessary. If you are satisfied that all is well, do keep going. Keep trying to inject excitement and interest into it. If you behave as if it is all a boring waste of time, then you cannot expect your child to respond well.

In fact, you can go even further than this by using humour and irony. It is certainly better to joke and have fun with your child instead of hoping she might behave better if she sees how miserable and desperate she has made you. Tell her to do the *opposite* of what you really want her to do. For instance, you might wail (but occasionally only, or this won't work), 'You're not going to eat up *that* mouthful, are you? Don't do it!' Or, 'You can't run quickly to your bedroom to get undressed. Bet you can't!' Do use your best acting skills to make sure your child understands that she is not meant to take your words literally!

How long you keep your child on a motivation programme depends on how fast she progresses, on the value to all if a plan is to be continued longer term, and on your willingness to keep it going. Some children will change their behaviour within days just with a reward chart. Others will need much more of the concrete rewards tied in; and take three or four weeks. Often, however, an action plan will require several weeks, and could require additional intervention, such as 'time out' (*see below*).

What should I do if my child is on a successful action plan but then misbehaves?

Even if your child is doing well on a positive-reinforcement action plan, it is to be expected that she might still do something very naughty that you can't just ignore, for example if she lashes out and hurts someone. For these kinds of behaviours you do indeed need to take action. The best way is not punishment (which means the infliction of something nasty). With very young children, also avoid negative reinforcement, such as the removal of something pleasurable like television, or 'fining'. You could, in some circumstances, use a consequence-oriented task, such as helping to clean up a mess. Rewarding children for their efforts and behaviours is generally much more effective than taking negative action. It is also much better for your relationship with your child. Often negative reinforcement comes across to a child as an unpleasant threat. For example, 'You do that again and I'm taking the computer away' or 'You won't be going to the zoo on Saturday.'

If all else fails, and for the most severe situations, you might want to consider removing your child from the scene to cool down. This strategy is known as 'time out'.

How to Use Time Out

Time out is a period when you do not interact at all with your child – it can be a very effective way of helping her change her behaviour (and for you to keep your cool and your sanity). However, it is best not to start using this method unless you have a positive reward plan in place. This is because it is so much better to work on the principle of *rewarding*, of noticing your child's efforts, of talking to her about what she has done right and not what she has done wrong.

1. Set up and explain, in advance, the positive reward plan. Remind your child that if she does X, Y and Z (your expectations of behaviour, positively phrased) she will get A, B and C (the rewards she has helped choose, and the stars or stickers).

2. Next explain to her that if she does certain things that she shouldn't be doing (yell, bite, hit, shout, refuse – be specific) you will put her into time out. It's fine to use the phrase 'time out' with her.

3. When your child next starts to misbehave (in any one of the ways you have decided in advance should be dealt with by time out), say to her, 'Please keep your cool/play nicely with your brother/ come and eat your lunch, it's on the table,' and so on. If your child responds positively, great. Just carry on as normal with whatever you are doing (and remember to reward later for having behaved as you have asked her to). If she continues to kick/shriek/refuse to do as you ask, say, 'I've asked you to keep your cool, etc., and will have to put you in time out if you don't come now.' This is your **one** warning to her. If she stops then fine, but if she continues with the same behaviour, say, 'I am going to put you into time out.' You can add a brief comment/explanation like, 'Kicking hurts people' (no more comments than that, please, so as not to enter into discussion or argument about what was wrong); you will already have explained to your child why kicking and hurting others is unacceptable.

4. Now put your child into the area you have chosen for time out. Make sure your child is safe (remove dangerous objects if you need to) and the area not too unpleasant. Think about this beforehand. Sometimes just putting her outside the door of the room you are in is the simplest, or even a special time out chair. Whatever you are comfortable with and works for you is fine. Some parents will want to use the child's bedroom for time out, whilst others

would prefer not to, as they feel it is better to keep the bedroom for sleep and play. The main thing to bear in mind is that time out is not a punishment – just a time away from rewarding and pleasant activities, and particularly away from attention given by others. If she walks by herself into the designated time out area, great. If not, use touch – as lightly as you can get away with, but firmly if you need to – to take her there (and keep her there too if you are using a chair in the same room as yourself and she refuses to stay). Do not look at her or say anything else. Some children are very clever at trying to make you change your plan, such as by loud screaming, door kicking or trying to leave the time out place. All kinds of inventive tactics may be employed. If your child removes herself from time out, immediately and firmly (without any discussion) return her, holding the door shut if necessary. Once your child is in time out, ignore what you can (like the door kicking or opening the door) until it is time for her to come out.

5. For a pre-school age child, aim to leave her in time out for around five minutes. Then, as soon as she is quiet, say in a neutral and calm tone of voice, 'You can come out of time out now,' perhaps adding, 'Well done for calming down.'

6. Repeat the process as often as you need to. Have lots of fun in between, and don't refer back to the time out or talk about the behaviours that led up to it. If you need to talk about things – fighting with a brother, hurting other people, not listening to adults – then do it when your child is calm and behaving well. It is fine to speak briefly about what is right and wrong when you are putting your child into time out, but remember not to carry on talking about it.

7. When you first set up a time out plan at home, some children might protest in the form of much shrieking and crying. You cannot let your child come away from time out until she is *quiet*. You have to

find only the smallest window of quiet for your moment to say, 'You can come out of time out now.' You will have told her when outlining the whole plan that she has to be quiet in time out for her to be let out. If you let her out while she is screaming, you will have taught her that, if she screams, you give in (for a quiet life). It is better not to use time out at all than let that happen. So, you need to be really quick to catch your child quiet. Young children can work themselves up into a very distressed state, and it would be best not to let the situation develop that far if possible.

8. Do not be alarmed or concerned if a child says she doesn't want to come out of time out. This is her protest – ignore it and she will emerge eventually. The point is that she is 'out of time out', and if she chooses to stay standing or sitting where she was put, then that's fine. If you start to beg her to come out because you are worried that you are doing something bad to her, then she is the one in control.

When your child's behaviour is annoying but not a terribly serious problem, it can be effectively dealt with by a mixture of reward and ignoring.

How to Ignore Your Child's Behaviour

'Ignoring' – which is more about ignoring a child's behaviour rather than ignoring the child – is actually more difficult than many people think. A look, a tone of voice, a comment can all convey to your child that whatever else you are doing, ignoring her behaviour is not one of your actions.

To ignore a child's behaviour, remember to:

- Say nothing about the behaviour, including comments such as 'I am ignoring you while you are …'
- Avoid eye contact with the child.
- Make no gestures or body movements such as throwing your hands up in despair that might communicate to your child that you have indeed taken note of the behaviour, just as she intended.

And Finally …

Now you have the tools to help you bring out the best in your child – and to cope when her behaviour gets difficult. If you have a plan to put into action, you are far less likely to shriek with despair yourself. Few parents do not feel like tearing their hair out at least occasionally. And if you have other things on your mind, such as other children or work worries, then it would be normal to feel this way more often. The information and principles about setting up reward/reinforcement plans are guidelines. Use your imagination and your drawing skills to think up new ideas that catch the imagination of your child. She will more readily internalise the things you are trying to teach her if you have a structure. Children who protest mightily about time out to start with have been known to walk to the allocated place without being told after they have committed some misdemeanour. They can see that it is a good way of cooling off, and that it is so much better than a nasty punishment or the removal of privileges.

When your child goes to school, if she is in reasonably good control of her behaviour, can respond to adults' requests without fuss, and can go about her business without regularly disturbing or annoying others, she will be in a fine position to cope well with all she has to face.

4
Social Skills

Human relationships provide the essential fabric of daily life. Although we gain satisfaction and pleasure from doing things, achieving things and enjoying beautiful art or nature, how we view ourselves – our self esteem – comes largely from how others see us. We need to be loved, to be accepted for what we are, to feel we matter. If we fail to make good relationships with others, if we feel unaccepted or little valued, then the way ahead is almost invariably unhappiness or worse.

Equally, how well our children enjoy school depends greatly on the social relationships they form. How well their mental health develops depends upon having good social relationships, though many other factors make a difference here. Your child's ability to form good social relationships with adults and other children is just too important to leave to chance.

How Do Relationships Develop?

The start of your child's social relationships skills and experience is with you, the parents, and then the wider family. The importance of establishing good relationships between parents and children has long been viewed as central to an individual's well-being. Of course, not every family situation is 'ideal', not every circumstance easy. There may be difficulties between parents that ultimately lead to separation or divorce, even as or before a child is born. There may be wider family difficulties, such as grandparents who do not approve of the parents' relationship. There may be additional stresses and strains on the parents, such as a heavy workload, financial difficulties and so on. The child himself may have early problems, perhaps with health or development; perhaps with his type of temperament (*see Chapter 5*). All these things affect how those early but all-important relationships might develop.

While the child's first relationships are normally with the parents, children also usually come into contact with a huge variety of other people before they start school. Those with whom they might develop close relationships typically include grandparents, siblings and childcare workers (such as childminders and nannies). At a slight distance away in terms of closeness and caring come neighbours, family friends and any professionals who may be involved in the child's life, such as doctors.

During these pre-school years, your child will take the first big step away from his huge reliance and dependence on you towards social contact with his peers. Most pre-school children have some experience of being with other children in playgroups and pre-school classes. Isn't this enough, you may ask, to pave the way for socialisation at school? Isn't it sufficient to go with the flow and see how things develop in the future?

In answer to that, for many children some help or guidance is useful. You will have been teaching your child about relationships from the word go, so he won't be starting from scratch at school. He will need to learn the social skills important for making friends, for keeping friends, for solving relationship conflicts and for generally being liked.

The relationships your child forms with the adults in his life will be different from those he forms with his peers. Different skills have to be learned too. Adults – especially those who are not the parents – expect:

- A non-equal relationship with children
- No overfamiliar talk and behaviour from the child
- An appropriate degree of respect
- Responsiveness to the adults' requests, ideas and demands
- Politeness

There is some leeway for individual differences, but by and large children will be expected to follow – or learn quickly – certain codes of acceptable behaviour and to know the boundaries between these and unacceptable behaviour. If they don't manage well in their relationships with adults at school, children will soon be viewed as difficult or a problem – and their behaviour and work as well as their self-esteem and happiness will be affected adversely.

Social Relationships: Your Child's Experiences So Far

The following three short questionnaires look at the extent of social contact your child has already had with other adults and children (in addition to you). How experienced with other people do you think your child is? Questionnaire 1 is about how *often* your child has contact with others. How *well* your child manages his social experiences is looked at in Questionnaires 2 and 3.

Questionnaire 1 – Early Opportunities for Contacts

Before looking at the social skills your child already has, take a look at how much opportunity he has had to develop these. Some children may have had a great deal of contact with a wide variety of other people of all ages; others very little. Tick the box for each question to show the degree to which each is true for your child.

How often does your child have contact with adult family members (grandparents/uncles/aunts)?

☐ daily   ☐ once or twice a week   ☐ occasionally   ☐ rarely

How often does your child have contact requiring some interaction with non-family adults – such as occasional visitors to the house, health professionals, and so on?

☐ daily   ☐ once or twice a week   ☐ occasionally   ☐ rarely

How often does your child have contact with family or neighbours' children (not counting siblings)?

☐ daily   ☐ once or twice a week   ☐ occasionally   ☐ rarely

How often does your child have contact with children in an organised regular setting, such as playgroup, kindergarten or other pre-school facility?

☐ daily   ☐ three or four times a week   ☐ once or twice a week
☐ not yet started

Do you feel, from your answers to these questions, that your child has had good opportunities to interact with others, or actually very little?

☐ good   ☐ adequate   ☐ little

Questionnaire 2 – Quality of Contact

Let's now turn to *how well* your child manages his contacts. Is it the case that:

Your child engages happily with known neighbours or professionals?

☐ certainly ☐ sometimes ☐ not really/never

Your child engages happily with new adults who come to your house?

☐ certainly ☐ sometimes ☐ not really/never

Your child plays happily with children he knows, with or without an adult needing to be present?

☐ certainly ☐ somewhat ☐ not really/never

Your child has other children he considers friends/a friend?

☐ certainly ☐ somewhat ☐ not really/never

Your child goes happily to play at other children's homes?

☐ certainly ☐ sometimes ☐ not really/never

Your child engages readily in play or talk with children he has just met?

☐ certainly ☐ somewhat ☐ not really/never

If you have ticked quite a few 'certainly' boxes in Questionnaire 2, and your child has had some reasonable experiences of being with peers and new adults (Questionnaire 1), then he is able at this stage to manage his interactions well. If you have ticked mostly 'not really/never' boxes in Questionnaire 2, then your child may find it rather difficult to join pre-school classes and to feel comfortable with both peers and adults. If you have ticked mostly 'rarely/not yet started/little' boxes in Questionnaire 1, then the quality of his social contacts may be largely limited by his opportunities.

Questionnaire 3 – Quality of Relationships

For children already attending a pre-school or playgroup facility, the following questionnaire looks at the *quality* and *extent* of your child's social relationships.

Does your child:

relate well to staff at his pre-school or nursery class?

☐ usually   ☐ sometimes   ☐ rarely

initiate play with other children?

☐ usually   ☐ sometimes   ☐ rarely

If so, is this to same sex only ☐ or both sexes? ☐

respond positively when other children make approaches to him?

☐ usually   ☐ sometimes   ☐ rarely

If so, is this with all or most children who approach ☐, a select group of known children ☐ or one or two other children only? ☐

Can your child share his toys?

☐ usually   ☐ sometimes   ☐ rarely

Can your child wait his turn happily?

☐ usually   ☐ sometimes   ☐ rarely

Does your child get into fights or disagreements with other children?

☐ most days ☐ once or twice a week ☐ once or twice a month
☐ very rarely

If you are not sure of the answer to any of these questions, try observing your child and ask the care staff/playgroup leaders for their opinions (they may not have been able to observe all these areas accurately, however). If you have mostly ticked the 'usually' boxes (and there are only occasional fights/disagreements), then your child is probably making a good start to socialising and will be well prepared when he starts school. If there are difficulties and conflicts around your child's interactions – with quite a few ticks in the 'rarely' boxes – then he would benefit from more preparation for socialising.

It's good to tackle any indications of a child's problems with socialising early on. First, however, you need to identify the clues to the problem so you know the areas in which to take action. Even if your child doesn't show any evidence of a major problem, and hopefully this will be the case, it's good to make sure he'll have the most enjoyable time with peers that he possibly can. And it's certainly better to start helping your child now rather than waiting until poor patterns of interaction become more fixed and habits harder to alter.

Social Competence and Moving into School

A recent review of the research on the development of peer relations in childhood by psychologist Dale Hay and others concluded that there is good evidence that even young children in the first three years of life show differences in their peer competence. Peer relationship difficulties don't just get better by themselves. Therefore if some young children do start showing behaviours that could single them out as socially inept or often in conflict with others or unable to make friends, that's a signal for you to get involved right away. It really is a good idea, shown clearly by many studies, that preparing your child to be socially competent before he starts school pays massive dividends.

At school, your child will experience different expectations from those of the pre-school years. These will affect how your child develops socially. For example:

- There are more demands on children and greater expectations from adults than in the more sheltered pre-school environments.
- There are many new faces – adults and children – to get to know.
- Children are expected to learn to be more independent.
- They start to have more formal lessons.

One of your child's big tasks is to learn to get on with his teachers and his peers. This can be a steep learning curve. He will of course learn much from those around him at pre-school and at school when he gets to that stage. From other children he will learn particular social rules and ways to make and keep friends. From the adults your child will learn other rules and how to meet their expectations. Getting on with both adults and peers is vital; difficulties in one area can lead to difficulties in the other. But even in those early school and pre-school days, children who find themselves not getting on well with their peers may feel unhappy, or react by showing difficult behaviour at home or in the class group.

The classroom can seem a brutal place where every child has to make his own mark, form his own relationships and stand up to tough children or even bullies. Many adults will remember some rough moments or times when other children were unkind or made their lives a misery. These days, teachers and classroom assistants are better trained to watch out for and promote children's social development, but sometimes things happen that they don't see. You know that. You may therefore be concerned, as many parents are, that your child settles in well at school and gets on with the other children.

The Skills Children Need to Get On with Others

Peer acceptance, friendships, popularity and social skills or social competence are all terms describing how well children get on with their peers. Teachers, parents, psychologists and journalists sometimes use the terms as if they mean the same thing. Sometimes they mean rather different things.

Acceptance refers to how well your child is accepted or maybe even tolerated by his peer group. It doesn't mean that he is especially liked, in the sense of being popular (*see below*). Nor does it include your child's view of other children.

In contrast, a *friendship* is a reciprocal relationship; your child likes someone who likes him back in return. Reciprocity is what makes friendships special. Both being accepted *and* having friendships are important for how well your child gets on overall.

Popularity refers to how well liked a child is. Those who are most liked or very much liked are described as popular. The term seems to imply that only a few make the grade into the popular camp, so giving them something of a 'star' status. This means that relatively few children are going to be in this position. However, being popular is not at all necessary for getting on perfectly well; general acceptance – and preferably having friends too – is more important.

Acceptance and friendship patterns have been shown to relate differently to the *social skills* or *social competence* your child shows. Researchers have found that children who are poorly accepted and who have few or no friends are different in their behaviour from children who also have few friends but are in contrast generally well accepted by their classmates. The overall finding seems to be that the children who are both poorly accepted by their peers and who do not have friends show behaviour that is less socially skilled than those who have few or no friends but *are* generally accepted. Both these groups of children, however, are generally less skilled than children who are both accepted and have friends.

As a parent, therefore, it is important that you foster the skills for both friendship and for peer acceptance.

A note about the negative side of peer relationships: 'dislike'. Even some generally well-liked and accepted children may be disliked by a few. It is not essential – at any age – to be liked by everyone; your child can happily keep away from those who do not like him (and whom he may well not like in return) and be happy because he gets on well with everyone else. However, things could be problematic for your child if those children who dislike him start to show their feelings. This could constitute bullying, and prompt action would need to be taken.

Pre-school Friendships

Being accepted, getting on well with peers and having friends is a complex process; however, preparing your child is not simply about coaching him in friendship-making skills, although this has an important place. For example, a child's general behaviour in the classroom and playground can sometimes affect peer accept-ance and friendships; some children may not want to associate

Pre-school Friendships

- Peer relationships – interest in same-age children – begin for many children even in the first year of life.
- Reciprocal friendships – that is, where both children like each other – develop during the pre-school years. Preference for particular peers can start from the second year.
- Gender: children initially make friends with others regardless of their sex. This gradually moves towards mostly exclusively same-sex friendships, before changing again in adolescence.
- Socially skilled toddlers have learned to gain attention, comfort, praise and get help from others; they can give the same to others and they can co-operate with others; they can engage in many games (including 'pretend play'), carry on conversations, resolve disputes and form and maintain friendships.
- Many four- to five-year-olds can distinguish 'best friend' from 'friends'.

with children who are always getting told off for being naughty, even if they like them otherwise. It may therefore be important to change the child's general behaviour to improve peer acceptance. Children who are emotionally fragile or 'immature' – often in tears or distressed – may also have problems with peers; here part of the solution would be to address the child's emotional needs. So, when planning how to help your child make friends and become more accepted, refer also to Chapters 3 and 5.

Can I Help My Child Make Friends?

When your child is young, you are the most likely person to be making contacts and arranging play opportunities for him. If you like a particular child, or a child's family, you will find yourself steering your own child in their direction. That's normal and good. But of course you may worry that another child is too boisterous or out of control, or allowed to do too much unsupervised, or allowed to do things you would not allow yours to do – so you try to keep that child at a little distance from yours. Again, that's perfectly understandable and reasonable. It's also fairly obvious that living close by another child makes fostering friendships easier.

The important thing is that you don't just leave friendships to chance. You do need to organise your pre-schooler's social life; make opportunities occur; ensure that your child's experiences of friendship are as wide as possible. You may be often busy with

How You Can Help Your Child Make Friends

- Pre-school children whose parents arrange informal contacts for them with peers not only have a far larger social network but also become more socially skilled.

- Children whose parents arrange their social contacts soon learn to follow their parents' example and come to do their own 'networking'.

- Mothers who take the initiative in arranging children's contacts with peers generally have children who themselves come to initiate such contacts and are accepted by their peers.

- The closer and bigger the parents' circle of friends, the more this encourages their children to follow their example. This applies particularly to the mother's friends.

- If you make an effort to get to know the parents of your children's friends too, it makes all your lives easier. For example, if you can't pick your child up from school one day, perhaps a friendly parent can do it for you and your child can go back to the friend's home to play for a while. This gives you the chance to do the same in return, so helping your child's friendships to grow.

work or with home responsibilities; you may have other children to look after; getting around may be a problem; and the unexpected always happens. Even so, the effort of helping your child make friends and get out and about with other children is hugely worthwhile in terms of later rewards for your child. If you can persist with helping your child in his social contacts throughout the primary school years, so much the better. After that, your chances of making a great deal of difference sharply diminish. Adolescents will only view your efforts as interference!

It's good to involve your child in making some arrangements, even at pre-school age, but do make sure that things happen. They may not if your child has to do the asking. Not only pre-school children but older children too can find it hard to make arrangements on their own. As 'play dates' get more frequent, it is wise for families on both sides to know what arrangements are being made if you wish to avoid awkward clashes of interests. However, keeping one's own diary may be difficult enough, but managing your children's social diaries as well adds plenty of stress. You have been warned!

The more actively you, as a parent, cultivate old friends and make new ones, the more your child is likely to follow suit and learn how to make friends and socialise. Some children may find relating to others tricky, despite your help, but it is still well worth persisting, even if it takes a while for your efforts to show.

Strategies for Coping with Everyday Social Situations

It will be helpful for you to discover just how much your child already knows about dealing with particular social situations. This will put you in a better position to help him devise good strategies. The scenarios below outline some common social relationships.

When you first observe your child in these scenarios, take stock of exactly what happens. When you have some time together with your child, you can talk about or act out some of the scenes with him as a kind of game. The scenarios also give you the opportunity to discuss strategies, feelings and relationships in general. They get your child to think about how he has behaved and give you the chance to help your child solve problems.

1 Choose the scenarios you are going to start with (it will probably be easier to tackle them in the order given). Find the toys and dolls or puppets you might need. You can of course change the toys suggested to ones more available or of more interest to your child.

2 Add to your list scenarios you have seen your child or another child struggling with. Note that the scenarios given cover a wide range of behaviours, but all of them involve skills that are useful for making friends and getting on well with others.

3 Go through the scenarios with your child and put ticks in the columns of the chart on page 110 to show whether your child has good coping ideas or whether he can't think of coping ideas. This is the **assessment** part.

4 After your assessment, start to teach strategies using some of the 'good strategies' suggestions given for most of the scenarios. This is the **coaching** or **teaching** part.

5 On your chart, mark in the dates you have 'teaching sessions' for particular scenarios. After some time of doing this you can reassess how well your child has taken on board the ideas by repeating the scenarios test. Mark in the column when he seems to have got the idea.

6 Keep going!

Using dolls or puppets to act out the scenario creates a distance between your child and the scenario. In this way your child won't feel criticised if he doesn't have good coping strategies as yet. However, as a pre-schooler, he is still likely to speak 'for' the doll as he would himself, in action or in words. Sometimes it is good nonetheless to ask your child what *he* would do if somebody asked him for a toy (or knocked over his tower accidentally or hit him) and so on. Feel free to try the scenario questions both ways, but start by asking your child what someone else might do or say before you check what he might do or say.

Listen to what your child says (this is true of all the scenarios). Be accepting of all suggestions, saying, 'Yes, that would be one thing you could do (or say). Can you think of anything else? And another idea?'

When your child has given you several ideas, ask, 'What do you think is the best idea?' From his answers you should get a reasonable idea of how well he knows what to do. If he's got some obviously good ideas, put a tick in the 'Shows Good Coping Ideas' column of the chart on page 110. On the other hand, if you feel he hasn't really got the hang of what is reasonable to do, tick the 'Can't Think of Good Coping Ideas' column.

Here are the scenarios, with suggestions of what you should say to your child, and examples of competent coping strategies and poor strategies. As you teach your child what to do, make sure you praise him encouragingly for all appropriate strategies he tells you about or acts out.

Scenario 1: Your child wants a toy another child is playing with.

Show two dolls (of the same sex as your child – call them, say, 'Max' and 'John'). Say, 'Here's Max. Max is playing with this fire engine. Now John wants a turn to play with the fire engine. Max has been playing with it for a long time. What can John do to get a turn to play with the fire engine? What can John say?'

Good suggestions from your child might include:

- I'd ask him nicely if I can have a turn.
- I'd say, 'I'll give you this toy and you give me yours.'
- I'd say, 'Can I have a go in a bit?' (Specific amounts of time are hard concepts for pre-schoolers to manage; 'have a go after you' could mean a very long wait or a short one, but in either case these are appropriate strategies.)

Poor strategies might include:

- I'd snatch it away from him.
- I'd hit him.
- I'd cry.
- I'd tell him he is mean and horrid.
- I'd tell teacher to make him give it to me.

You can then go on to suggest to your child that some strategies will be better (and more likely to succeed) than others and to show him how to cope even more effectively.

Scenario 2: Accidental upset – Lucy's built a tower. Kelly runs around and knocks the tower over by mistake. Oh dear. What can Kelly say or do so that Lucy won't get cross with her?
Good suggestions might include:

- I'd say sorry.
- I'd say sorry and ask if I can help build it back up again.

Poor suggestions might include:

- I'd laugh.
- I'd tell her it wasn't a very nice tower anyway.

There are many other good and poor suggestions your child might make, and plenty of good ideas you can devise for different scenarios. Here are three more scenarios, some version of which your child is almost bound to come across at one time or another.

Scenario 3: Joining in play. Tim and Jack are playing with some bricks. George wants to play with Tim and Jack too. What can George do or say so that he can play with them?
Good suggestions are:

- 'Would you like some yellow bricks from the basket? I'll get them for you.'
- 'Can I drive my car under your bridge?'
- 'You've made a great farm – can I build a field for the cows?'

Poor suggestions are:

- 'Those aren't your bricks.'
- 'I want to play with them now.'
- 'You are mean, 'cause you aren't letting me play.'

This joining-in scenario is quite a tricky one, and the skills required are complex and sophisticated. Young children need to learn that first 'bids' or 'initiations' or attempts to join others often get a negative response. This doesn't mean that your child isn't liked. He will need to learn that what he has to do is not give up but make another kind of attempt. Of course, other children can feel that too many attempts from one child are just annoying – at that moment. Your child needs to develop the self-confidence to say and feel, 'Okay, another time, perhaps,' and do just that.

Some good suggestions for making additional bids might be:

- To start with: 'Please can I play?'
- After watching a little, make a positive observation or interesting comment: 'That's a really cool tower' or 'You make the train go so fast.'

- After a while, again, new suggestions could be made by your child. For example, an exciting suggestion like 'I'm a wizard and we can fly to the castle. Are you ready to fly?' The 'are you ready' bit is quite adult and sophisticated, and young children might not get to this part. But the other children could nonetheless be enticed from their original plan by the idea of the wizard, so allowing the previously excluded child to join in. The key is for your child not to feel defeated or miserable at being left out if (when!) his first bids fail.

Mostly your child needs to learn that he should not just take over instantly and change the game (this is too bossy). Adding something exciting makes the other children think 'That's a good idea' and allows your child to join them. But this takes much skill and not a little patience and self-confidence.

Scenario 4: Helping to find something. Here are Emily and Jessica. Jessica can't find her pencil. What can Emily do or say?
'Helping' is an example of what is sometimes called a 'prosocial behaviour' (*see below*). These same behaviours are also called 'emotionally intelligent behaviours' in Chapter 5. Here the focus is on how these behaviours help build up social relationships. Good suggestions include:

- 'I'll help you find your pencil.'
- 'I'll ask the teacher to give you another one.'
- 'Here, I've got two, use mine.'

Poor suggestions are:

- 'Go away.'
- 'You are silly to lose your pencil.'
- I'd laugh.

Prosocial Behaviours

Prosocial behaviours have been defined as those that aid or are of benefit to others. This can cover a wide variety of behaviours involved in being kind, sympathetic and helpful, sharing and co-operative, listening to others and putting yourself out to rescue or protect another. These are important to teach young children. They help hugely with the development of relationships with adults and with peers alike. But they develop at different rates:

- Helping, sharing and providing comfort to others emerge between the ages of one and two.
- Showing concern for others' distress and comforting a companion can be seen in toddlers, though they are rarely motivated to do this.
- An increase in prosocial behaviours develops over the pre-school period in terms of giving positive attention and approval to others, showing affection, giving way and giving objects (such as toys) to others.
- Showing sympathy, sharing and altruistic behaviours (putting others before you, being concerned more about them than about yourself) develop only slowly during the pre-school years but much more rapidly in middle childhood.

Make a note of which prosocial behaviours you have observed in your child – and which ones you might consider teaching him.

Scenario 5: Making a new friend. This is Ed and this is Jason. How can Ed make friends with Jason?

When you have done this scenario, ask your child, 'Now, how can *you* make friends with Jason?'

Good strategies are:

- Go up to him and say, 'Hello, what's your name? My name is ...'

- Say, 'Do you want to play with the bricks with me?'
- Tell him he has built a really good model.
- Ask him to join in the game with me and my friends.
- Answer his questions.

Poor strategies are:

- Do nothing.
- Say, 'You look silly standing there.'
- Say, 'You are new. I don't like you.'

Here is a chart to record your assessment of how your child managed on the scenarios. You can also use the same chart to record your child's progress during the teaching part.

	Assessment		Teaching	
	Shows good coping ideas	Can't think of good coping ideas	Dates of teaching	Now seems to have better idea
Scenario 1 – wanting another child's toy				
Scenario 2 – accidental upset to another child				
Scenario 3 – joining in play				
Scenario 4 – helping find something that's been lost				
Scenario 5 – making a new friend				

List below other scenarios you come across and assess these too. Examples include: a child asks your child to borrow a toy; a child grabs your child's toy and won't let go; a child wants to join in your child's game.

Remember that everything you have done here with these scenarios is just the start. All these situations come up time and time again – perhaps in slightly different forms – as your child gets older.

You may have been thinking about your child's social relationships and putting into action some of the ideas above. However, once you see him among other children in a group, or you actually leave him at school, you might start to have some concerns. Here are some frequently asked questions on the subject.

I am worried that my child seems to be a loner. Does this matter?

This is an important question. A child can be a 'loner' or on his own because he prefers his own company whilst getting on with his activities. It is an entirely different matter if he is a loner because he has been left out by other children.

The good news is that for many children who interact little

with peers there is no problem, and nothing to worry about. Children don't have to play or be with others all the time to be getting on perfectly well. However, if the child is anxious, fearful or socially unskilled, then this is a different story because he might be, or become, unhappy. The same is true for a child who wants to make friends but is struggling to do so. But a child just wanting to keep himself to himself some of the time, by choice, is perfectly fine.

There is another group of children who may not interact much. These children are neither actively disliked not actively liked and are sometimes referred to as 'neglected' or on the edge of a group. They may, however, want more contact with other children but do not yet have the necessary skills or confidence.

Children do need to be able to initiate positive social interactions – and to respond to others who approach them – even if they like to do things by themselves; specialist professionals say this is an essential developmental achievement. Children who are not making any initiations would certainly need some help. Would you know whether your child is or is not able to make initiations of this sort? It can be hard because the adults in preschool and school facilities may not always notice; children who interact little are not generally disruptive of classroom activities, so don't draw attention to themselves. You may get a better idea if you can make some observations yourself.

I want to be sure my child is happy with other children before I leave him alone with them.
If you worry a lot about leaving your child alone with new peers, it could be that you are behaving in an overprotective way that is unhelpful for his social development. This is not meant to be critical of parents, and you will see that there are ways of moving on. First, if you are *worrying* about your child, your worry can

transmit itself to him. Furthermore, your *behaviour* can make him behave in more anxious ways. For example, if you stay with your child when he starts at nursery school because he seems wary or distressed, this gives him attention that may in fact be rewarding him for being worried. This in turn can lead to your child finding it harder to separate from you, harder to get used to peers and less likely to try things out for himself.

So what should you do? You need to encourage your child to join in social activities, but also take care not to reward or 'reinforce' him for being shy. In the boxes below are some examples of things you can say to your child to encourage him to join in with others. There are also some examples of what might be better avoided, as these could reinforce shyness and hinder his active attempts to become involved in play or conversation. Make sure that you are not *forcing* your child to interact but *encouraging* him to think that he is able to participate, that he can cope, and that he has the skills to do so. This will make him more competent and confident.

Encouraging Things to Say

'Look, that boy is making a Lego tower. You are really good at Lego. Perhaps you can help him. Maybe he'd like another tower.' Alternatives to suggest here might include, 'Maybe he'd like you to hold his tower so he can build it higher.' Or 'Why don't you ask if he'd like you to make a bridge between his two towers.'

'Look, do you think that boy might like to play with your ball with you?'

'What a cool model that girl has made. Why not ask her what she is making? Maybe she'd like this pretty ribbon to go with it? Or do you think she would prefer the fluffy wool?'

What to Avoid Saying

'Don't worry. You don't have to play with anyone if you don't want to.'

'I'll stay and play with you if you don't want to play with those girls right now.'

'Come on, James, don't just stand there. Join in!'

The issue of leaving children alone with other children to just 'get on with it' can have its place. If you have been preparing him well in the skills of getting on with others, it's reasonable to test out, before school, whether he can cope happily. To decide what to do, you will need to have been watching your child carefully. Leaving him for a short while could be beneficial if he seems confident and at ease with others. He will then learn for himself some more strategies for getting on with other children. Of course leaving your child doesn't mean there should be no adult present: pre-school children require careful adult supervision and protection at all times. The idea here is to stand back and keep a discreet eye open from a little distance.

Leaving your child alone with peers can be done in easy stages. At first you could be nearby talking to another adult. This gives your child the feeling that you are not intrusively looking over his shoulder and monitoring everything he does. At the same time you are available for him should he need you. You could, over time, make sure you move progressively further away; be out of sight for brief periods, until you and your child are confident about being separated or at a distance.

When children come to your home, it can be especially important for you to keep a close eye on them and be involved in some of the games and activities. Things can go wrong for young children. How a visit is managed and, above all, how it ends will affect how that child feels about coming again to visit your child. And it can, in turn, affect how your child feels he is liked by the other child.

Be aware that many children who are happy to engage with peers and do so well may nonetheless get upset by other children coming to their home, grabbing their toys, 'messing things up' or winning at games. It is not unusual even for 10- or 11-year-olds to feel upset in this way – but it is even harder for pre-schoolers to handle. Of course, children do need some experience in solving problems for themselves: important skills in negotiation, under-standing another's position and compromise are all to be learned from a disagreement during play. 'Conflict resolution' skills need to start early. You just need to help your child to manage, and gradually and gently give him more and more opportunities to try – that is, *succeed* – in managing independently.

For the more vulnerable child – one who finds friendships or being accepted and liked more difficult – it is especially important to build up out-of-school relationships with class peers, and for these contacts to go well. You have an extremely important role in ensuring that this is the case. Pay attention to the idea of 'over-protecting' described in the last section, but at home, where you are in a position of influence, you can do much to help.

My child finds it difficult to relate to people and there are some odd things about his relationships. What can this mean? Some youngsters may show marked differences to other children in their desire to relate to others or in the way in which they relate. There may be additional concerns about use of language and behaviour that can be considered 'obsessive' and repetitive. Children showing these behaviours may have a developmental disorder. Check this using the following questionnaire.

Have you noticed any of the following in your child?

	Yes	No
He shows little interest in people or does not try to engage with them like others do.	☐	☐
Sometimes he seems 'deaf' and doesn't react to things you say.	☐	☐
He rarely looks at you when you speak to him (poor eye contact).	☐	☐
When you ask him something like 'Do you want a biscuit?' he replies, 'You want a biscuit', not using the correct pronoun 'I'.	☐	☐
He is distressed by other children, or allows himself to be played with passively like a doll, or is ignored by them.	☐	☐
He insists on sameness and dislikes changes to routines.	☐	☐
He has fixations or obsessions with unusual things like vacuum cleaners.	☐	☐
He likes to do or say the same things over and over again and becomes distressed if stopped.	☐	☐
He seems to have no ability to 'mind read', that is, being able to view something from another person's point of view.	☐	☐
He says 'odd' things that are irrelevant to what is going on.	☐	☐
He may find it hard to keep a conversation going, including turn-taking and sticking to the subject without going off at a tangent.	☐	☐

If you have noticed a number of these behaviours, it might be that your child has a social-communication disorder. This would need further investigation, as some of these children also have difficulties with the use of language and may be described as having an 'autistic spectrum disorder' (*see Chapter 8*). A milder form of autistic spectrum disorder seen in the more able child is often referred to as Asperger's Syndrome. A different and rare communication disorder is selective mutism. This means that the child does not speak to others in selected situations, typically outside the home. Teachers may view such children as very shy, but unless they receive professional help the situation can be very difficult to resolve. If you are concerned that your child shows some difficulties in these areas, ask your GP to refer you for a specialist opinion, such as by a child development team.

Is it normal for my child to show aggressive behaviours?

Aggressive behaviours are negative behaviours that may be directed at peers, adults, property or a combination of the three. The behaviours that are seen as aggressive vary according to the age of the child. Younger children usually hit, grab toys and name-call. They show more frequent episodes of brief aggression compared with older children. Older children may use more subtle and indirect means of aggression directed at others (usually peers, although possibly siblings or even parents), such as intimidating or threatening behaviour. This can be referred to as 'psychological bullying'. Although it is not unusual for young children to show aggression from time to time, it is unacceptable when physical or psychological harm is caused to others. From a very early age, children need to be taught that causing such harm cannot be tolerated.

Conflict is different from aggression. Conflict is about being at odds with, or in disagreement with, another, where one person does something to which the other objects. Conflicts can occur either with or without aggression, and both are part of normal development. In the toddler years, girls and boys get involved in similar amounts of conflict. From the age of three to four, gender differences begin to emerge. Later on, boys are more likely to find themselves in conflict situations than girls. Conflicts have a positive importance because they provide children with the opportunity to learn the skills of good conflict resolution, essential for adult life.

Disruptiveness usually refers to behaviours in groups of children where a child behaves in ways that stop or prevent other children from doing what adults feel they should be doing. Aggressive behaviours are seen as disruptive, but other kinds of behaviours can also be viewed in this way, such as messing around in quiet times. However, many children seen as disruptive to teachers also have related difficulties with their peers. The behaviours resulting in disruptiveness in school or other group settings hinder children's progress and happiness, so need to be prevented or stopped.

Can I make sure my child doesn't become a bully or a victim of bullying?

The term 'bullying' rightly arouses strong emotions in adults; no one wants their child to be 'got the better of' and hurt by another. Likewise, if your child gets the reputation for being a bully to others, it may be unpleasant for the parents too. If you are the parent of a bully, do you support your child's position in order to back him up – or do you punish your child? If you are the parent of a victim, how do you tackle the adults who 'allowed' this to happen? Do you tell your child to hit back? Or do you speak to the bullying child yourself? It is very difficult to know which approach to take, either from the side of the victim or the bully. Each case is different. You have to be sensitive both to the circumstances and the personalities involved.

The following points come from research studies and should apply generally in cases of bullying.

- Early family factors are important and can predict which children will become bullies (or 'bully victims' – that is, children who bully others but are also bullied themselves). A study of five-year-old boys showed that those who experienced more hostile, abusive and punitive family treatment during the pre-school years were both aggressive to others and victimised. Therefore, be aware of the attitudes of your family and those around you. Ask yourself if there is an undue tolerance of aggression – is it seen as 'manly', a matter of training for self-defence in later life, part of an acceptable pattern of public displays of aggression? Are there few feelings of guilt or remorse around? Do you give a lot of weight to the importance of 'street cred' and the ability of the individual to take the law into his own hands?

- The bullying child has been shown to be dominant in manner, impulsive and energetic, perhaps too with a higher pain threshold than others (so seeming much 'braver'). However, they are usually less able to distinguish between real and play fights; they have fewer and less effective strategies for dealing with conflict, and a limited repertoire of appropriate social skills.

- Getting a reputation for being a bully is something to be avoided. It has been found that once a child starts to get such a reputation, he is likely to continue to be viewed as aggressive – and yet he may feel more lonely and depressed. This, unfortunately, results in a cycle that is likely to increase rather than decrease the chances of him behaving aggressively as he grows older. In a group where aggression is the norm, peer rejection does not occur because he is only behaving like everyone else, such as in some gangs of teenagers.

If you are already thinking about the prevention of bullying and victimisation, this is a good thing. Many children's lives have been made utterly miserable by being picked on, teased and consistently bullied. There is now much greater understanding of this in schools, and considerable attention has been given to the issue; active steps to prevent it are being taken everywhere.

The underlying behaviours of bullying are aggressive in nature, whether physical or verbal. There are of course situations in which you would want your child to stand up for himself, to make his views known. That can be fine. Being assertive can be a good quality. But a step too far and assertiveness turns into aggression, and here the trouble starts. However, there are things you as a parent can do to prevent your child from becoming either a bully or a victim of bullying.

Let's look first at those children who are bullied – the 'victims'; they need help to feel that the bullying is not their fault and that bullying behaviour by anyone is not acceptable. However, it is also helpful to make sure children have strategies to cope when they meet bullies and to take as much action as possible (you and your pre-school child) to avoid it happening in the first place. Of course, totally preventing bullying from happening to your child may not be possible, but it is worth trying.

Strategies to Help Prevent Your Child from Becoming a Victim of Aggressive Behaviour/Bullying

- **Do** role-play social situations (*see the scenarios, above*) and talk to your child about ways that he might deal with bullying children.
- **Do** teach your child prosocial behaviours (such as sharing and co-operating), the art of initiating interactions and other friendship-making skills.
- **Do** encourage him to try these initiations, to feel fine if he can't find

a way to join in a group he wants to join, and to feel self-confident enough to try other things.

- **Do** help him by ensuring he will have some allies – make friends with other parents and their children from your child's playgroup or kindergarten (friends from outside these groups will not do the trick in the same way).

- **Do** make sure you strike the balance in your parenting – try not to be too intrusive and controlling or too overprotective (*see Chapter 3*). These behaviours by parents have been shown to make children more anxious, more dependent and to have a low self-esteem. In turn such children appear to their peers as more fearful and so vulnerable to victimisation.

- **Do** help your child to learn the skills to avoid 'reinforcing' the bullies. If he reacts by 'giving in', crying, looking miserable or generally acting like a victim, this can reinforce or act like a green light to the bully to do it again.

- **Do** realise that some children have more anxious and fearful temperamental tendencies. Some look physically frail or small. These children might need much more input from you from an early stage to make sure they have the skills to cope, that they practise these skills, and that they have enough allies to protect them and help them become more confident.

As for preventing your child from being a bully, you do have to accept that some children sometimes behave in aggressive and unkind ways to other children, which causes the victims pain and suffering. 'Bullying' behaviour may not always be with the intention of hurting another. You may sometimes feel that your child has been wrongly accused, that he was provoked or that he just copied others. Whatever the case, however, there is the real suffering of the victim to be considered too. It can be as hard to be the parent of a bully as it is to be the parent of a victim, especially if you see no obvious reason why your child should be bullying others. It may be painful and shaming for you to be called in to face up to evidence that your child has caused suffering to another. So how can you prevent that happening?

Strategies to Help Prevent Your Child Becoming a Bully

- **Don't** give your child the message that it is okay to cause hurt. It is important that he can put himself in others' shoes so that he avoids saying or doing things that other children find hurtful. If you let your child think it is fine not to think carefully of others but only of himself then that is what your child will do.
- **Don't** be too angry and punitive with your child. If you do then you are modelling bullying behaviour. This will only lead to more bullying. An over-punitive style of family discipline can itself result in the child becoming hostile and aggressive.
- **Do** notice if your child calls other children names or behaves in ways likely to frighten or upset others. Do talk – gently – to your child about how upset the other child might feel.
- **Do** suggest something kind that your child could do or say to make the other child feel better, to repair the hurt caused. Get your child to think of helpful things for himself.
- **Do** praise your child for being kind, for saying sorry, for reacting in non-aggressive ways when the game does not go his way, and so on.

And Finally ....

During the pre-school years you can make your relationship with your child grow, and watch him develop relationships with others. Your influence can be considerable, so make the most of it. Beware the possible adverse influence of being over-controlling and over-disciplining your child (*look again at the section on parenting style in Chapter 3*). Your approach will make a difference to how well and appropriately your child behaves, but also to how he relates to you, to school and to peers. Look ahead to the next chapter on emotion; several studies show that where there is good child–parent bonding, the child is more likely to have good peer relationships. But most of all, relax and enjoy your child – and also, if you possibly can, enjoy his friends (or friends-to-be) and their parents too.

5
Emotions

Preparing your child emotionally for school is a major part of helping her to settle easily and happily. How she is going to *feel* at school is tied up with how well she is able to *cope* – behaviourally, socially and educationally.

The idea of your child being emotionally prepared for school means first and foremost that you will want her to feel comfortable about the idea of going to school, being left at school and to be ready to make the most of her time at school. It might mean too that, when things go wrong – where there's been an upset of some kind (a lost glove, a mean remark from another child, a perceived rebuke from a teacher) – your child gets over the incident reasonably quickly and smoothly without being unduly traumatised. You would like her to feel confident and at ease in manoeuvring herself in new situations and when meeting new people, without being anxious or afraid. You might like to feel that she is able to relate and respond to others' emotions and, in due course, be able to act in helpful ways.

Think about what you already know about your child's feelings or emotions:

- Which outward expressions of emotion have you already observed in your child?
- Does your child show a wide range of emotions?

- Does your child seem basically contented and to be developing well emotionally?
- As far as you can tell, are you at all worried about your child's emotions/feelings?

Take some time to reflect on your answers to these questions. If you are not sure, observe your child in different situations. When you are ready, fill in the chart below, bearing in mind the various situations you have noticed when your child shows emotions. Think about how you *know* that she is feeling a particular way. Make a mental note, too, of how much time you think your child spends in a state of feeling any of the emotions. The chart itself covers the most basic feelings, which you should be able to observe from your child's facial expressions and behaviours. For example, under 'Angry' you might write 'having toys snatched by brother'. If some of these expressions of emotion are never evident, make a note of that too.

Which situations (from your observations of your child) make her:
Angry
Happy
Sad
Interested
Disgusted
Sympathetic
Fearful/frightened
Surprised
Embarrassed
Ashamed
Proud

Excited
Worried
Other (list) ...
Think about your recent observations (say, over the last couple of weeks):
Has your child shown all the above emotions?
Are some more frequent than others?
What is the pattern?
How would you describe your child *overall*?

With these thoughts in mind, look at the possibilities below and decide which of them would, by and large, be most true for your child. Make a decision about which box (or boxes) to tick based on your general impression, taking everything into account. If the boxes do not cover the emotional characteristics of your child, then put your own descriptions in the 'other' section. Remember, this is only a general judgement to get you thinking about how easy or difficult life might feel for your child as she goes to school.

My child is:

a mostly happy, optimistic child ☐

a confident child ☐

an easily angered, frustrated or emotionally discontented child ☐

a sad, miserable, unhappy child ☐

a fearful/anxious or often worried child ☐

a timid/shy child ☐

other (describe) ☐

If your child is basically happy and confident, she is likely also to be reasonably easy-going and able to cope with changes. She should fit easily into school even if there are some problems for her to face. The easily angered, fearful or miserable child is likely to have a much harder time, so will need most preparation. Timid or shy children can feel miserable or anxious, even if they are potentially quite competent. The child with many worries on her mind may find it hard to relax and enjoy herself too.

Of course, this is simplifying things quite a bit. Even young children show and feel complex emotions. Some may even seem to change from day to day in how they *behave* – and so too, you might deduce, in how they *feel*. The 'Jekyll and Hyde' child who is loving and affectionate one moment and the next an uncontrollable, temper-tantrumming demon, apparently full of anger coming from nowhere, is not an unfamiliar figure. It is important to be able to try to understand where, emotionally speaking, your child is coming from. But it is also important – especially with two (or more) apparently conflicting 'personalities' – to deal with more than just the emotions (*see Chapters 3 and 4*).

To help with the practical aspects of what you might do to help your child emotionally, let's first consider the concepts that are important for emotional development.

Temperament

Temperamental differences – or the characteristics of a child's personal behavioural style – exist between children from the time of their birth. A classic research study by Professors Alexander Thomas, Stella Chess and Herbert Birch in the USA described three types: the 'easy' child, the 'difficult' child and the 'slow-to-warm-up' child. The easy child quickly learns life's routines, seems generally happy and copes well. The difficult child has problems with routines – such as sleeping and getting up – with adapting to new experiences and coping generally. She may react with strong negative emotions to express her feelings. The slow-to-warm-up child reacts slowly to new experiences; she tends not to be very active or responsive and to be fairly negative in her emotions, but copes reasonably well once familiar with people and situations. The difficult and slow-to-warm-up descriptions are useful because such children have been shown to find life more problematic in both pre-school and school years.

While there is evidence that personal style characteristics show stability over the life span, the eminent child psychiatrist Professor Sir Michael Rutter reminds us that 'development is simultaneously about change and continuity'. In an interview in 1999, he went on to say, 'We may have looked different at age twelve than we look now, but we are still the same person.'

Inherited and Environmental Influences

Temperament – which has traditionally been seen as genetic – is now known to be additionally affected by the child's environment.

The biggest environmental influence on your child's emotional development, especially in the early years, is *you*, the parent. Research has shown that for children to develop emotionally as well as possible, the type or style of parenting needs to be responsive to the particular child's temperament. This may sound all very well in theory, but what does it mean in practice? You may feel it is hard enough to identify the features of your child's temperament (don't worry – you are likely to be more expert than you think), but when you add your own and your partner's temperament 'type' or characteristics, things are likely to be even harder!

However, there are ways you could look at this for yourself.

You might start by thinking about your own temperament type, your partner's temperament type and your child's temperament type as they seem now. Some questions you might like to consider are as follows:

- Are you the sort of person who is very active, 'driven', always busy and working at something?
- Are you obsessively tidy and perfectionist?
- Are you relaxed, easy-going, laid back and even 'chaotic'?
- What upsets you?
- What are your chief vices?
- What pleases you?

The list can be pretty long, but it can help you to think about your day-to-day lifestyle and how your approach and characteristics might affect your child. When you have answered the questions and thought more about yourself, and perhaps added some questions of your own, ask the same questions of your child, your partner and any other children in the family. Write your responses in the box opposite. You can then look over this and add to your lists from time to time. Take your time and choose your moment carefully to do this exercise. Be honest about yourself and not critical of your partner. Try to recognise your own patterns – strengths and weaknesses – in your own eyes. It can help if you make sure that you include as many positive characteristics about yourself, your partner and your child as you can, and use these to help you all work around your differences. You will all feel better too if you have more than just a list of criticisms, even if these are intended to be used in a positive way.

From this exercise of listing and thinking about you and your family's characteristics/temperament types, you should be in a better position to analyse what happens in your family and where things go wrong. You will see more clearly what each

Parent 1
Parent 2
Child 1
Child 2

individual brings to the climate of the family and how each affects the pattern of the different relationships (such as mother–daughter) and the family as a whole.

The extent to which your parenting links well with your child's temperament will go a long way towards making life smoother for you and your children (who, if you have more than one, may be very different in temperament style, and so have very different needs).

When describing your partner, be aware that you might well write down different features from those they would use to describe themselves. You and your partner might also describe your joint child in very different terms. This is fine but could lead to problems if you do not handle this sensitively. To one person, being 'laid back' is a positive quality. To a partner who feels overworked it becomes a negative: 'lazy', 'unmotivated' or even 'uninvolved/uninterested in the family'. It would of course be good if you *and* your partner could look amicably together at your joint contributions, but first consider together how you are going to handle your disagreements! Done in a caring and careful way, this exercise can be great for the communication between parents. It is meant to promote better understanding of where you as parents are each 'coming from' and to help you manage your child more easily. There are no rights or wrongs, just differences – but how you handle these differences is important.

Remember, also, that it is not about how similar you are to your child. It is about how you adapt your parenting style – which will develop in relation to your particular temperamental/personality characteristics and experiences – to 'fit' your child more effectively.

You do not have to try to change your temperament – who you feel you are – to achieve this. However, you may be able to adjust your style and consider how you can become more tolerant of your child's or partner's differences from you; how you can perhaps modify your enthusiasms and interests (for example, get involved in your child's or partner's interests); and how you can protect yourself from feeling distressed or hurt because your family is different from you.

When you were thinking about yourself, especially if you are a mum, did you find that you are depressed, or do you have close family or friends who tell you that you seem depressed? If so, your low mood could also affect your child's emotional state. Studies have shown that babies of depressed mothers don't sleep as well and attend less well to their surroundings. Researchers have shown recently that depression in mothers affects how children – but boys especially – develop attention and intellectual skills.

Depression in mothers has also been shown to affect the level of 'attachment' between her and her child. For the sake of your child's emotional well-being and your own, if you – mother or father – suffer from constant low mood, then do seek some professional help.

Attachment

Another way of looking at parents' roles in the development of their children's emotions comes from the concept of 'attachment', as described originally by psychoanalysts Sigmund Freud and, later, John Bowlby. Attachment refers to the emotional links of affection a child develops towards those close to her. Usually, the mother is seen as the first and most important figure, but of course children form attachments to fathers and other family members or special friends as well. The idea is that those children whose principal attachments are 'secure' are also developing most healthily emotionally. Both the child and the parent contribute to how any one child's attachment relationships develop, but other features of the environment may also make a contributing difference.

From the descriptions of different possible 'levels' or 'types' of attachment (*see box overleaf*), you will see, once again, how important your role as a parent is in your child's development. It is of note that clear attachment appears and develops when the child is six to eight months to two years old.

It is worthwhile thinking about attachment in the sense of how well you relate to your child and how your child might behave when you leave. You are, after all, preparing your child to be left – at school – so the idea is a very relevant one.

Researchers have found more problems later on for those children who do not have an easy relationship with their parents

Secure attachment refers to the situation where the child becomes so attached to the parent that she knows she can use the parent as a safe base from which to explore her world. Also after a separation from the parent, the securely attached child will be able to be comforted by the parent, respond with a positive greeting or move forward towards the parent.

Avoidant attachment is the opposite of secure attachment. Here the child does not appear to use the parent as a safe base, nor is she very responsive to the parent. She will not be distressed when the parent leaves or returns. She will avoid or be slow to greet the parent.

Resistant attachment is another example of insecure attachment. The child shows angry, 'resistive' behaviour to the parent (like pushing the parent away) after a separation and cannot be comforted.

Disorganised or confused attachment is yet another type of insecure attachment used to categorise child–parent relationships that do not fit into any of the other categories of insecure attachment. The child may seem confused after separation and show contradictory behaviours like switching between outbursts of crying, then being flat and unresponsive.

than for those who have been shown to have secure attachments. Secure attachments to parents link to more responsive and harmonious peer interactions, larger peer networks and more rewarding friendships. It is important therefore to understand such aspects of your relationship with your child and to use this knowledge to help make it even better.

On the whole, the kind of attachment shown between parents (again, mostly mothers) and their children remains much the same as children get older. Of course, for some families there may be events or circumstances that can make the relationship with the parent more difficult. Disharmony between parents or family events (such as the birth of a new child or a death in the family) or problems with jobs and finances affect child–parent relationships (as can maternal depression, as mentioned above).

You might want to reflect too on the relationship you had with your own parents and how attached you were (and are still?) to them. Research shows that how you view and have reacted to your own experiences matters more than what actually happened to you. If you had an unhappy childhood in which you faced much sadness in your relationship with your parents and had to cope with difficult circumstances, it doesn't automatically mean you are not going to have a secure relationship with your own child. If your parents were hard to talk to or not very 'touchy-feely' – and you would have liked them to have been – you might want to respond to this by making sure you touch and cuddle your own child (and your partner too). This would be a good way of dealing with your experiences – for you as well as for your child.

How you deal with your child's attachments to others is important too. For example, if you are not able to spend much time with your child, for whatever reason, it may well be that she develops close attachments to the person doing the daily caring – often a childminder, nanny or au pair. You should not feel jealous of this; concentrate instead on strengthening your own bonds with your child alongside her other relationships.

You need to think ahead for your child's long-term emotional welfare. If she is attached to or dependent on a temporary carer, it will come as a great loss to her when they have to part company. Your help will be needed to enable your child to come to terms with the loss; the upset to the child can be offset in part by maintaining the continuity of the relation-ship by meetings, encouraging the exchange of cards or talking on the phone. Many changes of the main person caring for your child – with frequent making, then breaking, of attachments – can be particularly damaging. The 'safe' option taken by your child could then be to form no close relationships with people, for fear that getting close to someone means abandonment soon after. Full-time nursery care with multiple and changing carers and too many children in their care can lead, for some children, to behavioural problems such as aggression. If you need full-time care of this kind for your pre-schooler, make sure you know who will be looking after her and ask how they manage 'continuity of care'.

The value of knowing about attachment is that when relationships seem difficult you should not panic or become upset with yourself or your partner ... and certainly not with your child. There are active steps you can take to improve things. Use your observations and thoughts (of yourself and your partner) to take stock of the situation and to think through ways of helping your child by developing her emotional state to one where she can feel mostly relaxed and happy and not – or at least less – tense, angry or tearful.

Attachment is not the only way of considering how children and parents relate to each other. Some psychologists have used the concept of 'connectedness' to demonstrate how parents and children express themselves emotionally to each other. This in turn provides the basis for a growing bond between them. Connectedness for you and your child means that you are able to communicate with each other; you are able to express (and to understand the other's) feelings; and you are able to get around any disagreements you may have.

The idea of connectedness is really important, not only because it describes a key aspect of the parent–child relationship, but also because it has been shown to relate to how well children get on with peers. When the parent–child connectedness has been shown to be positive, the child entering school will have greater success in forming friendships and in being accepted by peers.

Emotional Intelligence

In preparing your child emotionally for school, you may like to think that you are also developing what is called her emotional intelligence. This is an increasingly popular concept. It is seen as the ability to perceive others' emotions, to understand the reasons for their emotions, and to be able to react with emotions that are intelligent and sensitive to that person's emotional state. You need to develop the ability, too, to understand your own emotions. Of course this all takes time, but emotionally intelligent behaviour starts in, and will increase during, the pre-school years. To have the skills equated with high emotional intelligence will make that person more sensitive to others, form the basis of being a good and understanding friend and be helpful in the workplace. For those with good skills – high emotional intelligence – there is a strong relationship to good self-esteem, sociability and satisfaction with life. Emotionally intelligent individuals are also less likely to show aggressive behaviour. Emotional intelligence is very useful for getting on well at school. It is worthwhile trying to develop this sensitivity before your child starts school.

Which types of behaviour are emotionally intelligent? We will look separately at emotionally intelligent behaviour in relation to *understanding others' emotions*, and emotional intelligence relating to *understanding oneself*. You might like to put a tick or the date beside each example in the checklist overleaf when you see your child behaving in any of these ways. Of course, do add your own examples to the ones listed below. The list may remind you how skilled your child already is while also suggesting areas you might like to concentrate on helping her with.

Understanding Others' Emotions	
	Observation dates and comments
Comforts someone who is sad	
Offers assistance to someone who is hurt	
Asks someone who is looking distressed whether they are all right or in need of help	
Notices someone is angry and correctly understands the reason	
Recognises that (say) you have shouted at the dog (or your partner or her or another child) when *really* you are cross because of something else (such as your work or you burned the supper or you had little sleep the night before)	
Understands the idea of trust and that people need to be trustworthy and keep promises (NB Some aspects of this are going to be hard for both parents and children – but that's another story!)	
Respects and tolerates others' privacy/space/ views, even when disagreeing with them	

These concepts are quite sophisticated, and some may not emerge until your child is rather older. What you are doing is preparing her to *understand others'* emotions. By doing this you will help her, other children and yourself avoid becoming involved in unnecessary conflicts. You will help your child feel better about herself as she is less likely to feel rejected or victimised.

Look now at how well your child can *recognise her own feelings*. Since this is harder for you to observe than the recognition of others' feelings, this is best checked by asking her a few questions.

- Can your child tell you what she is feeling when you ask her in situations that might make her angry, sad, disappointed, surprised, happy, frightened, amused? Ask: 'How does/did that make you feel?'
- For any emotions that she can't spontaneously label, prompt by saying: 'Did that make you feel ... (e.g. sad)?' Is your child able to agree or disagree, and if she disagrees, can she offer an alternative emotion? (Remember, just because you think she may or should feel a particular way in a given situation, it may not in fact be the case that this corresponds to the way *she* feels.)
- Can she understand that she might feel several different emotions at the same time? For example, can she understand that it is possible to feel both hurt (emotionally) and angry; jealous but wanting to be kind; happy but also sad? If she doesn't volunteer the information, ask. Say: 'I can see/understand that you felt .... (when that happened/when he did that to you) but did you also feel a bit ...?' This one is particularly sophisticated and you should not worry if your pre-school child is not able to do this just yet.

Your child should also learn that just letting her feelings show may not always be the most emotionally intelligent way forward. Let her know that if she knocks down her brother's brick tower because she's cross with mum for turning off the television when it's bedtime, it's fine to feel angry but not to annoy or hurt someone else. It's not naughty to *feel* jealous of a brother or sister – it's a natural human feeling – but it can be destructive to family life (and later, too, to friendships) to *act* in mean and spiteful ways to compensate for the nasty feelings and experiences. It's fine for your child to tell someone how she feels – like a caring parent or friend – and indeed important to have an opportunity to put her position forward and express herself. However, it is definitely not good to spoil everyone's day by making unkind remarks.

It's also fine for you, the parent, to feel some sympathy for your child's predicament when she feels angry – but *not* fine to let her go away believing it is her right to lash out when she doesn't get her own way. A quick but firm 'Come on now, it's really late, it's bedtime – but you can see the rest of the video tomorrow' will let your child see 1) that you mean business; 2) that you are trying to be fair and kind. If, alternatively, you engage in long discussions, you will just make your child more likely to resist bedtime in the future. Too much dialogue and you could be rewarding her for engaging in fruitless and upsetting (especially to you) exchanges where she 'gets at' you. If you find yourself in this predicament on a regular basis, preventative action is really the best course (*see Chapter 3*).

The emotions of sadness, fear and worry perhaps seem different from those of anger because their outward expressions do not impinge on others in a negative way. However, even this is not quite true as families can be ruled by one member's fears and phobias, needs for reassurance, rituals for avoidance or other coping strategies. For anger, fear, worry or sadness, it is important that your child gets plenty of opportunities to air and talk about her feelings and the source of these feelings.

When you are thinking about teaching young children to understand others' thoughts and feelings, the issue of timing is important. Children need to learn, for example, that telling another child his or her work is useless or terrible might hurt that child's feelings; or that when someone knocks into you it might be an accident and not a deliberate action. This kind of social understanding is a form of 'mind-reading'. From the time they start to speak, children are becoming more aware of others and what others are thinking and feeling, which may be different from their own thoughts and feelings. They can use this to understand others and to guide their own behaviour.

These skills are really important for forming good relationships. However, if you try to teach such skills too early there can be problems; researchers have warned that the child can become too sensitive to others' unpleasant comments and feel 'helpless'. Later on, at school, all children will have to learn to deal with criticisms. Many teachers of young children will praise all (positive!) efforts from a child, just to be on the safe side and to encourage them. Inevitably, however, someone will make a suggestion to a child about how to do something in a better way. This – however gently phrased – will be perceived and understood by some children as criticism. Most adults think that constructive criticism is a good thing but some young children are very sensitive and feel bad – some so bad that they react by giving up.

Therefore, as you prepare your young child emotionally, go slow on teaching her to understand others' intentions until she is nearly five or seems ready. Focus on helping her to feel *confident* about what she does and keep praising her for her efforts.

Preparing Your Child Emotionally

Bearing in mind all the issues discussed so far, you can now plan how to help your child develop emotionally to cope with school. The following summarises the different types of action you could take to achieve this:

• Understand the type of person your child is, her temperament, the triggers that result in negative and positive

emotions. (Look back at your notes on your child's temperament and general characteristics, pages 127 and 131.)

- Understand yourself and your partner, the triggers that result
in positive and negative emotions for you and for them. (Look
back at your notes on your own and your partner's temperament and general characteristics, page 131.)

- Organise your domestic routines so you can minimise the
potential for unnecessary conflict (*see Chapter 2*). This helps to
provide an essentially positive emotional climate in your home.

- Use rewards and positive praise to reinforce good behaviour,
and consider your parenting style (*see Chapters 2 and 3*).
Again, this will help towards creating a positive emotional
climate. Rewards and 'positive reinforcement', as outlined in
these chapters, will help you make your child feel good and
boost her self-esteem.

- Talk regularly with your child about experiences in which
emotions feature. Encourage her to express emotions, placing
a strong emphasis on positive ones. Acknowledge your child's
feelings. Note that expressing only negative emotions, especially anger, will not help your child feel positive, happy and
at ease with the world.

- Teach your child to be emotionally intelligent. (Look back to
the section on emotional intelligence to remind yourself of
the concepts, and look forward to the practical section on
identification of emotions, pages 146–8.)

- Teach your child emotional understanding by working
through some of the play scenarios described in the section
'Analysis of Others' Emotions', pages 148–50.

- Teach your child to use 'positive coping talk'. Encourage her
to remind herself of how well she coped in a previous situation, and how she can use her knowledge of one social
situation to deal with another. For example, 'Other children

came up and talked to me when I was new at the nursery so I'm likely to make friends here too' or 'I was brave and put a plaster on when I hurt my knee so I can be brave if I hurt myself in the playground of my new school.'

● Tell your child in advance of any forthcoming events what is going to happen, where it is going to happen and talk in a way that will reassure her that all will be well.

● Make sure your child has – and knows she has – some emotional supports in place at school. Meeting and getting to know beforehand other children who will be in her class would be a good way of doing this. Let your child know she will always have you to talk to about school and any worries she might have; and that the teachers are also there to help and talk to.

Research has shown that three- and four-year-olds whose emotional knowledge is poor are more likely to be aggressive later (especially boys). However, early awareness programmes have been found to help young children acquire good emotional and social skills.

Going to School

● **Do** tell your child about the school. Describe where it is and what it looks like. Tell her about the fun aspects (with emphasis on what you know she is going to like, but don't give an unrealistic, fairyland picture).

● **Do** tell your child *how* she is going to get to school (walking? bus?) and *who* will go with her (and who will pick her up).

● **Do** take your child to see the school beforehand – a visit to look around and meet the teachers and other pupils would be best; but even the outside is a help (if, for example, you know only shortly before term-time which school your child will be attending).

- **Do** tell your child about the school day, about lunch and timetables.
- **Do** encourage your child to ask questions about school – and answer as honestly as you know how.
- **Do** ask your child what she is looking forward to most – to get her thinking positively about school.
- **Do** ask your child – but take care on this one – if there is anything that might bother her about this new school; you will be better able to allay her fears if you know what she is worried about. On the other hand, it is very easy to put words into her mouth, to give her the idea that there are things for her to be worried about. It will also make you seem anxious, and this could make her even more worried. If she goes to school 'prepared' for there to be worrying things, she will be more likely to react to small events as though she had been proven right; that school is indeed a place to be feared or disliked. By contrast, if she is prepared for newness, an exciting environment and change (and has learned the skills to cope), she should enjoy school better.

Separation

It is often very hard for children and parents to move from the stage where they are together all the time to the child coping 'alone' at school. One of your aims in preparing your child emotionally for school is to get her to the stage of being able, happily, to separate herself from you.

Preparing for separation should start early, by allowing your child to feel secure and happy with you. When you feel she is able to take the next step, start gradually to move your attention and then yourself physically away from her. Try this out at a friend's house – can you stand and talk to your friend near your child without her worrying or demanding your attention? Can you move outside the room (bearing in mind that pre-school children shouldn't be left alone unattended)? What about at a playgroup? Start by talking to another adult, so removing the focus of attention from your child, then gradually move yourself physically further away. Of course, if you do this, you will need to have made sure first that 1) your child knows that someone else is in charge and will look after her, 2) you are coming back – and have agreed with your child when that will be. Do stick to what you have said and not try to trick her by staying away for longer. It's better to build up slowly and let her tell you when you can stay away for longer. You can help by commenting on how well she is getting on by herself; you are aiming to reinforce her coping, and to get her away from the idea that she needs you there to be safe and all right.

If, after all your efforts, your pre-school child hates to be left even for short periods, this is evidence of 'separation anxiety'. Important questions to ask are:

- Is your child feeling ill, or has there been a recent change in the family (a birth, a death, a house move) that might have unsettled her?
- Have there been arguments or problems within the family, or have you been stressed in any way? These can all worry a child and set the scene for feeling anxious or fearful generally.
- Could you have given her the 'message' that she cannot cope on her own?
- Does your child show any other specific fears (or phobias) that are preventing her from being left alone?

If any of the above points is true, you will need to deal with these alongside further attempts, if you can, to encourage her independence. On the last point about fears, it is not uncommon for young children to be afraid of specific things such as the dark, insects, animals such as dogs, or water (swimming pools, some-times even the bath). If your child shows any of the above fears to a marked extent, you might want to consider a specific plan (*see pages 153–5*) to assist her to be less fearful.

Identification of Emotions

The most obvious way we judge people's feelings is by observing their facial expressions. Of course, these do not necessarily tell us everything. A person's body language is important too. For example, many people 'hang their heads down' if embarrassed or ashamed, or thrust their heads forward if angry. Some of these complex expressions may be much too hard for pre-schoolers to pick up, but they will do so in time. The context of the emotion also gives many clues as to how people might be feeling. A half (but serious) smile when talking to someone who has been hurt is an indication that the person is trying to show sympathy.

You can now check for yourself to see what level of emotional knowledge your child has, and teach her how to recognise and identify what others are feeling. To help you, some faces have been drawn opposite. You might also like to collect pictures of facial expressions from magazines and newspapers. To make the situation even more realistic, put the cut-out pictures onto the face of a small doll or finger puppet. You can then act out some different situations to demonstrate the emotion. Look at the chart on page 148 and record what your child is able to do.

Show your child one of the dolls/puppets 'wearing' one of the following emotions and ask: 'How does he/she (the puppet) feel, do you think?' From your child's answer you'll know if she can *identify and name* the particular emotion/feeling. If she is unwilling or unable to do this, try asking, 'Show me the one that is sad/happy' and so on. This will enable you to find out that, even if she cannot perhaps name the emotion, she can at least identify it.

If your child can identify and label the emotions, next ask some questions about what would make the doll (or a named peer, sibling or parent) feel happy/sad and so on. This will help you identify the *depth of understanding* your child has. Does she understand that some things might make everyone feel a particular way – for example, that you might cry when a pet dog dies – and that some things are more important or distressing or thrilling to particular people – for example, Tammy used to feel especially sad when her security blanket was in the wash.

Sad   Angry/cross   Surprised

Happy   Afraid/scared   Excited

Hurt/tearful   Shy/timid

	Can identify and label	Can point to named emotion
Sad		
Happy		
Angry/cross		
Afraid/scared		
Hurt/tearful		
Surprised		
Excited		
Shy/timid		
Other (*see also your list of the emotions observed in your child on pages 126–7)*		

Analysis of Others' Emotions

As discussed earlier, understanding and knowledge of others' (and one's own) emotions are seen as important for guiding social behaviour. If a child knows what another child is feeling then she will be able to behave in a way that is appropriate to that situation. On the other hand, if your child misinterprets what others are really meaning, conflicts are more likely to occur. For example, if she thinks another child who is shouting at her is angry with her, she might react by crying, shouting back or even hitting out.

If, however, she considers that the other child is shouting at her for some other reason, she will behave differently. If she thinks the other child is really upset with someone else, she might ask what the matter is, or offer to play.

Consider the following scenarios and use them to teach your child emotional understanding and appropriate responses to others.

Scenario 1: Here is John. John gives Jill a present of a ... (name a toy your child would like). How does Jill feel?

Replies showing emotional understanding of the other are: 'Jill feels happy/excited/cuddly and warm.' If, however, your child says 'angry' or 'sad' or 'annoyed', ask her what makes her think Jill would feel like that when she likes the present. From her answer you may understand what she is feeling in general, or about some present-giving experience she has found difficult.

If you want to check on social knowledge, ask a second question: 'What does Jill say?'

Then ask, 'John gives Jill a ... (name a toy less exciting to Jill). Jill does not like this present. How does Jill feel? What should Jill say to John?'

This scenario will tell you whether your child understands that a) receiving presents gives pleasure; and b) when you receive something intended to please, but which does not in fact give pleasure, you have to hide your feelings so as not to hurt the giver. You might find it helpful to make the scenario personal to your child. Say: 'Now (your child's name), how do you (or did you, if you have an example that she would remember) feel when you get/got a present you didn't like? What did we do?'

If your child hasn't understood these concepts, you could repeat the scenarios to teach her appropriate things to say and to understand the reasons for saying them.

Scenario 2: Your child cuts her finger on a knife. Her friend Ben is also sitting at the table. Ben asks your child kindly if her finger hurts.

Now ask your child how she feels? Happier? Less frightened? And how was Ben feeling? Was he kind and sympathetic?

Then suggest that Ben's response is quite the reverse: he says your child was silly to play with the knife and it serves her right.

How does your child feel now? Sad? Angry? Unhappy that Ben isn't being nice? And Ben himself? Is he being unsympathetic? Is he perhaps jealous of all the attention being paid to your child? Can she think of any other reason why Ben isn't being nice?

Again, see if your child responds to your questions appropriately. You can enlarge the scenario if you wish to include other possible reactions from Ben ... and from your child. For instance, he says, 'I bet it didn't really hurt,' or 'That was a naughty knife,' and your child might have a number of responses.

Scenario 3: Here is Bill. He is building a tower. Jane comes over and knocks it down. What does Bill think? How does he feel?
You might wonder if your child thinks Jane knocked the tower over by accident or on purpose. Ask your child, too, how Bill might feel in both of these cases – and would it make any difference to what he did next?

Scenario 4: Here is Ellie. She has come to the playgroup for the first time and she doesn't know anyone. How do you think she feels? What would make her feel happier, do you think?

Scenario 5: Here is James. He has just broken a glass at his friend Luke's house. How do you think he feels? Here comes Luke's mummy. What do you think she says to James? How does James feel now? Has Luke's mummy made James feel all right, or is he still going to feel bad?

These are just some examples, so do add your own.

Acknowledging Your Child's Negative Feelings

Consider the following dialogue:

Your Child (YC): Katie (sister or friend) took my doll this morning.

You: Did she, sweetheart?

YC: (silent)

You: Did you mind that? Was that okay with you? Were you playing a game together?

YC: No, she just took it. She hurt it.

You: Oh dear. Do you want to show me?

YC: (gives doll)

You: Poor doll. How did *you* feel?

YC: (silent)

You: Did it make you feel upset? Sad?

YC: (nods)

You: And angry too perhaps?

YC: (nods) She was really mean.

You: Yes, I can see why you were really cross. But you hit Katie afterwards, didn't you?

YC: She was horrid.

This mum has acknowledged her child's feelings – but she will now need to take the conversation further to explain why it is not good to hit another child, even if she was right to feel very cross.

You want your child to be able to express feelings rather than bottle them up. Those who have no outlet for their angry feelings can be like a volcano – quiet for a time then boil over with some kind of (often hurtful, physically or psychologically damaging) outburst. Or if the feelings are to do with being hurt or sad, your child can become very low or depressed or start to show psychosomatic symptoms like tummy aches or headaches caused by her feelings. Sometimes you can observe other signs such as 'tics' (involuntary movements of the eyes or mouth) if your child is under pressure, although these can come and go in childhood with no real connection to underlying worries. In extreme cases, you should consult a specialist.

A further avenue to explore is the acknowledgement of the feelings of the person who might be on the receiving end of your child's negative, angry emotions. You could perhaps continue the earlier dialogue with your child about Katie in this way:

> You: How do you think Katie was feeling?
>
> YC: Horrid Katie.
>
> You: Mmmm. But do you think perhaps she felt she was left out of your game?
>
> YC: (silent)
>
> You: She loves playing with you, you know. Maybe that is why she snatched your doll? Do you think that is how she felt – left out by you?

A word of caution: there is a potential danger in using – or rather using without being sensitive to all the consequences – these kinds of dialogue with your child, as in the examples just given. You could be rewarding or reinforcing your child's expression of negative emotions by spending a lot of time talking to her, alone, in a kindly way, after she has hit her sister. This could make her more likely rather than less likely to hit again. Turn to Chapter 3 for discussions on reinforcement, praise and reward. So long as you are aware of what can happen, it seems reasonable to acknowledge your child's feelings. It is also helpful to have a strategy in place to deal with feelings when your child starts school.

Fears and Worries

Children who are fearful can develop strong fears or 'phobias' about many things, such as water (in swimming pools or baths), loud noises, animals seen as threatening or even being at school (school phobia – although this could be more about separation anxiety). To get your child to understand and talk about feelings, you may need to encourage and explore them together. Be careful, of course, not to put words into her mouth. When a child says little at first, you can ask gently if this – or that – is what she might be feeling, and then see what she has to say. This is a good opportunity, too, for you to connect with your child.

Children can become 'sensitised' or so over-aware of certain triggers that they react with the emotion of fear. For example, a child frightened of going swimming may show a general fear of swimming pool buildings or even her own bath. You need to get your child accustomed to the feared situations or objects gradually but systematically. For example, for the common fear of swimming pools you could take action along the following lines:

1 Make lots of opportunities to do water play with your child at home.
2 Model enjoyment of water and swimming yourself or using a favourite doll.
3 At the same time, make trips to go past your local pool. Gradually get your child to go to the door ... and inside (this may take several trips). Find out what has been worrying her about the water or the pool. If possible, go inside the pool building for a treat of something from the vending machine or snack bar – and watch the other children enjoying themselves. Bring dolly or teddy or Spiderman along too.

4 Take a trip to the shops together to choose some 'cool' swim gear.

5 When your child is ready, take her with you to the pool wearing her new swim gear to watch you swim.

6 Encourage her to dip one toe in the water – then another, then a foot – then to sit on the edge.

7 Encourage each stage, using praise and reward as necessary, until eventually she can get completely into the pool.

To help your child overcome any fear or phobia:

- Never get impatient.
- Reassure where needed that she will be fine (but without engaging in long reassuring discussion as this will probably only 'reinforce' or strengthen her fears).
- Praise and even reward her for each step forward.
- Make each 'step' towards the final goal only very slightly harder than the last.
- Don't be tempted to go too fast as you don't want her getting frightened all over again.

Fears or phobias are not the only behaviours children can show in response to distress. Some children can have worries that they express in the form of physical pain, such as tummy aches or headaches, or in lack of appetite or poor sleep. It may be important for you to consult your GP in order to reassure yourself first that these symptoms do not have a physical basis. Once you know that there is no physical cause, take care not to reinforce the idea that your child needs to be worried about her pains. Drawing too much attention to these by constantly asking how she is feeling may prolong the problem. Find out with a gentle chat if she has any special worries, if you can. Try to help with possible sources of worry – for example, teaching her how to make friends or to cope with her younger brother, or how to be brave going to her own bed at night. Keep talk about pain to a minimum, but occasionally reassure her that her pains should soon, perhaps gradually, go away. Give your child plenty of attention in other ways, maybe even using a reward plan to reinforce coping. However, if you find that these simple measures are insufficient and that your child is continuing to suffer, then you may need some professional help from your GP, health visitor or a psychologist.

Jealousy between Siblings

Sometimes it must seem that you can't please one child without annoying the other and making her feel jealous. Jealousy is a common childhood emotion, usually viewed as negative. It is especially evident when there are brothers or sisters around demanding your limited attention, and it is often called sibling rivalry. 'It's not fair' must be a cry heard at some time or other by every parent in the land where there are two or more children. But can you treat all children equally? Can you be 'fair'? Is it enough just to say, 'Life isn't fair!' And can you allow one child who is nasty to the other to get away with it?

Well, of course, it is not easy; children's personalities and needs may be very different, or, if similar, equally demanding on your time. So what should you do?

Prevention is a good way to start – a process that should begin even before your second child is born. Help your older child to feel a useful part of the newcomer's arrival. Get her to help you prepare. Of course, she will continue to need lots of special time and attention from you; she can't be only 'mummy's special helper'. Tell her that the baby will admire and look up to her – and how wonderful it will be for you to have your big girl with you to help. When the baby arrives, give your toddler a special present 'from' her new brother or sister.

As the baby gets older, help your older one think with you about how to deal with the 'nuisance' of the younger one taking or spoiling toys. This approach is much better than you getting angry after the event – either with the older (for hitting the younger) or with the younger (for being destructive).

At a later stage too you can reward both children 'for getting on well together' or 'for helping each other'. This will make them more likely to be kind – at least more frequently – to each other than to squabble. Of course, some disagreements are entirely normal between brothers and sisters – and even desirable. Some research has shown that the disagreements and squabbles between siblings provide them with good 'practice' opportunities in a safe environment to deal with conflict in the wider world. But it can be very wearying for the poor parents if children fight a lot, especially if they have several children.

Extra problems for both parents and children can arise if one of the children is disabled or sickly; much adult attention and worry have to be devoted to the needy child. Many of the siblings of such children feel neglected. These children may well be harbouring strong emotions – of jealousy and even hatred, of sadness for the sick sibling but also the wish for more attention for themselves. It is very important to acknowledge these feelings in your well child and to try to find ways to help compensate, however needy the sick or incapacitated child.

If a younger child is brighter or more generally able than an older, the older child can easily feel inadequate and unhappy. Strong feelings of jealousy and years of having 'a chip on her shoulder' can be the result. Children who are close in age and of the same sex may find this especially hard – as the competition is so much more visible to the less able child. You may need to work very hard and continuously over many years to prevent this from becoming a life-long problem. Conversely, a younger child may find it very hard to follow in the footsteps of the older one. You need to bolster the morale of the one feeling most disadvantaged; give practical help to acquire or compensate for the lacking skills; provide opportunities for the needier one to develop special interests and skills – in sport, music or drama, for example. Use that child's skills and interests to help you make your choice. You may feel it is bad to deprive the more able one, but maybe you can find different things for them. Your aim is to reduce the easy comparisons of differences between the children and to give each things they can feel good about. The more able child has feelings too, so do take care that they do not end up feeling unloved or less favoured.

Parental Conflict

Strife between parents is very likely to have a bad effect on children. If your child witnesses rows – or is 'used' by parents in their arguments – then they are going to suffer more. She will feel bad; may have angry feelings directed at one or both parents; may become clingy and fearful or show problems with behaviour.

Acknowledging your child's feelings is important. If you do this, however, beware of trying to make your child take your side against your partner. You may see the problems that you and your partner are experiencing as being largely or wholly the other's 'fault', but your partner – or ex-partner – is still the parent of your joint child. Your child carries genetic similarities to her other parent as well as to you. She will be better off thinking well of or at least understanding the problems of both parents. For your child's emotional benefit you need to think carefully about her feelings towards both of you.

Parental conflict (which may lead to separation or divorce) and its impact on children's behaviour and development is obviously a huge area, and beyond the scope of this book. If this situation applies to you, however, it will be strongly in your child's interest emotionally, as well as socially and behaviourally, for you to find every way possible to minimise its potentially damaging impact on her. Do consider counselling and family conciliation if a separation (or divorce) seems to be where you are heading. If you, the parents, can maintain an amicable relationship with each other, your child is likely to be happier and to cope better.

Additionally, you may worry that being a single parent will in itself have a bad effect on your child's development. However, research has shown that the main problem for single parents is not so much that they are without a live-in partner. Rather, what causes problems for children is if the sole parent is isolated and without support.

And Finally ...

The most important point about preparing your child emotionally for school is that both you and your child can find ways together for her to feel contented and happy. This is likely to be much assisted if you also feel the same way. There may well be problems of one sort or another – life events or circumstances, the nature of your child – that make things difficult, but a way can be found to get around the problems. As the researchers have said, do not – especially in difficult circumstances – leave this to chance. Teach your child to develop her understanding of emotions – her own as well as those of others. Teach her to understand and cope with situations that can give rise to sadness or anger. Deal with fears and phobias in small, graded steps. Prepare your child for specific experiences she is likely to encounter as she starts school. The more prepared she is emotionally, the more likely she will be to settle easily into school, to make friends and to progress well educationally.

PART B
LEARNING TO LEARN

6
Play

Play is what all children do, what we expect them to do, what we want them to do: activity or games entered into for the sake of it, for enjoyment, for no particular purpose and 'just because'.

You may ask if starting to list play amongst other skills to be taught will take away from the pleasure of children playing. A more interesting question, though, is: do children need to be prepared for something they already do, something they do with considerably greater skill than adults? As we mature we lose some of our inventiveness, our ability to be carefree and just seize the moment, to make something out of nothing, to make a world from berries and grass, an airport from blocks of plastic. What need is there to formalise this?

Play is the medium, the means, of acquiring much knowledge in early childhood. There are many aspects to play, all important for the developing child and the basis of many different skills. Play should be fun but it also has practical benefits. The skills children learn through play may be physical, creative or social; they may also be educational. Your encouragement of play will do much to prepare your child for school, and there is no doubt you are already doing it.

It is easy to associate the idea of play with the modern toys and equipment that toy manufacturers so thoughtfully tempt us (and our children) with – Batman, Barbie, GameBoy, PlayStation and, of course, computer games galore. Is all this bad because it leaves nothing to the imagination? Does it foster greed because children always want more or to be like other children they see? Television and other advertising has done much to promote the need and desire for such toys, and many parents worry about that. But there may be less to worry about than some might think.

That's because the toys and equipment themselves are only part of the story. How children use them and the way you and others involve yourselves in your child's world of play are important other parts. Yes, of course there are many other influences too, such as your child's cultural environment and his experience of life and fantasy, from the media and elsewhere. The things he says and does in play will reflect these experiences. For example, children will invent games based on favourite television programmes or characters … or on their parents' jobs; they will use places in gardens or parks to make dens in or play hide-and-seek; they will use whatever materials are to hand to act out roles or play games with.

Skills Children Learn Through Play

Physical Play

Through physical play with various types of indoor and outdoor equipment and materials, children can practise and improve their gross motor skills (whole body movements) and their fine motor skills (co-ordination of the hands and fingers). At the same time they will learn to improve their balance, stamina, speed and hand-eye co-ordination. These skills form a vital part of the child's physical development. Where games, such as football, require co-operation with others, another skill is thrown in for free. Patience and turn-taking are added extras from physical play. 'Rough and tumble' play – the friendly side of fighting – is a physical kind of play that permits the expending of energy. However, children can also learn about boundaries from this type of play (you don't try to hurt people nastily) and that appropriate physical touch between human beings is fine. It is much like the 'puppy fighting' seen in young animals. Mostly it is boys who engage in this kind of play; girls are more likely to run around and chase each other with briefer moments of physical contact.

Construction Play

This type of play involves a wide range of building materials to create shapes or objects. Materials include blocks, bricks, straws and many commercial sets. Also included in this group are puzzles and inset boards, where pieces have to be correctly placed together or in a board.

Construction play is good not only for physical skills but also lends itself to the development of educational skills.

Construction activities all involve and so develop fine motor skills that are important for writing. Children who are clumsy or poorly co-ordinated may have difficulty with tasks such as building a tall tower. Some of these children may grow out of this problem with a little practice. Others may in fact have a 'developmental co-ordination disorder' (or 'dyspraxia', where the problems also include 'motor planning' – the skills of moving the body or parts of the body to the right position for a particular task). For a more detailed discussion of dyspraxia, its impact on children's written work and suggested solutions, see Chapter 11.

Another set of skills achieved with this kind of play is in the visual sphere: children learn visuo-spatial skills that are needed for writing and for maths – they become aware of how objects relate to each other in two dimensions, as in the flat puzzles, and three dimensions, when building towers or stacking boxes.

Whilst children play with constructional toys, they will learn the words to describe what they are doing. They learn skills important for language, reading and numeracy, for example by matching shapes, colours, sizes, and making patterns and counting.

Creative Play

Creative play is play using materials, but there is more scope for creativity than in constructional play. Creativity is the inventive side of play and the outlet for children to express their thoughts and feelings, and to develop their thinking and reasoning skills. Creative play is therefore vital for both emotional and intellectual development. Much of it involves language, even words that are not spoken out loud. Children will be learning to distinguish features of the materials they are working with, such as colour or form, and will be learning the words for these. Therefore creative play is essential, too, for language development.

There are three main types of creative play, depending on the materials that shape the skills acquired:

- Pens/pencils/paint
- Modelling/sculpting materials
- Music

Pens/Pencils/Paint

Most young children love to pick up a paintbrush, dip it into pots of thick, brightly coloured paint and daub it onto fresh, clean paper. It can be a very satisfying moment. Taken further, children can try to create patterns, shapes or versions of people, animals, events or even moods from the colour and style. Children learn hand-eye co-ordination – they need to be able to 'tell' the brush where to go on the paper to obtain the effect they want. Crayoning and drawing offer much the same but also help develop the skill of pencil control. These are very important skills for starting to write.

Modelling/Sculpting

Children can get a wonderful experience of modelling and sculpting with a wide variety of materials. They can make models with clay, and recycle foil or plastic bottle tops, wool or pasta pieces for constructions or collages, and so on. Some materials give quite a sensual pleasure, such as wet hands and moulding clay. With less structured materials than, say, building blocks, children can be much more inventive in their designs and productions. As they manipulate materials they learn science – how glue works, how to balance objects or change the form of materials (like soft newspaper to hard papier-mâché). They learn how things fit together in three dimensions (the visuo-spatial skills). They learn how to make things decorative and useful, or simply decorative. (Well, they will … in time.) And, of course, they have fun.

Music

Music is much more on the agenda in schools than it used to be, which is wonderful because it has so much to offer children. For thousands of years, music has been a feature of self-expression and communal closeness – think of African drummers, Welsh and Russian folk singers, Scottish pipe players. 'Play' with music from an early age will provide the foundations for such higher achievements. Children play with sound from a very early age. Babble is a baby's way of experimenting with sound – repeating, testing and changing sounds. Babble involves copying – babies imitate the cooing and booing noises their parents playfully use in 'talking' to him, but they also create and elaborate as they try out their own sounds. The exchanges between mother or father and child are social but they are also about hearing and listening to sounds as well as giving meaning to sounds. These sounds and games involve pitch and rhythm as well as meaning. Therefore, in addition to the voice being a major instrument for language and for creating and developing social relationships, it is also the first musical instrument.

Most very young children soon find pleasure in banging or knocking objects together to produce sounds. They will be starting to learn about pitch and quality of sound, that different objects produce notes that are higher or lower, and with a different texture to them; they need to learn to listen. Rhythm is another important part of music that children learn through nursery rhymes as well as through movement and dance. As they try to keep to a particular rhythm, they develop physical co-ordination.

Music links with mathematical thinking. As they try to copy a sound, children learn order and sequencing, distance between intervals, counting and matching. Good listening skills require concentration and attention (essential for good progress at school). Children can 'compose' their own music and in this way learn to express themselves and be creative. Many pre-schoolers have an array of sound-making instruments – sticks, rattles, bean-filled pots, shakers – to have fun with. More formal instruments such as recorders or violins may be started successfully in the pre-school period if the child seems interested, and this can be a great asset for later years.

Imaginative or Dramatic Play

This type of play has several aspects to it: it can be fantasy play where the child pretends to be something or someone, such as an alien or Batman, and may like to dress up in the right costume. Or it may involve the use of symbols – objects that stand for something else. Dolls' houses and play with small farm animals come into this group. Children's use of symbolic play is strongly associated with their development of language comprehension. Children may play different roles in a joint game. Fantasy play doesn't always need to involve materials, nor does symbolic play, such as with finger games like 'This little piggy went to market'.

Children learn to put themselves in others' shoes and develop their social and emotional skills through role play (when they pretend to be someone else) and symbolic play (including play with miniature people and animals). In this way they can learn about specific aspects of others' lives – like those of nurses and doctors in hospitals, police on the beat, fire fighters, postmen and women, builders and teachers. As they act out their games with other children playing different characters, they learn to co-operate and share. They learn to think logically. For example, if someone says or does a particular thing, what would be the consequences for another person? Or if a 'child' in a make-believe 'school' falls and hurts himself, does the 'teacher' take charge, and what could she ask another 'child' to do to help? And so on. They learn to problem-solve and improvise. When one 'character' has a problem to solve, they have to find a 'solution'. When one prop won't do, they have to find or make something else. So many things are learned by seemingly unstructured play of this kind; children come to understand much by playing things out themselves – they do not learn only from you, teachers or others telling them.

Formal Games with Rules

Into this category come all the more formal games such as card games, board games or battleships. It can also include team sports such as football or cricket.

This type of play involves very sophisticated abilities. Children have to learn not only the particular skills of the game, but how to relate to the other players as well. This involves skills of sharing, waiting for a turn, anticipating others' reactions, perhaps giving in to or helping another player, coping with losing – and how to be a good winner.

The Qualities of Play

Dividing play into five categories depending on the materials used as just described, is only one way of understanding play. It is useful to look at other ways play can be described, as this makes it easier to observe and understand the ways children learn through play. The use of materials in play can be further classified according to the actual use to which they are put and the **degree of symbolism** involved:

1 **Symbolic** play *with the child himself as the only material*. The child uses himself or parts of himself to be something, such as marching to be a soldier.

2 **Symbolic** play *with materials*. The child treats the materials he is using as something other than what they are. For example, to be a soldier he marches with a plant pot on his head and a stick under his arm.

3 **Non-literal (but not symbolic)** play *with materials*. The child uses materials simply in a way they were not designed for, such as putting building blocks into his mouth or chucking them; pummelling or squeezing dolls rather than playing with them. This kind of play has also been called 'partial play' because it doesn't make full, or appropriate, use of the materials.

4 **Literal** (or 'appropriate') play *with materials*. This is when materials are used as intended, such as building a tower with blocks.

Children can move very swiftly from one category to another, for example into a fantasy game whilst building a tower of bricks.

A completely different way of looking at play is in terms of the degree of social participation – how much and in what way the play involves others. Six categories of a child's **social involvement** in play have been distinguished:

1 **Unoccupied**: watches anything of passing interest; twiddles thumbs or wanders around.
2 **Onlooker**: more involved in observing others but does not join in.
3 **Solitary play**: the child plays alone and independently from other children around him.
4 **Parallel play**: the child is essentially playing on his own but doing the same thing as his neighbours – he may talk to them but the play itself is *beside* rather than *with* the others.
5 **Associative play**: the child plays with others and there is talk, and borrowing and lending of materials. However, each child is largely doing his own thing, acting as he wishes.
6 **Co-operative play**: this is the highest level. Labour is divided. Roles are allocated. The children have to co-operate for the whole to work, such as with board games and hide-and-seek.

From this social classification of play much can be learned about a child's skill in relating to others, but it also gives clues as to how the child views himself.

The Development of Play

In examining the sophistication of your child's play, it is necessary to take age into account. To remind yourself of how play skills develop, and so put your child's skill level in context, look at the box below. The list shows the order in which different types of play generally appear, and some of the ages at which they typically start. If your child is younger than four-and-a-half, he may not have developed some of these more sophisticated levels of play, particularly games with rules. This is perfectly normal, though you may see many differences between children of the same age.

The Developmental Progression of Play

1. **Functional play:** simple repetitive movements such as running about, pushing a car back and forth, kneading clay but not making anything: mostly for the first two years of life.

2. **Construction play:** creating or constructing something like a house out of blocks, drawing a picture or doing a puzzle: mostly from ages three to six.

3. **Make-believe/fantasy play:** acting out imaginary roles in different situations, such as playing house, nurse and doctor or characters from television: from around the age of three.

4. **Games with rules:** understanding and following rules in play activities such as board games, cards, hopscotch or cricket: by four many children can engage in games with simple rules. Games with more complex rules are not usually understood by children until after they have reached school age.

A child's gender also makes a difference to play. Different styles of play have been shown to exist between boys and girls – as you have no doubt already noticed. Boys in general prefer to run around more, to climb things and to play-fight. Girls in general prefer symbolic play, role-playing and side-by-side or social games. The difference in the physicality of play in turn affects children's choices of playmates. Quieter girls are more likely to choose other quieter girls. A lot of boys like to play in larger groups, such as to play football.

Many of you will have opportunities to watch your child at play with others of the same age. If you make a detailed observation over a continuous period of time, you will be able to learn much about your child's social skills, his range of play skills and his general ability to cope in an environment similar to school.

Observing and Assessing Your Child's Play

If you can make an opportunity to observe your child at play, do so from as close a distance as you can without disturbing the children. Try to look busy and not obviously staring at your child. It helps to be close so that you can hear what the children are saying to each other. It can be fascinating as well as instructive. Try to observe continuously for at least half an hour at a time. If your child has just come into a new group of children, he is more likely to be a bit shy and hesitant at first. You might find it helpful to record what you see. The Play Observation Chart below can help you to do this. Your observations can easily be recorded in terms of the categories from the three sets of classifications (*see pages 162–9*). This is explained in more detail below. Take a new column on the chart for each play activity you observe (if it is very fleeting, you may find it easier to skip over rather than record). Head the column with a brief description of the play, for example in the space under 'Activity 1' write 'Jigsaw at table', then note:

1 The **materials** or toys used (such as puzzles, dressing up, play dough, tricycle), marking 'none' if no materials are used.
2 **Use** of these materials – a judgement about the appropriateness of the use to which the materials are put. Say whether the play is appropriate, partial, or only fingering/fiddling.
3 The **type** of play (whether physical, construction, creative, imaginative or formal games with rules).

Play Observation Chart

	Activity 1	Activity 2	Activity 3	Activity 4
1. Materials None: Type of materials: **2. Use** Appropriate: Partial: Fiddles or fingers only: **3. Type** Physical/gross motor: Construction: Creative: Imaginative/symbolic: Formal games with rules: **4. Social category** Non-social (unoccupied/onlooker/solitary): Parallel play: Associative play: Co-operative play: **5. Time spent on activity**				

4 The **social category** showing the extent to which your child is involved with other children in his play. Say whether the play is non-social (and, if so, whether unoccupied or as an onlooker or solitary) or social (and if so whether parallel, associative or joint).

5 The **time spent** in the play activity. If the activity lasts for only a few moments (say less than a minute), mark with a tick (or cross if you prefer) the appropriate column each time you observe it. If your child spends at least a few minutes in any one type of activity, you can write down the actual amount of time spent.

You might need several pieces of paper, as children can involve themselves in many different activities over half an hour or so. There is one blank chart for you to fill in opposite.

Once you have observed your child at play, complete the three-part checklist below by ticking the appropriate column. You may be able to complete the checklist without the observations but you will have a more accurate picture and understanding of your child if you get a chance to observe with a more focused eye.

Play Checklist (Part 1)

	Regularly	Sometimes	Rarely/ never
Does your child make appropriate use of toys and materials, such as building with bricks, modelling with play dough?	☐	☐	☐
Does your child engage in fantasy or symbolic play, using himself or materials to be something different from what he is (like being a fireman and putting out fires)?	☐	☐	☐

	Regularly	Sometimes	Rarely/never
Can your child use miniature toys (such as animals, tea sets, garages and cars, tool sets) in symbolic play (such as playing farms, making tea, driving to the shops)?	☐	☐	☐
Can your child select toys/materials for himself and settle down independently to play?	☐	☐	☐
Can your child concentrate on one activity or game for a substantial period of time (at least ten to fifteen minutes at age four)?	☐	☐	☐
Does your child settle with or near other children and engage in parallel play (largely on his own but doing the same activity as his neighbours)?	☐	☐	☐
Does your child settle with or near other children and engage in associative play (child largely playing his own games but with more talk or exchanging of materials with neighbours)?	☐	☐	☐
Does your child engage in more complex play with other children, involving different roles and co-operation including turn-taking (such as witches and dragons, 'school', shops)?	☐	☐	☐

Play Checklist (Part 2)

	Much or most of the time	Some of the time	Occasionally/ rarely
Does your child engage in non-social activities of hovering and onlooking?	☐	☐	☐
Does your child seem to be in a world of his own?	☐	☐	☐
Does your child seem confused about what he could or should be doing?	☐	☐	☐

Play Checklist (Part 3)

Of the five categories of play below, how much of your child's play-time does he spend on each?

	Much or most of the time	Some of the time	Occasionally/ rarely
Physical	☐	☐	☐
Construction	☐	☐	☐
Creative	☐	☐	☐
Imaginative (role or symbolic play)	☐	☐	☐
Formal games with rules	☐	☐	☐

If you have ticked mostly the **Regularly** column in Checklist Part 1, the **Occasionally/rarely** column in Checklist Part 2, and at least **Some of the time** for the first four types of play listed in Checklist Part 3, then your child's play is coming along very well. He is able to play with a wide range of toys and materials appropriately; he includes some symbolic and fantasy play; and he can interact with other children in play. If you have ticked mostly the **Rarely/never** and a few **Sometimes** in Checklist Part 1, or if you have ticked mostly the **Much or most of the time** column in Checklist Part 2, then you may have some concerns or further questions. Your child may be having difficulty knowing how to play with materials or engage with others.

Concerns about Play

Bear in mind that your child's age and previous experience with various toys and activities and also with other children will affect his capabilities. Don't get worried unduly if you feel he is having some difficulties. By the time your child starts school he is likely to have had a lot of experience with the different kinds of play, be able to play socially and to engage in imaginative or symbolic play. However, if your child is around four and

- Spends much of his time hovering and looking on (or 'onlooking') rather than joining in with others' play
- Or seems unable to settle and engage in activities
- Or is unable to make appropriate use of toys/materials despite having had lots of opportunities to try them out
- Or doesn't seem to understand or engage in symbolic play

then you might need to check out other things (these will be explained more below) and put into practice some 'preparation' teaching.

Your Child Engages Little with Others, but Hovers and Only Watches

If you child seems to have no other problems with manipulating materials – he can play by himself on bikes or slides, can do jigsaws and build, can paint and draw – then his main difficulty seems to be a social one. He may be a little shy, biding his time thinking about and learning how best to join a group. This is fine. Children do need to learn to wait and not just push in. They need to understand about turn-taking. If your child cuts across other children's play or conversation, he risks being seen as taking over and bossy. However, it is of concern if hovering behaviours look like they are becoming a persistent pattern. This might suggest that your child doesn't know *how* to join a group; he may feel, even at such a young age, left out and lonely. This is of concern for his social and, ultimately, emotional development.

As mentioned in Chapters 4 and 5, it is advisable to take active steps to help improve your child's interactive social skills. You could teach him how to join a group in play, perhaps using dolls or puppets. Also introduce him gradually to being with other children at home in addition to the interactions he may be having in playgroup or nursery.

Your Child Flits around Constantly

If your child never seems to settle to any one activity long enough for you to see if he is able to make appropriate use of the materials, then there are two things to consider.

First, if he is with others in a nursery or playgroup, is there a policy of ensuring all children get to sit down for at least some of the time to do a structured activity, or do the children choose freely for themselves the whole time? There is no doubt that, given total freedom, a number of children – boys in particular – will choose rather physical, rushing-about games such as chasing, play-fighting, rough and tumble, using wheeled toys such as trikes and scooters and large apparatus like climbing frames. Mostly this is fine. The drawback is that your child may not, therefore, get as much experience of other kinds of play, such as symbolic or creative play. He is also not improving his attention/concentration as there is no need to focus in the same way for physical activities as for structured tasks. Furthermore, the type of social interactions can be more limited. Girls with the choice usually manage to engage in more structured play activities than many boys.

With purely physical play, there may be compensatory social skills learned – turn-taking, for example, or sharing the toys and the space. However, there is less opportunity for listening to others and exchanging views, and certainly less opportunity for talking about friends and feelings. Therefore nurseries and play-groups that ensure children get opportunities to engage in a wide variety of different types of play activities are giving children a better preparation for school and life skills in the long run.

Second, is your child on the go in almost every situation? Is he like that at home? Is he unable to settle to anything? If the answer is 'Yes', you need to consider the issue of attention difficulties. You might find it helpful to turn to Chapter 7.

Your Child Fails to Make Appropriate Use of Toys and Materials

If he only fingers or throws toys rather than playing with them in more creative ways, then this is likely to indicate that his general development is progressing at a slower rate than expected. Check out first that he is not just being 'naughty' – deliberately throwing toys in order to annoy or tease others or gain attention – rather than truly unable to understand what to do. If his behaviour is the real concern, then turn to Chapter 3 to see how to deal with it. If you feel concerned about the development of his understanding, thinking and learning, then do see your GP who may refer you to a paediatrician and/or a psychologist for a more detailed assessment.

Your Child Rarely Gets Involved in Symbolic Play

First check whether this is because he is unable to do this or whether he is much more interested in other things. Some children are good at many other kinds of play activities but don't seem to understand that objects can be used to stand for or mean something else – that they are symbols. What happens if you sit him down with some miniature toys – farm animals, say, or a tea service for a teddy bear's picnic? And what happens if you attempt, in the (planned) absence of toy cups, to ask your child what he would inventively use instead? Could he believe that a leaf is a saucer and an acorn a cup?

If your child has difficulties in the area of symbolic play, it is likely that he also has trouble with language and with relating to others (*see Chapter 8*). It may be that your child has a language or social communication problem. It is important – both for your child and the whole family – that you sort out the reasons for any difficulties at an early stage so that you can get the best help for your child – and much can be done.

Your Role in Your Child's Play

Parents are really important playmates for their child. There are many reasons why this is true:

- You give your child the chance to have fun in a safe, caring environment. If you are playing with him you can see and make certain for yourself that he is having a good time and feeling happy.
- You will help to shape your child's ideas of what is enjoyable. You can introduce him to a wide range of experiences and types of play that are helpful for learning and for developing a wide range of skills.

- You can help him to acquire any skills that do not yet seem to be present but are important for school. From your play observations, remind yourself what kind of play your child engages in and so which areas are being missed (look back to Play Checklist Part 3 on page 175). Consider below any skills or types of play he might still need more experience with, and then note some activities you might try to achieve this.

Planned Activity to Extend Skills
Physical: gross motor
Physical: fine motor
Creative: pens/pencils/paint
Creative: modelling/sculpting
Creative: music
Construction
Imaginative: role play
Imaginative: symbolic play
Games with rules:

- You create an environment that teaches your child much about social relationships. Involving yourself in your child's play teaches him how to interact with others. You enable your child to acquire many of the social skills needed to relate to both adults and peers. Playing together is, of course, what peers do. You will be able to show your child how interacting involves warmth; you teach him to take turns, to negotiate, to apologise when necessary. A number of studies have found that children's behaviour towards their peers is similar to their parents' towards them.

- You can give him opportunities to act out and so prepare for new situations (like starting school or even a visit to the dentist) or to express emotions about things that could be bothering him (like the arrival of a new baby). 'Rehearsal' in play is a great way of helping your child prepare for school. Together you can act out what has to be done before school starts (the clothes, the school bag, the journey) as well as all the many exciting things that can and will happen during the course of the school day (meeting his teachers, quiet time, activities, lunch, playground and so on).

- You could be helping to prevent behaviour problems. Low levels of mother-child joint activity have been shown to be associated with behaviour problems in pre-school children. Children of mothers who did more activities of various kinds with them – from playing to more 'educational' tasks to domestic routines – showed far fewer problems. So do 'play' your way through the chores, whether shopping, cooking, tidying or cleaning, with your child – in addition to the obvious play with toys and materials.

- You will feel better yourself if you have enjoyable time with your child and are not involved only in the caring, cooking and disciplining part of child-rearing.

It is also good to teach your child to play independently, as this skill will be required when he starts school. Encourage him to develop independence and to play and do things on his own. However, don't do this by leaving a pre-schooler for long periods to amuse himself. If you do, you are likely to get annoyed about the mess he ends up making or the mischief he gets up to. It is far better to encourage very short periods of activity without your full attention or your direct presence. Even when he is playing alone or with another child or children at home, you can still offer the odd suggestion or interesting prop to try to assist him as you pass by. Do praise and reward him for 'getting on with things' on his own, however short the period, and keep on doing things together with your child, both play and ordinary activity.

Above all, remember that play is not only about providing structured activities or expensive toys. Some freedom, relaxation, daydreaming, boredom and creativity are all part of the real play experience. So, too, are cheap toys; there are lots of stores selling good materials at reasonable prices. And the toys made by your child, perhaps with your help, can also give much pleasure, as well as being instructive.

Suggested Toy Materials to Have at Home

- Materials for making things – set aside some boxes in which to collect useful materials such as cardboard boxes, plastic bottles, scraps of material, egg cartons, bubble wrap, bottle tops, straws and buttons for model making (including making toys).
- Paper, pens, crayons, felt tips (washable), thick paints (water-soluble), large pieces of paper of different colours, glue (of the safe variety), glitter, sticky paper, stencils, etc., for creative play. Child-friendly scissors will be needed too.

- Modelling materials such as play dough or Plasticine, together with accessories including rolling pins and cutting shapes.

- A dressing-up box of old clothes and materials for fantasy play. Also useful to encourage fantasy play are spaces organised as a kitchen, hospital, school, etc. Big boxes (preferably home-painted) for furniture, such as stoves, can be just as good as commercial equivalents.

- Sets of small farm animals, small dolls (perhaps with furniture and a dolls' house), miniature tea sets for dolls, small tea sets and cooking utensils for domestic play; trucks, trains and cars (with accompanying tracks, garages, etc.), tool kits and so on; also a range of dolls, teddies, puppets, Action Men, etc. to promote symbolic play.

- Jigsaw puzzles, blocks, marbles, coloured discs (good for matching skills), beads and strings, sewing cards, Sticklebricks, Duplo/Lego, inset boards, stacking toys (towers and nesting kits) for fine motor control, spatial abilities and so on.

- Depending on what space you have available, tricycles, scooters, climbing frames, trampolines, etc., for gross motor development.

- Sand tray and facilities for water play, plus shapes and containers for sorting and measuring, toys for floating in water, etc.

- Musical instruments, homemade and bought, such as maracas, tambourines, bells and shakers.

- Picture and story books, letter and number friezes, plastic letters and numbers; picture cards of common objects (good for matching and naming).

- Dot-to-dot books and colouring-in books, paper-and-pencil mazes, for developing fine motor control.

Whether your child is a boy or a girl, try to have a range of cross-gender and unisex toys available at home. Many girls may like pink-coloured toys, and boys – at some point – toy guns. But it is good for children to cover the range without boys being labelled as sissy or sad for playing with dolls, or girls as being in some way brutish for liking rough-and-tumble play.

And Finally ...

Remember play is about fun and relaxation and not just a means to promote learning (although it does that too). Your child's life does not have to be – and indeed should not be – structured the whole time. Children need time to reflect, to explore, to think, to daydream, just to be themselves. We all need to 'allow ourselves to daydream more', says the psychoanalyst Adam Phillips. If children are encouraged to 'do something' – even if it is 'play' (with a structure and of someone else's choosing) – all the time, they won't take the initiative to think for themselves. Don't worry that your child might be bored sometimes. Of course, you might want to make sure that there are stimulating things around to tempt him. You will also not be expecting your child – especially a pre-school child – to initiate all play activities himself.

Try to steer your child away from *only* computer games, electronic games and television. These games can be a useful way of developing good hand-eye co-ordination, and some are wonderfully sophisticated and imaginative, but often they are little more than a way for your child to pass the time. In other words, make sure your pre-school child has not already become an addict of electronic games and television. Remember that your chances of getting him to experience a wide range of play, toys and materials are best in the early years.

7

Concentrating

Being able to pay attention and to concentrate is extremely important in the early as well as the later school years. Without this
ability, children cannot take in what the teacher is saying, and so
will find it harder to learn. Concentration or attention skills (these
two terms are often used interchangeably) are also very important
for behaviour. If your child fidgets a great deal and cannot sit still,
she distracts herself, distracts other children, disrupts classroom
activities and makes adults cross. Relationships with peers, siblings
and parents will certainly be affected when the child doesn't listen
to what is being said, or when she is being impulsive or overactive.
Children who have poor skills in these areas can also place themselves in great physical danger (for example by running into the
path of an oncoming car).

Attention is so important to school life, it is well worth
preparing your child for the listening and concentrating demands
of the classroom.

There are many terms used to describe concentration/atten-
tion and the difficulties associated with it, as outlined below:

- **Attention** – this refers to the child's ability to focus on what
someone else is saying (*listening* attention) or doing (*visual*
attention). She needs to show through her words or actions
that she is attempting to *take in* the information. For listening attention, she needs to try to do what is asked of her. For

visual attention, she needs to try, for instance, to follow and copy a demonstration. What a child does with her eyes is an important clue to whether she is attending. Is she looking at the person who is talking to her? Is she watching the activity that is being demonstrated? Do her eyes stay focused on the object of her attention?

- **Concentration (or attention) span** – this refers to the length of time a child can engage in a task or spend listening to someone talking. Obviously, younger children have shorter concentration spans than older children, and their concentration span may be different for various activities. Most pre-schoolers can concentrate for far longer when watching a cartoon than they can when doing a structured activity such as a hard puzzle.

- **Distractibility** – this means the ease with which the child is distracted from the task in hand by outside or minor irrelevant events. For instance, if she is easily distracted by another child talking in the background, or by another person walking past.

- **Overactivity** – most young children are active. At times they may be 'overactive', especially if they are very tired, exuberant or excited. Although you may find this behaviour wearying or annoying, so long as it is not occurring most of the time, then this may be regarded as a not unusual pattern of early childhood.

- **Hyperactivity** – this term is best used to describe children who are almost *constantly* and *persistently* overactive and cannot contain their level of overactivity. This is very much more than occasional high spirits. Hyperactive behaviour can create enormous disruption at home and at school. The management of this level of activity may require professional help, as most schools find it very hard to cope with persistent hyperactivity.

- **Impulsivity** – this is the child's inability to hold back from saying or doing something that is either inappropriate or even dangerous. For example, the child who frequently shouts out during playschool story-time, when she is expected to be listening quietly. Or the child who runs away from an adult and across the road without looking first. Or the child who 'jumps in', grabbing toys or giving an answer before you have told or shown her what to do.

What Can we Expect of Pre-schoolers?

Between the ages of three and six years, you can expect to see huge developments in your child's attention, including:

- An increasing ability to engage in structured activities.
- An increase in the length of her concentration span from a few minutes at age three to around half an hour at age six (at least in structured one-to-one activities with an adult).
- An increasing ability to stay with the task and not become easily distracted.
- An increasing ability to work on her own for short periods.
- An ability by the age of four to hold back from an action she wants to do but has been told not to.

Development of attention is not always smooth. Do not expect to see your pre-schooler concentrating all the time, never being distracted or never giving in to impulses. These behaviours are normal. When children are tired or sick, their concentration and attention may take a dive. Also, if they have any worries at home or school, they will find it harder to concentrate. Generally speaking, boys are a little slower to develop their concentration skills and may be more easily distracted than girls. However, as long as there is a general move forward in the direction of improving attention, you do not need to worry unduly.

How Well Can Your Child Concentrate?

The checklist below will show you how well your child can attend. Remember, the older the child, the more you can expect of her. However, even if your child is younger than four, you can still complete this checklist. It will give you an opportunity to chart her development and progress over the next few years. For each item tick the box that best describes your child's level of attention in Part A and level of activity in Part B.

Concentration and Activity Checklist
Part A – Attention and Concentration

Can your child:	Regularly	Sometimes	Almost never
Listen and respond appropriately to simple instructions?	☐	☐	☐
Concentrate on a structured activity for 10–15 minutes (not television or GameBoy)?	☐	☐	☐
Watch cartoons for 20 minutes or more?	☐	☐	☐
Sit at the table during meal times (until she has finished eating)?	☐	☐	☐
Finish (short) tasks or games once started?	☐	☐	☐

Part B – Activity

Does your child:	Often	Sometimes	Almost never
Run around and appear to be always on the go?	☐	☐	☐

	Often	Sometimes	Almost never
Interrupt others or intrude inappropriately (for instance poking or prodding)?	☐	☐	☐
Make a lot of noise or talk constantly?	☐	☐	☐
Have difficulty taking turns?	☐	☐	☐
Fidget and squirm?	☐	☐	☐
Appear to act 'without thinking'?	☐	☐	☐

If you have ticked most of the items as 'regularly' in Part A or 'almost never' in Part B, this means your child is developing good concentration skills, and concentration is a pre-school skill you won't have to be too concerned about.

If you have mostly ticked the 'sometimes' column, your child is doing quite well, but you could help bring her along a little further in readiness for school.

If you have lots of ticks in the 'almost never' column in Part A, or the 'often' column in Part B (*and* your child is four or older), you have some way to go to prepare your child for what is needed in school.

How to Prepare Your Child to Concentrate: a Comprehensive Action Plan

This action plan will help you to help your child:

- Listen attentively
- Look attentively
- Finish tasks
- Work towards a longer concentration span
- Think before acting

Before You Start

You need to think about the following points before starting the action plan.

Who?

Who is going to run the programme (mother, father, carer, grandparent)? Even though you might see this as a formal programme, try not to think of it as too big a deal to manage. Remember, formal means regular and structured, not complicated. You can even continue this programme into the school years, if it is needed, working together with your child's teacher.

Where?

You will need a quiet corner away from other family members or children (this is really important, even though it may be difficult). What you need are:

- An uncluttered desk or table.
- A place where there are no distracting noises, such as the radio or television, people talking and mobile phones ringing.
- A place where there are few visual distractions. A simple, even bare, setting is best.
- Somewhere comfortable but at the same time quite 'formal'. The floor or sofa may make the activity appear more like a play or leisure situation and may put the child in less of a frame of mind to concentrate.

When?

- It is best to pick a time when your child is not hungry or tired. Shortly after returning from pre-school or even first thing in the morning may be best.
- Make sure your child is not missing out on her favourite television programme or anything particularly special to her.

How Often?

- Short teaching sessions are much more effective than long sessions.
- In general, regularly and often is best.
- Daily sessions are best, but at least three times a week would be needed for useful progress.

What You Need to Do

First, collect all the materials you will need:

- Kitchen timer.
- For the **Concentration Tasks** and **Quiet Activities** (*see later in this chapter*) it is a good idea to mix play activities with tasks described in other chapters (such as on reading and number). So prepare paper, pencils, crayons, scissors, glue, sticky papers, puzzles, books, etc. Whatever you choose, get all your equipment and materials ready before you go to get your child.
- Red cards and green cards. Red for 'stop and wait' and green for 'go ahead' (see *box overleaf.*)

How to Lengthen Your Child's Concentration Span

1 When you start the first concentration session, make sure you choose a session length that is right for your child's concentration span. If you think her concentration span is very short, it is perfectly fine to start with only five minutes. This is especially true for children as young as three to four years. A child of five to six years could probably manage about 15 minutes (with activity changes). The starting session length is called the 'baseline'. The aim of the programme is to increase the session length bit by bit. You can measure progress by comparing the latest (and hopefully longest) session length with the baseline. Think of your programme lasting weeks

Red Cards and Green Cards

Get some coloured cardboard (in red and green). Cut this up to make cards that can be held up in front of your child when required. For a pre-schooler, make them bigger than the ones a referee holds up at football matches – around six inches high would be enough to make an impact.

Tell your child that you will hold up the **Green Card** when you want her to start something or to go ahead.

Tell her the **Red Card** will be held up when you want her to stop whatever she is doing instantly – and to look at you for the next instruction.

Practise a couple of times before you bring the cards into use – to make sure your child understands the idea.

rather than days. You should aim for a concentration span of around 30 minutes by the time your child is five or six.

2 Try to make your child (as well as yourself) stick to the time limit. For instance, suppose you set five minutes and she wants to stop after three (yet you know from experience she is capable of five minutes' work), try not to let her pull out of the session. Encourage her to sit at the table with you for the full five minutes, even if she refuses to work. She needs gradually to come to understand that you, the parent, are directing the situation (like a teacher), not her. However, this needs to be done in a very calm way, certainly without you raising your voice. In the beginning, it is a success for some children if they stay sitting, even if they are not doing the set activity. These children should be praised highly for just sitting at the table. If five minutes seems difficult for your

child, you might need to set your activity period for only two minutes. Your child needs to experience success so that she will want to do it again. Don't be discouraged if you have to start with a short time period, or have to back-pedal (briefly). Remember, developing your child's ability to co-operate is really important for learning at school and for getting on well with her teacher.

3 Once you have decided on the length of the session, stick to it. You should time it carefully. Do not overstep the time limit, even if your child is working well.

4 Most young children are uncertain of concepts of time and don't know how long five or ten minutes is. If this is the case, it may be helpful to use a kitchen timer with a buzzer or alarm which can be set to signal the end of the session. The timer will help your child not to focus on the time passing but on the task in hand.

5 Ideally the session should be ended while your child is still interested and co-operative, not when she is bored, frustrated or having a tantrum. She is more likely to want to work again with you in the future if the session finishes on a happy note.

6 Before you think of lengthening the session, your child needs to be working consistently and confidently for the baseline time period for *at least a week*. When you do increase the length, do so by a very small amount. For instance, if the baseline is five minutes, increase it to about six or seven minutes. If the baseline is 10 minutes, increase it to about 12 or 13 minutes. For moving on again, the same process applies – your child must be able to concentrate on work for the (new) time period for at least a week before the next increase.

7 Before you start giving instructions, make sure your child is looking at you. If you are demonstrating something, get your child to look at what you are doing, not just at you. (Say,

'Katie, listen'; then, when she is looking at you, say, 'Katie, look' and point to the materials.) Physically touch your child on the arm if needed, as this can help you get her attention. Make sure you work alongside your child at her physical level, not towering over her.

8 Make sure that the activities you do with your child are interesting and enjoyable. For instance, if she's mad about dinosaurs, choose dinosaur materials when you start out.

9 Make sure the activities you choose are not too hard for your child – you want her to feel pleased with herself afterwards. Certainly start with easy tasks and then build up slowly, in small steps, to more challenging ones as her concentration improves.

10 Make sure you keep on telling your child how well she is doing when she is working nicely with you. Praise her by saying, 'Good girl,' 'Well done,' 'You did that really nicely,' or 'You're really concentrating beautifully.' Avoid urging her to 'concentrate' or 'try harder' or commenting critically, such as saying, 'You're not listening' or 'That's wrong.'

11 Do use a reward programme (*see Chapter 3 for more detail*). As always, ongoing praise is important, but stickers can also be given for staying on task until the timer buzzer goes.

How to Cope with Impulsivity

If you are trying to get your child to do something and want to stop her 'jumping in' or cutting across what is being said to her, this is what you need to do:

- Before you start an activity, first make sure your child is **looking** and **listening.**
- Keep your instructions and demonstrations **short and clear.**
- Praise your child for listening or watching carefully: say, 'Well done – you watched really carefully.'

- If your child jumps in, work out with her a special signal that means 'stop and wait'. You could use a red card as described earlier, or touch the child gently on the arm and say 'Hang on' or 'Cool it' – whatever you think will work best for her. Praise your child for waiting, then carry on with the instruction or activity.

How to Cope with High Activity Levels

Is your child one of those who is always rushing about, climbing over everything, getting under your feet and never sitting still? Here are some general ideas on how to get your child to calm down and have more frequent quiet periods.

- First, organise your day – as best you can – so there are **Active Times** and **Quiet Times**. Build Quiet Times into daily routines, such as before bed and after lunch. Remember that you still need to keep an eye on your child whatever she is doing; don't expect her to get on with it by herself.
- Active Times are important. Young children need lots of opportunity to be active and run around freely. Try to give your child a daily active time – or times. She will have something to look forward to, which may help to keep her calm at other times.
- Quiet Times are important. At school, your child will need to be able to sit quietly on a mat for story-time and not be running around the classroom. Quiet times also help cut down on destructive rushing or high activity levels when your child should be quiet. Try to give a Quiet Activity (like a puzzle or picture book) or instruction for a 'rest'. Watching television or a video is fine for half an hour or so – but ensure this doesn't get out of hand. It is much harder to stop older children from watching television (or playing with a computer game) when it becomes a habit.

- Remember to praise your child for sitting quietly/completing the activity. You can also give stickers or small treats if you need to.

Charting Your Child's Progress

It will be helpful to keep a record of what you have done. This will encourage you and your child, and you can see how far both of you have come.

It is easier to measure progress if you have a visual aid or a chart you can look at together, such as the one below. In this example, each smiley face shows that the child has concentrated successfully on the task for the time set her. With three sessions per week of training she progressed from two minutes in week one to seven minutes in week six. Note that this child does not move up to a longer concentration span until she has earned three smiley faces in a week.

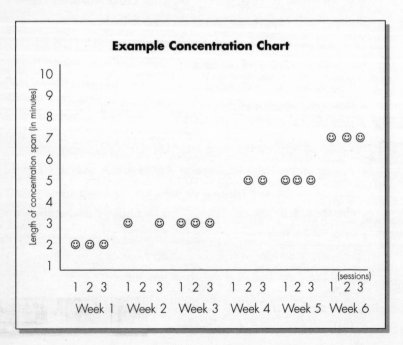

Example Concentration Chart

Here's a chart for you to fill in for your child.

A blank chart for plotting the child's length of concentration span (in minutes), from 1 to 15 on the vertical axis, against sessions (1, 2, 3) for Week 1 through Week 12 on the horizontal axis.

Should your child fail to earn a sticker at any one time, she might become upset. To help avoid this, a) praise her for what she did manage to do successfully; b) talk to her about whether she thinks she might keep trying the longer time or go back to a shorter time if necessary; and c) increase her motivation to continue by offering her an additional reward (like a bumper sticker) for, say, every three smiley faces she earns, however long she takes to earn them.

At intervals (say every two or three months), you might like to go back to the Concentration and Activity Checklists given earlier in this chapter. Is there any improvement? Over a period of a year you would expect to see very noticeable changes as your child's concentration matures. However, if there seems to be very little change over six months, then you may need to intensify your action plan – or persist for rather longer.

Dealing with Severe Attention Problems

If you have tried to follow the action plan closely over a period of several months and your child is not improving, you may have to take alternative action. A very small number of children have severe attention deficit problems, which may be genetic in origin. If this seems to be the case for your child, you should consider seeking formal professional help. You will need to go to your GP or paediatrician to obtain a referral to a hospital or clinic, if appropriate. The following terms are used to describe persistent difficulties with attention and concentration:

● ADHD (Attention Deficit with Hyperactivity Disorder) refers to children whose 'behaviour appears impulsive, overactive, and/or inattentive to an extent that is unwarranted for their developmental age, and is a significant hindrance to their social and educational success'. (British Psychological Society Working Party on ADHD, 1996).

- ADD (Attention-Deficit Disorder) describes children who have poor attention but without a high level of activity.

Here are some findings about ADHD from recent studies:

- Around five in a thousand children in the UK are diagnosed with full ADHD, more often boys than girls.
- For a diagnosis of full ADHD, problems must appear before the age of seven, be persistent and also evident both at home and at school.

A number of other problems seem to go together with ADHD – typically, marked non-compliance, learning problems (especially dyspraxia and, less commonly, dyslexia) and social problems including making friends.

And Finally ...

Concentration is a vital part of learning to learn: without good attention children will find the learning of educational skills very difficult. Most parents should not, however, feel unduly worried about a young child whose concentration and attention seem poor. For some children, this aspect of development just takes a little longer. Putting into practice the teaching techniques recommended in this chapter should, however, speed things up. Even if your child has an attention deficit disorder, be reassured that many children with this problem do outgrow their difficulties, and much can be done to help them to learn.

8
Language

Acquiring spoken language has to stand out as the single most important feat of pre-school development. Note that we have said 'acquiring', not learning, language. Parents don't teach their children to understand and use language like teachers teach children the alphabet and eventually how to read and spell. Rather, children *acquire* language.

Acquiring language is no mean achievement. Adults carry around the knowledge of tens of thousands of words: how they sound; what they mean; how we join them together to make sentences; how they are read and spelled and so on. Apart from the reading and spelling part, all other aspects of language are acquired before children set foot in school on their first day. How on earth do they manage it?

Children learn language by acquiring 'rules of grammar'. You as a parent will not need to teach these rules explicitly. No parent ever said to their three-year-old, 'Today we are going to learn about plural endings. Generally speaking, to make a plural you put an "s" on the end of the word. However, there are exceptions to this rule – like "man–men", "sheep–sheep", "foot–feet". Now see if you can remember that!' Rather, children 'create' or 'reinvent' their language. This is why, when they're in the process of acquiring a new rule like plural endings, they get the general idea that you put an 's' on the end of the word. But before they learn the exceptions, they over-generalise the rule and so produce grammatically incorrect plurals like 'mans' and 'foots'.

For children to acquire rules of grammar, they have to *hear* and *imitate* language. This means that you and those around your child have a vital role to play in shaping and supporting his development of speech and language. From birth, you will provide him with opportunities to imitate your speech, which in turn will act as a springboard to enable him to develop and expand his own language.

Spoken Language: the Sum of Many Parts

It is important to look at the *components* or *structure* of language, then the *developmental milestones* of pre-school language and finally *individual differences* in language development. You will need to have this information so that you can judge if your child is achieving the milestones in all the components of language as he should.

There are essentially four components that make up the complex language system that develops before your child starts school.

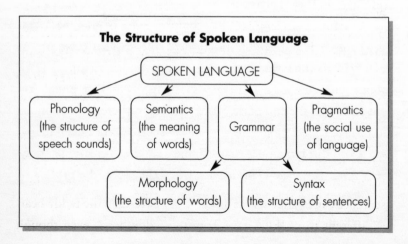

The Structure of Spoken Language

SPOKEN LANGUAGE

Phonology (the structure of speech sounds)

Semantics (the meaning of words)

Grammar

Pragmatics (the social use of language)

Morphology (the structure of words)

Syntax (the structure of sentences)

Phonology

This refers to the *speech sound* structure of our language. Each language has its own set of speech sounds that may or may not be shared by other languages. Indeed, it can be very difficult when we come to learn a second language to get to grips with its different sound system and to learn to pronounce the words correctly.

Semantics

Semantics concerns the *meaning* of language. In the case of pre-schoolers, this refers mainly to the development of their *vocabulary*. Your child may be able to understand the meanings of many words (his *receptive* vocabulary) before he is able to use these words correctly or meaningfully in his own conversation (*expressive* vocabulary). The rapid acquisition of a vast vocabulary is one of the great feats of the pre-school years.

Grammar

Grammar consists of two separate components, *morphology* and *syntax*. Morphology is about word structure, in particular the use of grammatical *markers* to indicate tense, gender, active versus passive, plurals and the like. These grammatical markers can be added to many 'base words'. For instance, we may talk about one dog or two dog**s** where **s** is the grammatical marker indicating plural for the base word 'dog'. In relation to verb tense, the regular past tense grammatical marker is **ed**; so for the base word 'walk', which denotes present tense, we can add the grammatical marker **ed** to make 'walked', indicating past tense.

Syntax refers to the arrangement of words in sentences – how words are put together or ordered to make a sentence. This tells 'who did what to whom'. Changing the order of words in a sentence can change its meaning: 'Tom gave Ellie the teddy bear' is different from 'Ellie gave Tom the teddy bear', even though the two sentences are made up of the same words. In the first sentence, Tom does the giving, while in the second sentence Ellie is the giver.

Pragmatics

This is the use of language in its social context. Pragmatics includes a range of skills centred around interacting and conversing with other people. Your child needs to be able to tell a story or a narrative that makes sense; he needs to be able to take turns in conversation; he needs to recognise that the language he uses with his teachers is different from the language he uses with his friends. Pragmatics also includes intended meaning, which may be different from what is actually said. Metaphors are good examples of this: a four-year-old might say, 'Daddy cross – he's going whoosh.'

Developmental Milestones for Language

Phonological Development

You will see great changes in your pre-schooler's phonological (speech sound) development from the time he produces his first words to when he actually starts school. In fact, phonological development is largely complete by the time children are five years of age. What this means is that your child should be able to pronounce all the different speech sounds accurately by the time he goes to school. In general, children will be able to produce individual sounds like 's, m, t' before they can accurately produce blended sounds or clusters like 'sh, th, fl, tr' (though there are a few exceptions to this). Also, they may be able to say a sound in isolation but not produce it correctly when it appears in a word. This is all quite normal for pre-schoolers.

What you will hear between the ages of one and four years is your child making 'substitution' errors when he speaks (these are very common in pre-schoolers). He will try to say the sound correctly but come up with the wrong sound. He might say 'yap' for 'lap' or 'weddy' for 'ready'. Three- to four-year-olds also commonly leave out sounds from words so you get a 'reduction' error. For instance, he might say 'nana' for 'banana'. This is nothing to worry about. It is only if reduction and substitution errors (apart from in odd isolated words) persist after your child starts school that it could become a problem – then you might be concerned that these may affect his ability to make himself understood or that other children might tease him for sounding 'babyish'.

Semantic (Vocabulary) Development

In the early years, semantic development is really about vocabulary development. You will have noticed when your child was a baby or toddler that he could understand many words that he had not yet begun to say. Children's *receptive* vocabulary runs ahead of their *expressive* vocabulary. Your child will be able to follow instructions and to demonstrate an understanding of many words before he can express all the words he understands in his own speech.

First spoken words usually appear around the age of 12 months. You may be surprised to hear that by the age of six years, children have a vocabulary of around 10,000 words. Between the ages of 18 and 24 months, children experience what is usually referred to as the *vocabulary growth spurt*. During this period they add new words to their vocabulary at a remarkably rapid rate. Some pre-schoolers can add up to 10 words per day! A child may have heard a word used only once before he adds it to his 'mental dictionary of words' (or 'lexicon'). Children add these words to their lexicon through an automatic and unconscious process called 'fast mapping'. Of course, nobody has formally defined the new word for the child. Rather, he has to *infer* the meaning somehow through how it is used within the structure of the sentence. The context in which he hears the word said helps him do this.

The first words children say are words for *objects* (doggy, mummy, car) followed by words for *actions* (go, more, out). Later on, they begin to use *state* words, which tell more about the object words (big, dirty, mine). Two further categories of words that appear during the pre-school years are *personal/social words* (please, ta, no) and *function words* (to, what, where).

You need to bear in mind that when children start to learn words they do not necessarily use them in the same way adults do. They may use them too narrowly (*underextension*); for instance, your child might use the word 'bear' to refer only to his own specific teddy bear. Probably more common is *overextension*, when children apply a word to a wider collection of objects or events than is appropriate, for example, using the word 'car' for all vehicles including buses, bicycles and trucks. These errors gradually disappear as the child's vocabulary increases.

Children as young as two will 'invent' new words based on ones they already know. He might say 'flower-man' to describe a gardener. These fascinating invented words demonstrate very clearly how language acquisition is *rule-based* and not merely a matter of imitation. Another good example of how creative young children's language is comes from their use of metaphor, which begins to emerge at around three years of age. For instance, a four-year-old who has a headache may say, 'Mummy, someone's banging in my head.'

Grammatical Development

Once a child has developed a small vocabulary of object and action words, he begins to join them together. This *word combining* begins at around 18 months of age and takes the form of short 'telegrammatic sentences'. He will put together what are called 'high content' words to make a two-word sentence but without use of connector words like 'the, to, is'. Therefore you might hear your toddler say, 'Go car' or 'Mummy shoe,' meaning 'Are we going in the car?' and 'Mummy put my shoe on.' Most three-year-olds can produce three-word sentences following subject-verb-object order, like 'Me go car' and 'Mummy put shoe.' Gradually, over the next year or two, your child will add on to his three-word sentences other parts of speech like adjectives and prepositions; he will say 'We go in the car,' 'Mummy put my shoe on.' In this way, his language eventually begins to resemble adult language.

Once children are able to form three-word sentences, a grammatical explosion takes place and they begin to introduce grammatical markers. As described earlier, these are small sound units attached to words to change their meaning. The use of grammatical markers follows a particular order of development. Regular endings ('s' to indicate plural, 'ed' to mark past tense) usually appear before irregular forms, so don't worry if your child over-regularises (as in 'two foots' instead of 'two feet').

Negatives begin to develop at two to three years of age and gradually become used in a more sophisticated way. At two, a child might say, 'No bickies,' but at three-and-a-half say, 'There aren't any more bickies.' Similarly, with asking questions, a two-year-old will simply use voice inflection to indicate a question, 'Where daddy going?', but by the age of three-and-a-half will add the auxiliary (the 'is' part of the verb 'go') to turn the same sentence into a true question, 'Where is daddy going?'

Between the ages of three and six years, children begin to develop increasingly complex grammatical structures. They will start to use connectives like 'and', 'then', 'because', 'but' and 'if'. They begin to use passive sentence constructions like 'The dog was patted by the girl' in addition to the active sentences they're already using ('The girl patted the dog'). As the pre-school years draw to a close, children can be seen to use almost all of the grammatical structures they will need for the rest of their lives.

Pragmatics

This is about using language to communicate to others and to engage in social interaction. Obviously this becomes very sophisticated in later childhood and in adult life, but you will notice your pre-schooler beginning to be aware of language used in social contexts. Even children as young as two-and-a-half use language for polite social interaction – they might say 'ta' (for thank you), 'please', 'hello' and 'bye-bye'. They begin to understand that they might have to elaborate on what they say if, for instance, an adult doesn't understand; early on they may just repeat what they said before, but when they're a little older they can rephrase what they've said to help the other person understand.

Pre-schoolers also understand about taking turns in conversation. After they've said something they will look to the other person to respond or they may finish what they've said with a question to encourage the other to reply ('I like custard – do you?'). Pre-schoolers can even begin to understand that you can change a topic of conversation by slightly altering the focus of the discussion ('I like your picture – come and see my train'). Their language begins to be expressed in a more subtle way – they may, for instance, express a desire but not use direct speech to do so. A four-year-old might say, 'I need a pencil', instead of 'Can I have a pencil?'

Watch out for these pragmatic features of your pre-schooler's speech – they indicate that he is using language in a social way. He is not just communicating his own views and needs. Rather, he is beginning to understand that he has to say things in a certain way so that people understand him, will be nice to him and (in relation to his peers) want to become his friend (*see Chapter 4*).

Individual Differences in Language Development

'Individual differences' refers to how rates and patterns of language development vary from child to child. From the previous section on developmental milestones, you may have gained the impression that all young children acquire speech and language at the same time and in the same way. However, this is not the case. There is quite a lot of variability from one child to the next, particularly in terms of speed and type of vocabulary acquisition. When we talk about children's vocabulary knowledge, we describe the average (or mean) number of words children understand and use – but we also need to take into account the *range*. Some 16-month-olds can understand 250 words; others of the same age only 100. Similarly, one 16-month-old may be able to say 130 different words, while another may use only two or three words. You need to be prepared for these individual differences. It doesn't necessarily mean that your pre-schooler who perhaps has fewer words than his friend is necessarily going to have long-term difficulties with language.

However, in spite of this apparently normal variability, it is still useful to know if your child is showing signs of a language difficulty that you should do something about. Are there things you can look at which will help you distinguish between normal variation (which isn't anything to worry about) and the early stages of a possible language delay or disorder?

Although not all children produce words by 18 months, most will understand a considerable number by this age. This suggests that a good starting point is to look at the number of words your child *understands*. If he understands a lot of words but is saying little, this is much less to worry about than if he seems to understand very few words. If you think it would be helpful, write down a list of words he appears to understand and compare it with a list of words that you hear him use.

Another clue as to whether or not a child is having problems with vocabulary development is to look at the relative number of 'object' to 'action' words he uses. Pre-schoolers seem to be able to build up their vocabulary much more quickly if they use lots of object words like 'daddy, dog, cup' than if they use mainly action words like 'go, more'. So if your child is going round naming lots of objects, there probably isn't too much to worry about. However, on a cautionary note, don't get too carried away with saying to him, 'What's this? What's that?' Your child needs both object and action words to join together to make phrases (and, later on, sentences). Don't just talk about names; talk about actions too. Later on, we'll come to the issue of what to do if your child's language development seems to be behind.

Gender Differences

What else contributes to the rate at which children acquire a pre-school vocabulary? One factor is certainly *gender*. Girls are usually slightly ahead of boys in their initial vocabulary development. After the age of two, boys start to catch up. One possible explanation for this is that the left side (the language centre) of the brain tends to develop earlier in girls than boys. However, there may be an environmental factor as well; it has been shown in a number of studies that mothers speak more to their daughters than they do to their sons. This means that girls may hear a richer vocabulary than boys. Do bear in mind, however, that these gender differences are small and lessen as children get closer to school age.

Temperament Differences

Another factor that can affect vocabulary development is *temperament*. There is some evidence that shy and cautious children understand much more than they are prepared to say. However, once they do finally get going, their vocabularies catch up very quickly.

Multilingual Children

The final, very important, individual difference when it comes to language development is that of *bilingualism* or even *multilingualism*. Increasing numbers of children in the UK are now being brought up with two, and sometimes even three, languages. There are two ways in which children may be raised bilingually. One is where both languages are acquired at the same time – so, for instance, a mainly English-speaking mother might speak to her toddler only in English from the very beginning while his mainly French-speaking father might speak to him only in French. The second route to bilingualism is by learning one language first, and then bringing in the second after the first is well under way. For example, Gujerati-speaking parents within the UK might talk to their child only in Gujerati, but after he starts nursery school (say at four years), where he mixes mainly with English-speaking children, he will begin to acquire English.

In general, children who are taught two languages together have no particular language difficulties, though for some years their vocabularies in each language may be smaller than for children learning only one language. Bilingual pre-schoolers often mix their two languages, but this is to be expected; most bilingual adults tend to mix their languages too! Indeed, up until three years, bilingual children may not even realise they are speaking two languages. In the long term, one of the two languages is likely to be used more than the other.

There is some evidence that bilingualism can have advantages for language and other aspects of development. Studies have shown that children who speak two languages well are often advanced in their attention skills and their ability to use language for learning new concepts. Additionally, bilingual children often have more advanced 'metalinguistic' (language-awareness) skills; they may be better at noticing errors of grammar and they are often more 'speech sound aware' than their single-language peers. Their improved awareness of sounds can help with their early reading development (*see Chapter 9*).

There is one possible problem with bilingualism, and that is when the child has an underlying language difficulty. If so, bringing him up bilingually could create added pressure on his language development. Do seek advice from a speech and language therapist about this.

Speech and Language Checklist

The best time to fill in the following checklist is when your child is turning four years of age. However, if your child has had serious language delay, you will very likely have already realised that there is a problem – and will have sought help by now.

The checklist breaks up language into the four main areas described above, and then asks you to answer four questions from each, ticking where appropriate. Before you fill in the checklist, glance over it and see if you are able to answer the questions easily. In any case, it may be a good idea to do a short

observation of your child's speech and language, say over a two-
to three-day period. Use a notebook and write down sentences
he says; make notes about how he uses language in various situations; and see how clear his speech is to you and others. If it is
easier, make a recording of you and your child talking together,
and play this back while you are filling in the checklist. As you
work through, you may need to look back at some of the earlier
sections in this chapter from time to time to remind yourself of
some of the terminology.

Phonology

Is your child's speech understandable to you and other family members?

Almost all the time ☐

Most of the time ☐

Some of the time ☐

Almost never ☐

Is your child's speech understandable to people who don't know him well?

Almost all the time ☐

Most of the time ☐

Some of the time ☐

Almost never ☐

Is your child able to produce most single sounds (such as s, t, m) correctly in his everyday speech?

Almost all the time ☐

Most of the time ☐

Some of the time ☐

Almost never ☐

Is your child able to produce most sound blends or 'clusters' (such as /st/ as in 'stone', /fl/ as in 'flower', /th/ as in 'thing', /sh/ as in 'shoe') correctly?

Almost all the time ☐

Most of the time ☐

Some of the time ☐

Almost never ☐

If you've ticked 'almost all the time' or 'most of the time' to these questions, your child's speech seems to be developing quite nicely.

If you've ticked 'some of the time' or 'almost never', it may be that your child's phonological development is delayed. Bear in mind that *you* may be able to understand your child's speech (because you're used to it), but if people who don't know him well can't understand what he's saying, this can cause a lot of difficulties (and frustrations) for him – and could be problematic when he starts school.

Vocabulary (Semantic) Development

How large is your child's spoken vocabulary?

Thousands of words – I've lost count! ☐

Between 500 and 1,000 words ☐

A couple of hundred words ☐

Less than a hundred words ☐

Does your child use many more object words (such as 'dog', 'mummy', 'car') than action words (such as 'go', 'eat')?

Yes, very definitely ☐

A few more object than action words ☐

About half and half ☐

Mostly action words ☐

Does your child use state, personal/social and function words (such as 'please', 'ta', 'no')?

Yes, a lot of the time ☐

Most of the time ☐

Some of the time ☐

Almost never ☐

Does your child use words very specifically (as opposed to making over- and under-extensions; for instance using 'doggy' to refer to all animals or, at the other extreme, using it to describe only his own dog)?

Yes, his vocabulary is very specific ☐

Mostly specific ☐

Specific some of the time but some over- and under-extensions ☐

Lots of over- and under-extensions ☐

If your child has a very large and specific vocabulary that makes use of lots of object words (but brings in other sorts of words as well), he is well on the way to good semantic development.

If he has a small vocabulary, says the same words over and over again and uses them incorrectly (over- and under-extensions), this could be an indication of a language difficulty.

Grammar

Does your child produce sentences of at least five to six words in length (such as 'Mummy please put my shoes on')?

Yes, almost all the time ☐

Most of the time ☐

Some of the time ☐

Almost never ☐

Does your child get the words in the right order when he speaks?

Yes, almost all the time ☐

Most of the time ☐

Some of the time ☐

Almost never ☐

Does your child use grammatical markers (such as regular plural 's' and past tense 'ed' endings), even if occasionally incorrectly?

Yes, almost all the time ☐

Most of the time ☐

Some of the time ☐

Almost never ☐

Does your child make appropriate use of negatives (such as 'not'), questions ('why', 'when', 'how') and connectives ('and', 'but', 'because') in his speech?

Yes, almost all the time ☐

Most of the time ☐

Some of the time ☐

Almost never ☐

If you've ticked 'almost all the time' or 'most of the time' to the above questions, your child is doing well in terms of his grammatical development.

If you've ticked mainly 'some of the time' or perhaps more worryingly 'almost never', then your child's grammar is not developing as well as it should.

Pragmatics

Does your child make appropriate use of 'social' or greeting words and phrases (such as 'hello', 'please', 'thanks')?

Yes, almost all the time ☐

Most of the time ☐

Some of the time ☐

Almost never ☐

Does your child either repeat what he's said or describe further when you make it clear you haven't understood him?

Yes, almost all the time ☐

Most of the time ☐

Some of the time ☐

Almost never ☐

Does your child 'take turns' in speaking when he's talking with you or one of his friends?

Yes, almost all the time ☐

Most of the time ☐

Some of the time ☐

Almost never ☐

Does your child indicate with a look or a question when he wants you or a friend to reply or take their turn in a conversation?

Yes, almost all the time ☐

Most of the time ☐

Some of the time ☐

Almost never ☐

If you've ticked 'almost all the time' or 'most of the time', your child is beginning to understand the social rules of language that will enable him to communicate easily with others – and which will help him make friends.

If you've ticked 'some of the time' or 'almost never', your child has not yet begun to understand the give and take of language. Although it's still early days with regard to his pragmatic development, you will want to keep an eye on this as it is important for settling socially into school.

If, after filling in the checklist, you're happy with your child's language level, you may need to do little more than feel reassured that he is well prepared for the language demands of the classroom. However, if you are concerned that your child's language is not quite what it should be, here are some general hints for helping support his language development.

Supporting and Promoting Your Child's Language Development

There are two main ways parents can influence their child's language development. The first is *expansion* and *recasting* (they usually go together). The second is *reflection* and *reinforcement*.

Expansion and Recasting

Expansion and recasting means that, when your child says something, *you* expand what he has said into a longer, and probably more complex, sentence. You may also recast (rephrase and correct) what he has said if he makes a mistake, such as getting the wrong word order or making a grammatical error. For instance, your child could say, 'I gotted new blue coat,' to which you might respond with something like 'Yes, you got a new blue coat with shiny buttons.' What you're doing here is expanding what your child has said by putting in the indefinite article 'a'; you've also added a further description of his coat. Note that you have corrected his grammatical error by recasting – he has over-generalised the regular past tense ending 'ed' to the irregular word 'got', so you have supplied the correct (irregular) verb. This expansion and recasting will seem obvious to some parents, but if you haven't been doing it very much, why not try it with your pre-schooler? It really is a very easy and natural way of giving feedback that helps extend his vocabulary and grammar (while also correcting it when needed).

Reflection and Reinforcement

In reflection and reinforcement, when your child produces a well-constructed sentence, you simply repeat it back to him and then continue the conversation based on what he has already said. Your child might say, 'I had brownies at nursery today,' to which you could reply, 'Great, you had brownies at nursery today. Did they taste good?' This provides positive feedback and reinforcement to your child, which reassures him that what he has said is correct *and* has been understood and responded to.

These feedback techniques can be used regularly in all sorts of everyday situations. Try them out, see how easy they are to use, and watch your child extend his vocabulary and grammatical development.

Learning to Listen

Some children find listening and responding to what others say very easy – others do not. If you feel your child doesn't listen well, try the following (*see also Chapter 7*).

● Say to your child, 'What do we use our ears for? We use them for listening. I am listening with my ears. What can I hear in the kitchen? I can hear the fridge humming; I can hear daddy emptying the dishwasher; I can hear the clock ticking. What can you hear?' Try this 'what can you hear?' game in other situations too, like when out in the car or at the shops or playground.

- Collect some things to listen to, like a musical instrument, marbles in a tube, a cup with a spoon in it, a book. Get your child to shut his eyes and ask him to listen hard while you play the instrument. – now get him to guess what sound it is you're making. Do the same for jangling the marbles in the tube, stirring the spoon in the cup and turning the pages of the book.

- See if your child can listen and respond to your instruction:
  - touch your nose
  - step backwards
  - put your hands in the air
  - close the door

- To take listening a step further, you can ask your child to **listen hard, remember** what you've said and then **do it**. This is, of course, not just about listening and understanding but also remembering. Start with short sentences and build up to longer ones. Here are some examples:
  - touch the plate and then the cup (two ideas)
  - walk a step, then jump and turn round (three ideas)
  - give me the book, the pen, the cup and the fork – from a selection of objects (four ideas)

Learning Some Difficult Words and Concepts

Some words have a complex meaning. Children need to hear these words quite a few times before they grasp their meaning – for example, words like 'big', 'little', 'on' and 'under'. These take a little longer for children to understand fully and then use consistently. Object or action words like 'dog', 'car', 'run', 'jump' are much easier to understand because all the child has to do is link the word with the object he sees or the action he's doing.

Here are some examples for helping your child get to grips with these more complex words:

- *Up and Down:* Put a teddy bear on a high shelf and say, 'Look, Teddy's *up* high on the shelf.' Then put it on a lower shelf and say, 'Now Teddy's *down* low on the shelf.'

- *On and Under:* Use dolls' house materials, including a table and cups. Say, 'Let's put the cup *on* the table. Now let's put the cup *under* the table.'

- *Big and Little:* Point out to your child objects that are *big* like buses, trees, houses and ships, and things that are *little* (or *small*) like buttons, leaves, peanuts and coins. Ask him to point to *big* things in the living room and then *small* (or *little*) things.

- *Top and Bottom:* Get your child to walk to the *top* of the stairs and then to the *bottom* of the stairs. See if he can tell you which is the *top* of the saucepan and which is the *bottom.*

- *Behind and In Front:* Again, use little dolls' house or maybe even farmyard toys and ask your child to 'put the horse *behind* the pig', 'put the spoon *in front of* the cup'. If he finds this difficult, do it for him while saying, 'Look, I'm putting the horse *behind* the pig. Shall I say it again and this time you do it?'

- *Feeling Words (happy, sad, scared, sorry):* Use these words in context so you're giving examples like, 'I feel happy when we have ice cream for tea,' 'I feel sad when my friend falls over and hurts himself,' 'I feel scared when there's a thunderstorm.' Relate the words happy, sad and so on to people's facial expression (*see page 147*).

Asking Questions (who, where, when, why)

- *Who:* First, help your child to understand what *who* means by giving him the answer: 'Who came first in the race – it's Susie'; 'Who spilled the milk on the floor – it's daddy'. Look together at pictures that show people doing things and then ask your child, 'Who's chasing the dog, who's playing with the ball?' Later on, ask your child to come up with his own question using the 'who' word.

- *Where:* Similarly with the *where* word, you may need to use 'where' and then follow up by giving your child the answer. 'Where is your bike? Look, it's out in the garden.' Then ask him questions: 'Where are we going now?'; 'Where's the cat?'

- *When:* When (and *why*) are difficult and abstract words for pre-schoolers to get to grips with. As a result, the use of when and why questions develops a little later than the use of who and where questions. Use the *when* word to ask about every-day events in your child's life. You may need to give him the answer the first few times: 'When do you go to bed? Yes, you go to bed at 7 o'clock'; 'When is your birthday party? It's next Tuesday.' Go on to ask him questions like: 'When do you go swimming?'; 'When do we start our holiday?'; 'When do we go to visit granny?'

- *Why:* You may have noticed that your child asks questions using the 'why' word over and over again – often to the point of driving you mad! Sometimes this is just a way to get your attention, but there may be more to it than that. While your child's use of 'why' is often appropriate ('Why is the doggy wagging his tail?' 'Because he is happy'), sometimes it is not. On occasions, your child's question appears nonsensical, or it may not be possible to give a meaningful reply. You might comment, 'Look, it's a lovely sunny day,' to which your child asks (inappropriately), 'Why?' Some linguists believe that young children often over-generalise the use of the word 'why'. This is because its complex meaning requires them to 'test it out' in lots of different situations. They take note of the responses they get (such as an appropriate explanation as opposed to a puzzled look or an 'I can't answer that' reply) to gradually narrow down the meaning and correct use of the word 'why'. If your child uses a 'why' question appropriately, you might say, 'That's a good question,' and then go on to give the relevant explanation. If his 'why' question is inappropriate, you may point out (gently) that there is no answer to that question. You will notice that, as your child gets older, he asks 'why' questions less often but more appropriately.

Beginning to Develop Narrative

- *Telling Stories:* Tell your child a little story about a family member or use one of his toys like a teddy or a doll. After he's listened to the story, ask him to tell it back to you. Now ask him if he can make up a little story of his own – he could use the same character like the teddy, but something different has to happen to teddy in his story.

- *Sequencing:* Of course, part of story-telling is getting ideas and events in the right order. To help your child develop a sense of sequence, get him to describe everyday life events that have a definite order – like what he did in the morning after he got out of bed up to when he came home from nursery school for lunch. You will probably have to use quite a lot of prompt questions like, 'What did you do first ... then what next ... and then ... and then ... and after that ... and what was the last thing you did?' You and your child might want to count on your fingers as he tells you the events step by step.

- *Reading Stories to Your Child* is one of the easiest and most enjoyable ways of helping facilitate your child's language.

There is very clear evidence that reading stories to your child helps expand his vocabulary, makes him aware of language structures, and improves his listening and comprehension skills. Try to read to your child every day if you can – a bedtime story is one of the best times to cuddle up together, share a story he enjoys and introduce him to the wonderful world of language and books. Point to pictures in the book as you go along; ask him questions about what's happening in the story; and see if he can show you he understands sequence and narrative by asking him questions like, 'What do you think teddy will do next?'

Children's Speech and Language Problems

Unclear Speech

Sometimes children have good understanding and appear to be producing sentences of their own but their speech is so unclear it is hard for others to follow. Some children have marked and persistent difficulties with speech sound production; they make lots of speech sound substitutions, they leave out parts of words or fail to finish off word endings. This is referred to as a *phonological* problem. An example of a speech sound substitution is a lisp. This is when the child substitutes the 's' sound with 'th'; it is common in early childhood and little to worry about unless it persists. Quite commonly, phonological difficulties occur alongside expressive language problems.

When the difficulty is caused by the child having problems in co-ordinating and sequencing speech sounds, he may be described as having *developmental verbal dyspraxia*. Not making yourself understood is very frustrating, especially for the bright child who has a lot he wants to say. If he can't get others to understand him, or he has to repeat himself all the time, he may become upset and angry.

If you are concerned about your pre-schooler's speech, ask his nursery teacher and other family members whether they can easily understand what your child says. Talk to your health visitor as well. If everyone agrees there is a real problem that doesn't seem to be improving with time, then your child should be assessed by a speech and language therapist. It could be just a case of mild immaturity (caused by a *delay* in the development of his phonological system). Then it is usual to keep an eye on his progress. Your child will be called back for a check after, say, six to twelve months. If, however, the speech therapist assesses him as having a *disorder* of his phonological system – it is not just developing slowly but also in an abnormal way – then he will be seen for regular speech therapy. In addition to helping him produce the correct speech sounds, you will be given some exercises to work on at home so that he has lots of practice in saying the sounds correctly.

Most speech problems will improve with appropriate therapy. Watch out for your child's future literacy development. Children with unclear speech are at risk of becoming poor spellers. This is because they cannot accurately produce the speech sounds to which they have to 'connect' the letters when they come to spell words.

Stammering (or Stuttering)

Between the ages of two and five years, it is common for children to repeat words (or sounds), to hesitate, and to say 'um' and 'er' when they are sorting out what to say next. This is nothing to worry about. Short periods of 'dysfluency' are part of normal speech and language development for many pre-schoolers. If you notice your child repeating words, hesitating or just struggling to get the words out, try not to see this as a problem – but do observe closely whether this is just a passing phase lasting a few weeks or whether it is continuing for longer (and maybe even worsening). If, after a few weeks, this period of dysfluency hasn't resolved itself, or if your child is becoming frustrated and distressed by it, it would be wise to take steps. This persistent problem might then be referred to as either stammering or stuttering.

Stammering is not an uncommon problem; 5 per cent of children will stammer at some stage in their development. However, on an encouraging note, four out of five pre-school children who show a definite stammer are speaking fluently by the time they are teenagers.

Parents do not cause stammering. You should not feel guilty or worry that you might have caused your child to stammer by putting pressure on him to speak or by sometimes being too busy to listen to what he has to say. Like many speech and language problems, stammering does appear to have a genetic basis; that is, it runs in families, and boys are more likely to be affected than girls.

Theories about the causes of stammering suggest that it is to do with mistiming or an error of 'feedback' during speech. Environmental and personality factors, though not actually causing the stammer, may contribute to its persisting – for instance, a very fast-paced family lifestyle or the child having a sensitive, perhaps even anxious, temperament.

Don'ts for when your child is dysfluent or stammering:
- Don't tell him to slow down.
- Don't tell him to say it again.
- Don't tell him to think before he speaks.
- Don't look away from him when he is struggling with his speech.

- Don't ask too many questions of him when he is in a dysfluent phase.
- Don't label your child's speech as a 'stammer'; if you have to describe it in front of him for some reason, use words like 'bumpy speech'.

Do's for when your child is dysfluent or stammering:

- Do spend some special time each day to talk with your child in a quiet and relaxed way, away from other children so your child doesn't feel he has to compete with them for your attention.
- Do listen to the *content* of what your child is saying and not *how* he is saying it.
- Do slow your own speech a little.
- Do make sure you give your child plenty of time to say what he wants to say.
- Do allow your child to finish what he is saying – don't finish it for him.
- Do look at your child when he talks to you.

And, more importantly than anything else, even if you are anxious about your child's speech, don't show it. Try and present as relaxed a front as you can. If he becomes very frustrated and distressed when he is struggling to get a word or sentence out, just say to him something like, 'Those words are hard to say aren't they? Don't worry – it can be like that when you're learning to talk.'

If you're concerned that your child doesn't seem to be getting over his stammer – maybe you've noticed that it's getting worse or that he is becoming upset and embarrassed by it – you need to see a speech and language therapist. There are also some specialist centres that deal only with stammering – for instance, the Michael Palin Centre in London. Rest assured that lots can be done to help stammerers become more fluent. Certainly, if your child looks as though he is going to be one of those children who have a definite stammer, then it is wise to start treatment sooner rather than later. The earlier the intervention, the more likely the child will be to overcome his stammer before he starts school; and the less distress caused to the particularly sensitive child who may want to withdraw from speaking situations because he finds them stressful and embarrassing.

Specific Language Impairment

From completing the checklist, you will have a good idea as to whether your child is developing speech and language as he should – and also which particular aspects of his language are better developed than others. As mentioned earlier, it is more worrying if your child has problems in both understanding what others say to him (receptive language) *and* producing language of his own (expressive language) than if he has mainly an expressive language difficulty. If, by the age of two years, your child is not responding to simple instructions and requests, it is time to act. If, at two, he understands and responds to most of what you say but isn't talking, give him a little longer. However, if he is saying no more than single words by the age of two-and-a-half to three years, you should take action.

It has been demonstrated that around 6–7 per cent of pre-schoolers show delays in their speech and language development; however, at least half of these children will be delayed in other aspects of development too. There will be others who have marked hearing problems that will affect their speech and language. Excluding these children leaves 1–2 per cent who have a 'pure' specific language impairment or SLI. These children have difficulty in acquiring spoken language, but in other respects their development is normal. They have no obvious physical problems and they will have been brought up hearing language around them. Yet in spite of this they are late to start speaking; they have difficulty putting words together to form phrases and sentences; and they may have unclear speech which others find hard to follow.

Children with pure SLI still form a mixed group. Some have difficulty in understanding and using language; others understand what is said to them but have difficulty putting words together to express themselves; and some have problems in producing the speech sounds clearly. For many children with SLI, their language is slow to develop but nonetheless follows a normal pattern or sequence. In such cases, the *timing* of language development is the problem – we call this *delayed* language development. Other children with *disordered* (or *deviant)* language development may show not only slowness in learning to talk, but also an unusual *pattern* of speech and language development. They may produce abnormal speech sounds, or oddly constructed sentences, or use language in a strange or inappropriate way. These will be described in more detail later on.

There have been attempts to describe *subtypes* of SLI; child professionals talk about receptive disorders, expressive disorders, semantic-pragmatic disorders, phonological disorders, and so on. However, it is not easy, and probably not helpful, to slot an individual child into a single subtype – real people, including children, are just not like that. There is a lot of overlap and blurring between the different sorts of speech and language difficulties. Each child with SLI needs to be described in his own individual way that recognises his particular problems with speech and language (while not forgetting that he might have strengths in other areas, like being great at doing complicated puzzles or fantastically musical).

Environmental Factors

There is very good evidence that (except in rare cases of extreme neglect and deprivation) the pre-school child's language development is fairly insensitive to the amount or richness of the language he hears. So, if you have a child with SLI, you should not feel that it is your fault. Some parents of children with language difficulties worry that they may not have talked to their child sufficiently. However, we know that most children with SLI come from caring homes with parents who have provided all the language stimulation needed.

Hearing Problems

So, if the environment is not the answer, is it something within the child that is causing the language difficulties? Could it be a hearing problem? Children who are born with a permanent and significant hearing impairment (usually called sensori-neural hearing loss) will have long-term speech and language difficulties – but we would not describe these children as having SLI. However, some parents worry that middle ear hearing problems (otitis media, often called glue ear) might affect their child's ability to listen and, therefore, to acquire speech and language. This is a short-lived (though often recurring) problem. If it does not resolve itself, it may be successfully managed with antibiotics, insertion of grommets (tubes that allow the ears to drain) or even hearing aids. It is remarkably common in pre-schoolers, with as many as 40 per cent of children having suffered glue ear at some point in their pre- or early-school years. Recent studies have suggested that glue ear results in no more than a temporary hiccup in language development, if any is observed at all. Glue ear seems to be a 'risk' factor in SLI only if it occurs in combination with other things, such as prematurity. At any rate, most children with SLI do not present with a history of unusually severe or frequent glue ear.

Genetic Factors

There is increasing evidence to show that SLI runs in families and may therefore be inherited. One important strand of evidence for this comes from studies of twins; if a child who is one of a set of identical twins is found to have SLI, then the probability that his twin will have a similar difficulty is more than 80 per cent (in contrast to non-identical twins, where the probability would be around the 50 per cent mark). This suggests that genes have a strong influence in determining which children develop language difficulties. If your child has a language difficulty that runs in your family, you shouldn't think that there is nothing you can do about it. Even if it is genetically caused, it doesn't mean it cannot be helped.

It is important to identify speech and language difficulties as early as possible, preferably during the pre-school years. However, you should feel reassured to learn that around half of children who have delayed speech at age three are speaking normally by five-and-a-half. But there are some children who do have persisting speech and language impairments. They are then at risk for later reading problems, and also for social and behavioural difficulties. Not being understood by others because your speech is unclear, or not being able to express your thoughts, can be very upsetting and frustrating, even for very young children. Many parents of youngsters with SLI comment on their children's frustration over their communication difficulties that can, in turn, make them socially isolated. The frustration can also set the scene for behaviour problems, including temper tantrums.

If your child's progress in speech and language is causing you concern, the time to act is now – during these important pre-school years. Much can be done to help improve your child's communication difficulties before they begin to have an impact on his classroom learning, his behaviour and his relationships with his peers. Consult your GP, who will make a referral to a child development team or a speech and language therapist.

Disorders of Language Use

There are a small number of children who seem to have clear speech, a wide vocabulary and are able to produce sentences that are grammatically correct – yet what they say sounds 'odd', inappropriate or irrelevant to the situation. If this is true of your child's language, it is possible that he may have a *pragmatic language disorder*, in which case he can be helped by speech and language therapy. It has been estimated that 10 per cent of children with SLI have this kind of language difficulty. Some children who have pragmatic disorders also have a *social communication disorder* – they may even be autistic or have Asperger's syndrome – but there is no complete overlap between pragmatic disorders and autism/Asperger's. A child may have difficulties in using language appropriately, but not the severe social isolation and marked obsessive behaviours characteristic of autistic or Asperger's children. (*For a fuller discussion of children with social communication disorders, see Chapter 4.*)

And Finally ...

Language is an important and complex topic. Acquiring good spoken language is the biggest feat – and, for some children, challenge – of the pre-school years. Your child's language will drive many other skills, both social and educational (especially reading, but maths too). Being a good 'model' for language and giving your child plenty of opportunity to build his vocabulary and practise conversation are the main ways you as a parent can help to develop this vital skill. Watch out for any difficulties with speech and language development your child might have – caught early, most can be successfully remedied before your child faces that important first day at school.

PART C
EDUCATIONAL LEARNING

9

Reading

Learning to read is the single most important *educational* skill children learn during their first two years at school. Learning to read is not the same as 'learning' to talk. Reading is different. Children have to be *taught* how to read.

You may imagine that your child's teachers will show her how to read and that, apart from doing a bit of reading practice with her after school, you as a parent have no real part to play. However, this is not actually the case. The building blocks for reading are developed in the pre-school years. These consist of *foundation skills* and *specific skills*. You as a parent can do a lot to ensure that these are in place for day one of your child's school life.

Foundation Skills

The *foundation skills* relevant for reading are:

- Building up a spoken vocabulary
- Enjoyment at looking through books and listening to stories
- Concepts of print (such as what are letters, what are words, where is the top of the page, in which direction we read i.e. from left to right)

Spoken Vocabulary

Children can't learn to appreciate stories or to read before they have a sizeable spoken vocabulary. Having a good spoken vocabulary is needed for the development of *listening comprehension*. This means they come to understand and remember what has been said (or read) to them. If children don't develop good listening comprehension skills, it follows that they will not develop good reading comprehension. That means they will be reading without understanding – they will be 'barking at print'.

Awareness and Enjoyment of Books and Stories

Children start to become aware of the existence of books at a very young age. Toddlers will turn the pages of storybooks, and look at the pictures in them. Soon afterwards, most parents will begin to read to their children – often a bedtime story to end the day quietly – so pre-schoolers become aware of books and begin to enjoy stories long before they start school. It is this realisation that books can tell fantastic stories that encourages young children to want to learn to read. Soon they won't have to wait for mum or dad to read them a favourite story. They will be able to do it for themselves. Finally, reading stories to your child provides another valuable opportunity to strengthen your emotional links with her.

Concepts of Print

This rather technical-sounding term describes children's developing understanding of what a book is and how to handle it; how the book is constructed and organised; and what print looks like. Concepts of print would include:

- Recognising that print looks different to pictures
- Knowing the front and back of the book

- Being able to say where the top of the page is
- Realising that we read from left to right

One study in Australia has shown that one of the reasons why girls seem to get off to a faster start in learning to read than boys is because they have better developed concepts of print when they start school.

Ready to Read Foundation Checklist

Check to see if your pre-schooler has these foundation concepts by answering the following questions:

Spoken Vocabulary and Listening Comprehension

	Yes	No
Does your child point to pictures in books and name them?	☐	☐
Will your child name a pictured object in a book when you point? For instance, if you say 'What's that?', will she tell you what the picture is of?	☐	☐
Can your child describe in her own words the story sequence in a picture book as you go from page to page? For instance, you might ask her: 'What happened to the children after they set off to the shops?'	☐	☐
Can your child remember or 'fill in' some words or phrases from familiar books? If you said, for instance, 'And then they all went to the ....', could she fill in the correct word from her knowledge of the story?	☐	☐

Awareness and Enjoyment of Books

	Yes	No
Does your child:		
Enjoy listening to you read a short story?	☐	☐

Look at picture and storybooks for herself? ☐ ☐

Like to listen to story tapes? ☐ ☐

Talk with you about what's happening in the
story while you're reading it? ☐ ☐

Have favourite books she asks you to read to her? ☐ ☐

Attempt to 'mimic' reading, for instance, 'reading'
a book to a teddy bear? ☐ ☐

Concepts of Print

Does your child know: Yes   No

How to hold a book correctly? ☐ ☐

That print is different from pictures? ☐ ☐

Which the title page is? ☐ ☐

Where the front of the book is? ☐ ☐

Where the back of the book is? ☐ ☐

Where the top of the page is? ☐ ☐

Where the bottom of the page is? ☐ ☐

To turn the pages at the right time and in the
right direction? ☐ ☐

That the pictures relate to the text? (Does she point
to the pictures as you read?) ☐ ☐

That we read from left to right? ☐ ☐

That each printed word corresponds to a spoken
word? (Can she point to words as you speak them?) ☐ ☐

If you answered 'yes' to many of the questions, then your child
is well prepared to move on to the more specific pre-reading skills
(*see below*).

If you answered 'no' to quite a few of the questions, take
note of these areas and work on them following the exercises and
pointers given below.

Linking Spoken Vocabulary to Print

Building a spoken vocabulary is covered in detail in Chapter 8. Having a good spoken vocabulary is needed for learning to read, and reading storybooks is critical for helping to develop spoken vocabulary. When children come across printed words in books, they need to relate them to the words they have in their spoken vocabulary. Also, research has shown that parents who read to their children help broaden their spoken vocabulary. Here are some suggestions for how you can use your story reading to link spoken vocabulary to print:

- Use the pictures in books to help your child develop her vocabulary. Ask her 'What is that a picture of?', 'What's the girl holding?'
- When you come across a word in a book that you think your child might not know the meaning of, check first if she can tell you what the word means; if she can't, talk to her about it in simple words – maybe you could draw a picture together that shows its meaning.
- Keep your definitions simple and child-friendly, perhaps accompanied by a gesture or an example.
- New words need to be repeated a number of times and in different contexts before they are remembered and 'fitted into' your child's vocabulary. When you and your child come across the 'new' word for a second or third time, draw her attention to it again and ask her if she remembers what it means.

Developing Listening Comprehension

Listening comprehension develops naturally from having your child listen to, share and tell back to you stories that you are reading together. Not only is listening comprehension important for later reading comprehension, but it is also needed when your child is being taught in the classroom. Teachers teach by talking to children, and your child needs to be able to listen and to understand so that she can learn new skills and follow instructions.

Use the shared reading experience to help your child develop listening comprehension by:

- Asking her to tell back to you what happened on a given page of the story; begin by letting her look at the picture (as a prompt), but later on, turn the page over and ask her to describe what has just happened (when she doesn't have a picture clue in front of her).
- Asking her specific questions about what happened in the story, such as, 'Can you remember what was special about Jenny's magic hat?'; 'Why is Pussy hiding in the toy box?'
- Asking her to tell the whole story back to you. Say to her 'Can *you* tell me the story now?' She can look at the pictures in the book as prompts (together with occasional 'cue' questions from you) while she is 'being the parent'.
- Helping her to *draw conclusions* by *making inferences*. This means going beyond what is specifically described in the story and working out what might happen next or how people might be feeling. For example, 'How do you think Jenny felt when she saw that her mummy was cross with her?'
- Helping her to develop a sense of the *main idea* of the story by asking her 'What do you think this story tells us?' This is hard for many pre-schoolers; it may be that you will want to talk to her about the main point or theme of the story, but not necessarily expect her to work it out for herself at this stage.

Improving Book, Story and Print Awareness

Here are some tips on how your child can get the most out of your shared reading experiences:

- Read together while snuggling up on a big chair, in bed or with your child on your lap (or even while your child is enjoying a bath!) Make sure your child is comfortable and easily able to see the pages of the book and touch the pictures and words.

- Choose short books that can easily be read in one sitting; the print should be large, well spaced with simple sentences (no more than one or two sentences to a page for the very first books you read together).

- Read the book yourself before reading it to your child – you can then plan ahead how you want to present certain sections of the story.

- Before starting to read the story, look together at the cover, read the title and the author's (and maybe illustrator's) name.

- Say something brief about what the book is about, such as, 'This is a story about a little girl called Jenny who goes to play football in the park.'

- Turn to the first page and say, 'This is the beginning of our story,' and when you reach the last page, close the book and say, 'That's the end of our story.'

- Every so often, stop to make a comment or ask a question: 'What do you think Jenny will do next?'; 'That's a funny hat! What colour is it? Would you like a hat like that?'

- Give your child experience of handling the book by letting her hold it some of the time, and encourage her to turn the pages.

- Point under the words with your finger and glide your finger along the line as you read; this helps your child become aware that we read sentences from left to right, that sentences are made up of words and that we read the page from top to bottom.

- Encourage your child to join in rhymes or repetitive phrases, or to fill in missing words in books with which she is already familiar. For example, 'Jenny clapped, Sam clapped and then all the children … (clapped).'

- Encourage your child to 'read' the story to you or to a favourite stuffed animal – she can then practise holding the book, turning the pages, looking at the pictures and following print with her finger.
- From time to time, test your child's print awareness by asking her to show you the beginning and end of the book, the top and bottom of a page and the beginning and end of a line.

Specific Skills for Learning to Read

This may surprise you, but research has shown us that for children to begin to make sense of print, just two very specific skills need to be in place – these are *phonological awareness* and *knowledge of alphabet letters*.

Phonological Awareness

This refers to children's awareness that the spoken words they hear and use are made up of sequences of sounds. The main sets of sounds in words are **syllables** and **phonemes.**

Syllables

Syllables are units in a word that consist of a vowel flanked by one or two consonants. For instance, in the word 'carpet' there are two syllables: /car/ and /pet/. Syllables may be more easily understood by your child if you explain to her that they are about listening to the 'beats' in the word; you could tap on the table or clap your hands while you beat three times for the word 'bu-tter-fly'.

Phonemes

Phonemes are the smallest units of speech sounds. It is important not to confuse phonemes with letters. While there are three phonemes in the three-letter word 'dog' (/d/, /o/ and /g/), there are also three phonemes in the four-letter word 'chin' (/ch/, /i/ and /n/) because /ch/ makes one speech sound. Similarly, in the five-letter word 'sheep', there are also just three phonemes (/sh/, /ee/ and /p/) because /sh/ and /ee/ both make only one sound.

When working on phonological awareness exercises, it is important to pronounce the consonants as clearly as possible. When pronouncing 'b' and 'm', for example, be careful not to add an 'uh', like 'buh' or 'muh'; this 'uh' sound is called a 'schwa' – it does tend to distort sounds, so keep it to a minimum if you can. Pronouncing the schwa turns a word like 'dog' into something like 'duh-o-guh'. You should try to pronounce all consonants without the schwa; for example, 'sss' not 'suh', 'mm' not 'muh'.

As we have seen, children first develop awareness of syllables as 'beats in words'. At about the same time, they become aware of *first* sounds in words, especially the first sound of their own name. Your child might say, 'I'm Sophie – Sophie with a "sss".' You will also notice that, not long after, she will begin to show an awareness of rhyming, that is where two words sound the same at the end ('cat–mat', 'look–book' are pairs of words that rhyme). Awareness of rhyme is thought to be a foundation phonological skill that eventually leads to children being able to identify and manipulate phonemes in words (examples of 'manipulating' phonemes would be your child being able to say that the last sound in 'cat' is 't', and that 'cat' without saying the 'c' is 'at').

Letter Knowledge

This refers to how easily children learn the names and sounds of the individual letters of the alphabet, 'a' through to 'z'. Which should be taught first – letter names or sounds? Since letter names and sounds are quite closely related to each other, it probably doesn't matter too much which your child learns first. However, the current view (and indeed practice) of most schools is to teach the sounds first. How long it will take your child to learn the alphabet will be influenced by her individual rate of learning and, very importantly, the reading programme used at her school. There is a current trend in schools to teach the whole alphabet over a short period of time, even over just one term. This is certainly true for children who are being taught *synthetic phonics* (*see page 261*). While some letters will be learned before your child starts school, you should expect the remainder to be learned fairly quickly during her first school year.

The Alphabetic Principle

When children have enough phonological awareness to enable them to split words into sounds, and when they know most of the letters of the alphabet, they are ready to learn the alphabetic principle.

This is a term coined by the Australian psychologist, Brian Byrne. It is the idea that 'the letters that comprise our printed language stand for the individual sounds that comprise our spoken language'. Byrne goes on to say that for children to get the alphabetic principle they need to:

- Have sufficient phonological awareness so that they can split spoken words into sounds
- Know most of the alphabet
- Be able to put these two skills together – meaning that they can link or combine their sound awareness with their letter knowledge (what we usually describe as 'phonics')

Children come to grips with the alphabetic principle during their first year at school, and this provides the critical base upon which all later literacy skills are built. However, phonological awareness and learning the alphabet (on which the alphabetic principle depends) begin to develop during the important pre-school years. Supporting and encouraging the development of these pre-reading skills will place your child in an excellent position for learning to read after she starts school.

Test Your Child's Phonological Awareness and Letter Knowledge

Beginning, Middle and End Words

Does your child understand what are the beginning, middle and end words in a short sentence? Ask her:

		Yes	No
What is the **beginning** word in:	*My* red book.	☐	☐
What is the **middle** word in:	I *like* chocolate	☐	☐
What is the **end** word in:	Time to *play*	☐	☐

Awareness of Syllables

Is your child able to *beat out* the syllables in a word, by clapping them as she says them (or tapping on a table if she'd prefer)? Ask her to clap (or tap) with a beat the syllables in her own name and maybe her mum's or sister's name, before trying two-syllable words like (the answers are given in brackets):

	Yes	No
flower (beat-beat)	☐	☐
story (beat-beat)	☐	☐
picture (beat-beat)	☐	☐

Is your child able to *blend* (or join) syllables to make words? Say a two-syllable word, pausing for about a second between the syllables, and ask her, 'What word am I saying?'

	Yes	No
rain-bow (rainbow)	☐	☐

pen-guin (penguin) ☐ ☐
chil-dren (children) ☐ ☐

Maybe try some longer words that have three syllables: **Yes** **No**
el-e-phant (elephant) ☐ ☐
re-mem-ber (remember) ☐ ☐
di-no-saur (dinosaur) ☐ ☐

Is your child able to *segment* (or break) words into syllables? Can she
say what the **beginning** syllable is in **Yes** **No**
carpet (car) ☐ ☐
monkey (mun) ☐ ☐
spider (spy) ☐ ☐

Can she say what the **end** syllable is in **Yes** **No**
window (dow) ☐ ☐
postman (man) ☐ ☐
breakfast (fast) ☐ ☐

Rhyming

Can your child finish off a nursery rhyme that you've started?

	Yes	No
Hickory dickory dock, the mouse ran up the … (clock)	☐	☐
Jack and Jill went up the … (hill)	☐	☐

	Yes	No
Can she tell you words she knows that rhyme with **fan**?	☐	☐

Give her an example like 'tan'. Can she think of any others? Make a
note of the rhyming words that she says (even nonsense words like
'zan' and 'gan' are acceptable as long as they rhyme).

Phoneme Awareness

Can your child *blend* two or three sounds together to make a word? Make sure you say the *sound* (not the *name*) of each letter (*before you do this test, see page 243 on pronouncing sounds correctly*). Say each phoneme in the word with a one-second pause between each. Ask your child, 'What word am I saying?'

	Yes	No
s-o (so)	☐	☐
i-s (is)	☐	☐
t-ea (tea)	☐	☐
d-a-d (dad)	☐	☐
p-i-g (pig)	☐	☐

	Yes	No
Can your child play 'I Spy?'	☐	☐

Say, 'I spy with my little eye some things that begin with 'f'. Can you find them?' Your child may say, 'Flower, floor, finger', etc. Now try another sound, say 't' (for 'table, toy, teddy').

This leads in to working on the *segmentation* test below because you are drawing your child's attention to the idea of 'beginning with' or 'first', which some four-year-olds can find a little hard to get to grips with.

Can your child *segment* (or break) words into phonemes? Can she say what the **first** sound is in the words:

		Yes	No
cat	/c/	☐	☐
pig	/p/	☐	☐
top	/t/	☐	☐

Can she say what the **end** sound is in the words:

		Yes	No
cat	/t/	☐	☐

pig	/g/	☐	☐
top	/p/	☐	☐

Letter Knowledge

How many letters of the alphabet does your child know? Ask her 'What do these letters say'? Note that they're presented in random order, going from left to right. It helps to keep the left-to-right order as this is the case for normal reading, and is a skill to keep practising. Tick off each letter correctly identified, whether your child gives the name or the sound.

s m f t g a

l o r z p i

y b h k e w

c j n d q v

x u

Summary Table

Can your child:		Yes	No
Say the **beginning** word in a sentence		☐	☐
Say the **middle** word in a sentence		☐	☐
Say the **end** word in a sentence		☐	☐
Beat out a	**two-syllable word**	☐	☐
Blend	**two syllables**	☐	☐
	three syllables	☐	☐
Segment	**a beginning syllable**	☐	☐
	an end syllable	☐	☐
Finish off a	**nursery rhyme**	☐	☐
Say words that **rhyme** with another word		☐	☐
Blend	**two phonemes**	☐	☐
	three phonemes	☐	☐
Play	**I Spy**	☐	☐
Segment	**a beginning phoneme**	☐	☐
	an end phoneme	☐	☐
How many **letters of the alphabet** can your child say the name or sound of?		☐ /26	

If you've answered 'yes' to many of the questions, your child clearly has very good phonological awareness and is well prepared to get to grips with the alphabetic principle after she starts school.

If you've recorded quite a few 'nos', don't worry. It is not unusual for pre-school children to have difficulty with some of

PREPARE YOUR CHILD FOR SCHOOL

these skills. Opposite are some games and activities that will help your child build up her phonological awareness ready for school.

If your child knows around half the letters of the alphabet, that's fine. If she knows fewer than this, it would be a good idea to start building up her letter knowledge before she starts school. Some guidelines for how to work on the alphabet follow.

Help Your Child to Develop Phonological Awareness

When working through the phonological awareness test with your child, you probably realised that some tasks are much harder than others. Research suggests that breaking words into syllables is much easier for young children than breaking words into phonemes, and that rhyming games are in general easier than games that require children to, for instance, 'take away the last sound in a word'. In addition, blending sounds to make words is easier than breaking up words to make sounds.

In working on these suggested activities, you will be introducing your child to two different *levels* of phonological awareness. The first level is working on her *sensitivity* to sounds. These are the games that focus on words, syllables, rhymes and blending phonemes. Later on, you will be working on her ability to *manipulate* phonemes in words. These tasks include identifying phonemes in words and 'taking away' phonemes. They are much harder skills for pre-schoolers to achieve, and some children may not be ready to work on them until shortly after they have started school. Therefore, when you're helping your child build up her phonological awareness, don't run before you can walk! Start with the simpler games, such as the ones that work on syllables, rhymes and blending. When you're sure your child can do these games easily, move on to the harder ones that involve splitting the word into phonemes.

Games to Build Sensitivity to Words, Syllables and Sounds

Learning about Beginning, Middle and End

You will have realised from the test whether your child understands the meaning of these important words – *beginning, middle* and *end*. If she seems unsure, give her some practice in showing you which is the beginning, the middle and the end in these series of three. Say to your child, 'Point to the beginning picture, now to the end picture, and now to the middle picture':

	Beginning	Middle	End
Pictures	☺	♥	❄
Coloured counters	◯	◯	◯
Printed letters	s	t	p
Printed numbers	2	7	4
Words in spoken sentences		'My dog barks'	

Words and Sentences

As well as getting your child to tell you which is the beginning, middle and end word in a three-word sentence, get her to **clap** the words she hears in a sentence: so two claps for 'Bobby runs', three claps for 'Jenny is happy', four claps for 'My dog is big'. Encourage her to clap each word as she says it.

Another good game that helps your child begin to realise that words in sentences can be represented by symbols is to line up three or four coloured counters in front of her. Then ask her to **pick up a counter** for each word she hears you say – two counters for 'Mummy laughs', three counters for 'Sam is tall'.

A slightly harder game would be asking your child to **take away** a word from a sentence. You could say 'Can you say "Bobby runs", but don't say "Bobby"?' (answer: 'runs'); 'Can you say "I go home" but don't say "go"?' (answer: I home). Don't try this with sentences of more than four words; that would put too much load on your pre-schooler's memory capacity.

Work on Syllables

Start by **beating out** syllables in words. You could get your child to **clap** the syllables she hears (or even says herself) in a two- or three-syllable word (*see below*).

You say:	**picture**
Child says:	**picture**
Child does:	**clap clap**

You say:	**elephant**
Child says:	**elephant**
Child does:	**clap clap clap**

Now do some work on **blending** syllables to join words. You could use a puppet or doll for this. Explain to your child that the doll says words very slowly. Can she tell you what word the doll is trying to say? Start with two-syllable words like 'car-pet', 'bis-cuit', 'par-ty', 'pic-ture', saying the word with a short pause (around a second) between the two syllables. Once your child is good at this, move on to three-syllable words like 'di-no-saur', 'bu-tter-fly', 'al-pha-bet', and eventually four-syllable words like 'a-lli-ga-tor', 'ca-ter-pill-ar'.

See if your child can tell you which is the **beginning syllable** in words like 'car-pet', 'mon-key', 'trac-tor', and which is the **end syllable** in 'car-pet', 'mon-key', 'trac-tor'? If she finds this a little hard to begin with, use two coloured counters in a line, and point to them as you say each syllable to make it more concrete for her. Once your child gets the hang of this, you can take away the counters and see if she can do it just through listening to you say the syllables. Maybe you can try getting her to tell you the **middle syllable** of three-syllable words like 'bu-tter-fly' and 'al-pha-bet'.

Then see if your child can **finish off** the second syllable in a two-syllable word. Gather together some pictures of objects with two-syllable names like 'apple', 'monkey', 'circle'. Show your child the picture of a circle and say, 'I'm going to say the beginning of the word; you finish it off for me – here is a "cir-",' to which your child should respond 'cle'.

Hardest of all would be getting your child to **take away** a syllable from a two-syllable word. You'd say, 'What's carpet without saying "car"?' (answer: 'pet'); 'What's "monkey" without saying "mun"?' (answer: 'key').

Practising Rhyming

Children's awareness of rhyme is quite closely related to their early language (particularly vocabulary) development. Although rhyming skills are not thought to be necessary for beginning to learn to read, they may form a bridge between early vocabulary development and later phonological awareness skills. There are lots of easy, informal games you can do with your child to help her become aware of rhymes. Working on rhyming provides a base on which to build the complex phoneme manipulation skills that will be described later. Recite nursery rhymes together; read books that have rhyming verses; make up silly rhymes; ask your child to finish off the last word in a sentence from a familiar nursery rhyme, such as 'Hickory, dickory, dock, the mouse ran up the ...?' (answer: 'clock').

A more formal game would be to think up together words that rhyme with each other. Look together at a picture of a pig. You say: 'Here's a pig; I'm going to think up a word that rhymes with pig – what about "big"? Can you think of some words that rhyme with pig and big?' Your child might come up with words like 'dig', 'fig' and 'jig'. Then suggest that you both think of some silly made-up words that rhyme with pig, such as 'lig', 'zig', 'tig', 'mig' and so on.

For some inspiration, see the box below:

Which Words Rhyme with...?

lid	mat	rug	pot	pen
kid	pat	dug	hot	ten
did	sat	mug	dot	hen
rid	hat	jug	cot	den
bid	rat	tug	lot	men
Sid	fat	hug	tot	fen

And What about Some Silly Words?

fid	lat	wug	zot	ren
nid	jat	zug	fot	nen
pid	wat	gug	vot	sen

You can help your child **detect rhyming words** by showing her a picture of, say, a cat. You say, 'Here's a cat. I'm going to say two more words. Which of them rhymes with cat?' Then say, clearly and slowly, 'pat, bag'. Your child needs to pick out which is the word that rhymes, in this case 'pat'.

Here are a few more examples:

Star:	**jar**	pat
Face:	late	**race**
Box:	**fox**	pot

Help your Child Begin to be Aware of Phonemes

Awareness of phonemes begins in the pre-school years, but only at a fairly basic level. This skill continues to develop during the first year at school as your child builds up her reading vocabulary. The activities suggested here concentrate only on phoneme awareness skills that your child needs for starting school.

Blending Phonemes

This is a fairly easy task even for four- to five-year-olds, providing you keep the words nice and short, and of no longer than two or three phonemes. Use the puppet or doll again, and say, 'Our puppet says words very slowly – can you say it faster for her so it comes out sounding right?' You should begin with words that have only two phonemes to blend, like 'm-e', 'i-s', 'a-t', 'g-o', and then move on to three-phoneme words like 'd-o-g', 'p-i-ck', 'm-u-m', 'sh-i-p'. When you start teaching phoneme blending, stretch the word to emphasise the phonemes: 'cccaaaattt' (cat) and 'pppiiikkk' (pick). Once your child is working nicely on the stretched words, shorten the phonemes to 'c-a-t' and 'p-i-ck'. Your child is now ready to move on to the more difficult phoneme *identification* and *manipulation* tasks.

Games to Develop Ability to Identify and Manipulate Phonemes in Words

Remember that these are very much harder skills for your child to develop. Don't start on them until you've worked through the activities suggested in the previous section – and until your child is comfortable with them. When you think she's ready, try the following – but take it slowly. If she finds it hard, leave it for a bit and come back to them when your child is a little older, or back-pedal for a while using the games described above.

Identifying Phonemes: See if your child can **tell** which is the **beginning, middle** and **end** phoneme in simple three-phoneme words like 'd-o-g', 'sh-i-p' and 'c-a-t'. Again, use counters if that makes it easier.

Get your child to **clap** the phonemes she hears you say – two claps for 'go', 'me' and 'at', and three claps for 'dog', 'mum' and 'fish'.

Ask your child to think of words that begin with the same sound – what is called **alliteration**. Say to her, 'I'm going to say a word that begins with the /s/ sound – "sun". Let's try and think of some others. What about "sad"? Can you think of some more?' She may come up with 'sip', 'stick', 'sorry', 'sandwich', 'sock'. Then you say, 'Shall we make up some silly words that begin with /s/? What about "sut"? Can you think of some?' Your child may come up with silly words that you can laugh at together like 'saf', 'sog', 'sul'.

Here are some more examples of alliteration:

Can You Think of Words that Begin with the Sound:

	f	t	p	m	c
Your example	fun	tin	pat	mug	cap
Your child might say	fat	tag	pot	mine	cot
	furry	tiger	pink	mat	can
	fireman	tummy	pretty	middle	cut
	fizzy	tomorrow	pattern	money	cup

Get your child to **finish off** phonemes in words. Show her a picture of an object that has a single-syllable word, like 'cat'. Tell her you're going to say the first part of the word (ca) and you'd like her to finish it off. So, she says '/t/'.

Manipulating Phonemes: The hardest thing for pre-schoolers to do with phonemes is to *manipulate* them, for instance deleting or **taking away** phonemes from words. Children under seven can usually take away only beginning and end (not middle) phonemes from words. Pictures can be helpful for this, so gather together images of common objects with single-syllable names, like 'pig', 'dog', 'bun', 'cat', 'ball'. See if your child can take away the first sound from the word, so 'pig' without the /p/ becomes 'ig'. She may need quite a lot of practice and help with this, but if she doesn't seem to be getting it after a little while, leave it and come back to it when she's older. If she does get the hang of taking away beginning sounds, try asking her to take away end sounds from words, so 'meat' without the /t/ becomes 'me'.

PREPARE YOUR CHILD FOR SCHOOL

Games to Help Your Child Learn Some Letters of the Alphabet

One of the issues that sometimes confuses parents is whether they should introduce their child to the *sounds* or the *names* of the alphabetic letters. As mentioned earlier, the current practice in the UK is to teach letter sounds before letter names. If you're unsure about what to do, you might check with the school your child will attend as to whether or not they emphasise learning sounds or letters first. In this way you can go along with whatever the school will do once your child starts there.

Like most adults, you may be more comfortable with letter names, but if your child's school teaches letter sounds first, you will need to get to grips with how to say the sounds properly (*see page 243*).

Letters are not usually taught in alphabetical order, 'a' through to 'z', but rather by how common the letters are in words. Therefore, you might begin with six letter sounds that let you make up many three-letter words:

s a t i p n

Once your child has learned these six letter sounds, she has the basis for beginning to learn to read simple words like 'sat', 'pit', 'tan', 'tip', 'pan', 'sip' and so on.

The next set of consonants your child might learn could be:

d g h k

alongside another vowel, **e**.

Much later on (most likely at school), your child will learn the least commonly used letters, like:

q z w v

together with the vowels, **o** and **u**.

If you're teaching letter names first, your child will find it easier to learn the names of letters that are very close to the sounds they represent. Therefore, learning letters like **y, w, h** is harder and may take longer than learning letters like **s, b, t** and so on. This is because for the letter **s**, the sound /ss/ sounds very similar to the name 'es'. However, for the letter **w**, the sound /wu/ sounds very different to the name, 'double-u'.

Here are some tips about materials and activities you can use to help your child learn the letters of the alphabet:

- Look at colourful alphabet books with your child; there are lots of these available, so choose ones that you think your child will like most.
- Watch DVDs or television programmes that include alphabet games.
- Get some materials together to play alphabet games:
  - Either buy a set of plastic or felt letters (in lower case), or make yourself a little pack of cards with a letter of the alphabet written in large lower case lettering on each.
  - Make a collection of **objects**, for instance small toys or even everyday objects around the home, that begin with the letters of the alphabet you're working on with your child. You could use a plastic cow to represent the letter **c**, and a sock to represent the letter **s**. Use objects that begin with the common beginning sound for the letter; so a sock to represent the letter **s**, but not a shoe because its beginning sound is /sh/.
  - Also, make a collection of **pictures** of everyday objects beginning with the different alphabet letters.

Now play games with the letters, objects and pictures. These have been described assuming that you're working on letter sounds, but the procedures are essentially the same for letter names.

- Sort into little piles objects or pictures that begin with the same letter. For instance, when you're working on the letter c, pick out from your picture stack images of a cat, a cup, a clock and so on. After the pictures have been grouped together, put your plastic letter c next to it and say, 'Here is the letter c; /c/ for cat, /c/ for /cup/, /c/ for clock.' Gradually, your child will come to learn the letter, to associate it with its sound and to link it with the pictures and objects that begin with that letter.

- Use the pictures you've collected to help your child make her own alphabet book. Use one page for each letter, write it in large lower-case print at the top and then stick the pictures in place underneath the letter. Keep going back over the letters so that your child gets plenty of practice and doesn't forget them.

- Play games like 'I Spy'. Put out an array of objects and/or pictures, together with the alphabet letters you've been working on. Say, 'I spy with my little eye something beginning with /s/.' Your child then picks out the relevant object/s or picture/s. Encourage her to say, '/s/ for sock' or whatever she has chosen. Then see if she can pick out the letter that goes with the sound.

You can check on whether your child really knows the letters you've taught her by asking her to recall their sounds (or names) from time to time. Show her some of the letters in random order, then ask her to tell you which sound (or name) each makes. You don't need to work on all the letters before your child starts school, but it is a good idea for her to have a knowledge of around half of them.

Phonics

When your child does start school, she will follow a structured reading scheme that will include **phonics**.

It is generally accepted that any systematic reading programme should contain a strong emphasis on phonic teaching. The two main approaches to teaching phonics are *synthetic* and *analytic* phonics.

Synthetic Phonics

At the start of schooling, children are taught a small group of letter sounds very quickly, and are then shown how these letter sounds can be blended (or synthesised) to form words. Other groups of letters are then brought in later.

Analytic Phonics

In analytic phonics, children are taught to 'split' or analyse words into smaller parts to help with decoding. Teaching starts at the whole-word level and then works towards showing children patterns in the English spelling system. Alongside whole-word learning, Reception class children are typically taught one letter sound per week. The 26 *initial* letter sounds are taught over a two-term period. The children are then introduced to letter sounds in the middle and (later) end positions in words.

Both methods involve sounding out and blending, but there are fundamental differences between them. In analytic phonics, children analyse letter sounds *after* the word has been identified, whereas in synthetic phonics the pronunciation of the word is *discovered* through sounding and blending. In synthetic phonics, children learn to sound and blend right at the start of learning to read. In analytic phonics, children learn words largely as 'sight words'. Later their attention is drawn to initial sounds, and it is then that sounding out and blending are introduced.

There is recent evidence from studies in Scotland that synthetic phonics results in greater speed of learning to read than analytic phonics, and that these benefits are long lasting. However, it wouldn't be surprising if in the long run children learn best using a programme that includes both synthesis (to learn to decode) and analysis (to establish key sight words and to help children with spelling, especially of irregular words).

Specific Learning Difficulties

The term *specific learning difficulty* is used when a child has a problem in learning a particular skill, in contrast to her other abilities which appear to be developing well. It is used to distinguish between children who find it hard to learn a specific skill from those who have 'global' or 'generalised' learning difficulties and who are, therefore, 'slow at everything'. Children with specific learning difficulties may be very bright. In cases of dyslexia, for example, which affects reading ability, it is not unusual for children to be doing very well developmentally in other respects. They may have a very large spoken vocabulary, be good at doing puzzles or be doing well in number work.

There are a number of types of specific learning difficulty:

- Dyslexia – dyslexic children have problems with phonological awareness, which makes it hard for them to learn phonics when they start school; this affects progress in reading and spelling. Dyslexia is the most common specific learning difficulty, affecting 5–8 per cent of children.
- Dyscalculia – dyscalculic children have a specific difficulty with number concepts (*see Chapter 10*).

- Dyspraxia – dyspraxic children have poor motor skills that affect body movement and so sport and handwriting (*see Chapters 6 and 11*).
- Attention Deficit – this is sometimes thought of as a specific learning difficulty or at any rate as something that affects children's ability to learn (*see Chapter 7*).
- Specific Language Impairment (SLI) – again, this is not always considered a specific learning difficulty, but language problems certainly affect progress in learning (*see Chapter 8*).

Because so many children find it hard to learn to read, there has been a lot of research into how to assess and help dyslexic children. We now know what the 'at risk' factors in dyslexia are, even in the pre-school years. Are any of the following relevant to your child?

- Is there a family history of poor reading and spelling? Dyslexia is commonly an inherited condition and so runs in families.
- Was your child late to talk, or does she have unclear speech that other people find hard to follow?
- Has your child found it hard to learn nursery rhymes or to play rhyming games?
- Is your child finding it hard to learn and remember the letters of the alphabet?

If you have answered 'yes' to at least two out of the four questions, your child is at risk for reading difficulties. There are two things you should do:

- Keep up the exercises in print awareness, phonological awareness and alphabet learning described above. There is a lot of evidence that many reading difficulties can be prevented (or at least reduced) if they are identified early, and steps taken to remediate them. Working on sounds in words and on letters is the best preventive action you can take (along with reading books to, and with, your child). But two words of warning! First, take it slowly, and make sure your child can do the simpler activities before you move on to the harder exercises. Second, remember to make the exercises enjoyable for your child – keep it relaxed, make it fun, and if you are anxious about your child struggling, don't show it! If it's less stressful, or just for a change, get somebody else to do the exercises with her – a grandparent or other close relative, or a family friend. You may find it helpful to use some of the reward strategies outlined in Chapter 3, together with some of the ideas addressed in Chapter 7.

- Let the school your child will attend know about your concerns. If there are any 'at risk' difficulties, tell your child's teacher in advance. That way, they can keep an eye on your child, and specialist help can be given if needed.

If your child's difficulties persist during the first two years at school, it will be important to arrange for her to have an assessment of her difficulties. This might take place with a specialist literacy support teacher or psychologist.

And Finally ...

Don't forget that reading with your child is not just a question of teaching her about print. It's also about introducing her to the great pleasure of reading. Reading newspapers, magazines and books may become a source of both relaxation and enjoyment for the rest of her life. And, importantly in these early years, reading with your child is a great way for the two of you to share a special experience that will help you bond emotionally and communicate with each other.

10
Number Work

Children begin to develop an awareness of numbers from a remarkably early age. Babies as young as six months can distinguish between groups of objects that differ in number size. There have been some very interesting experiments to demonstrate this. For example, a baby is shown a picture of three balls. At first the baby focuses keenly on the balls, but then begins to lose interest. At this point, a picture of four balls is shown, and the baby shows interest again. It is assumed that it is the 'threeness' which the baby no longer finds interesting. Some two-year-olds can count, though not necessarily in the right order. Many three-year-olds can recognise quantities of one, two and three objects and say how many there are. By the age of four, children are beginning to understand one-to-one correspondence of number – for instance, linking the sound of three taps of a finger with three dots.

Young children develop their awareness of numbers through play, exploration and basic everyday activities. Pre-school children are at a 'concrete' stage of mathematical development. This means that they learn about number concepts through manipulating and playing with objects. This is of course great fun, and there is a lot that you can do with your child at home to develop these important foundations for what will eventually become 'abstract' maths. When children enter the abstract stage, it means they will be able to use just the numerical symbols (for instance, $2 + 5 = 7$) in their mathematical working – but these do not develop until the child is well into formal schooling. You and your child can together work on the early concrete number skills so he is well prepared for learning about abstract maths when he starts school.

The Five Pre-school Number Skills

Maths teacher, Ann Montague-Smith, describes five different early number skills that children develop in the pre-school years:

1 *Counting* – being able to count objects develops from around the age of three years, and leads to children acquiring an understanding of numbers, and even of number operations like addition and subtraction.

2 *Number Concepts* – children's ability to recognise numerals (in written form, such as 2, 7, 9), to use language like 'more' and 'less' to compare numbers, and to begin to relate addition to 'combining' two groups of objects and subtraction to 'taking away'.

3 *Patterns* – recognising that a sequence of objects (like alternating red and blue bricks) makes a pattern helps children make sense of the world and enables them to make predictions (about what happens next); children need to be able to recognise and continue patterns of objects in order later on to understand number patterns and relationships.

4 *Shape and Space* – being able to recognise, sort and categorise objects by size and shape (such as big and little, circle and square) is important in mathematics (for instance, doing geometry later on), as well as for other educational skills such as handwriting.

5 *Measurement and Making Comparisons* – pre-schoolers' concrete experience of simple measurement is important for them to be able to develop the language of measurement such as heavier/lighter.

Ready for Number Work Checklist

Counting

Can your child:	Yes	No
Look at three objects and tell you instantly how many there are?	☐	☐
Recite numbers in the right order (1, 2, 3, etc.) up to at least 10?	☐	☐
When counting a series of objects, count each item only once?	☐	☐
Co-ordinate the touching and counting so that these happen at the same time?	☐	☐
Count up to 10 objects in a series (fingers would do) without making a mistake?	☐	☐
Realise that the last object he counts in a series represents how many there are in all? After he's counted the objects, ask him 'So how many are there in all?'	☐	☐
Realise that counting applies to all objects, not just blocks or counters, even if they are not all the same? See if he counts correctly to four when you put out a spoon, a cup, a doll and a toy car. Can he then tell you how many there are altogether?	☐	☐
Realise that the order in which the objects are counted does not affect the number of objects present? Given the set of spoon, cup, doll and toy car, can you change the order of the objects with your child realising that there are still four objects? Put them in the order cup, toy, car, doll and spoon, and ask, 'How many are there now?'	☐	☐

Number Concepts

Can your child:	Yes	No
Recognise and name the written numerals 1 to 9?	☐	☐

Name numerals (1–9) when these are presented to him in random order? For instance:

2   5   1   4   7   3   9   6   8   ☐ ☐

Say which is the *bigger* and which is the *smaller* number when asked to compare two numbers? You could try this first by *saying* the numbers to your child:

2 (and) **5, 6** (and) **3, 7** (and) **4**   ☐ ☐

If your child can do that, can he tell you which is the bigger and which is the smaller when you *write* the numbers for him:

1 4, 5 2, 3 6   ☐ ☐

Tell you what is one more and one less than any number between 1 and 10? Again try this by *saying* the numbers to him first:
'What is one more than'

3 (answer 4), **7** (answer 8), **5** (answer 6)   ☐ ☐
'What is one less than'

7 (answer 6), **5** (answer 4), **2** (answer 1)   ☐ ☐

If your child can do this quite easily, show him the numbers in *written* form.
'What is one more than'

4 (answer 5), **6** (answer 7), **2** (answer 3)   ☐ ☐
'What is one less than'

7 (answer 6), **2** (answer 1), **9** (answer 8)   ☐ ☐

Do addition and subtraction with very small numbers (up to around 5) using his fingers or by counting in his head if he can? Ask him questions like:

'Susan has two blocks and mummy gives her one
  more – how many blocks will she have altogether?'   ☐ ☐
  (answer: 3)

'Danny has four toy cars and he loses two of them – how many will he have left?' (answer: 2)

☐ ☐

Show some ability to write down numbers? For instance, if you show your child three counters, can he represent them either by *drawing* three circles or by drawing 'tally marks' to represent them (I I I) or even *writing* the number itself (3)?

☐ ☐

Patterns

Can your child:	Yes	No
Copy a sequence of objects you've created for him, using, for example, beads of different colours or shapes?	☐	☐

For instance

	Yes	No
Continue (or keep going) a pattern or sequence you've started for him – for instance like the one above?	☐	☐
Create a pattern of his own and then continue it?	☐	☐

Shape and Space

Can your child:	Yes	No
Recognise and *name* **lines**, **squares**, **circles** and **triangles** when these are shown to him?	☐	☐
Sort objects according to **colour**, **shape** and **size** (so all the blue items are in one group, the red in another; and similarly, the big objects are in one group and the small objects in the other)?	☐	☐
Match objects by **colour**, **size** or **shape**; for instance, showing your child a blue object then asking him to choose an object of the same colour from a group of objects of different colours?	☐	☐

Use differently shaped objects to *create patterns* or other objects, such as putting triangles, squares or rectangles together to make a house?

☐ ☐

Measurement

Can your child: **Yes**   **No**

Say which line is *longest* and which is *shortest* in the following?

☐ ☐

_____

_____

_____

Say which is the *heavier* or *lighter* of two objects you ask him to hold?

☐ ☐

Order three objects according to length from shortest to longest, such as, these lines:

☐ ☐

_____

_____

_____

This becomes

_____

followed by

_____

and finally

_____

If you have answered 'yes' to most of the above questions, your child is clearly well prepared for learning about abstract maths at primary school.

If you have answered 'no' to many or even a few then it would be helpful to focus some attention on developing these less secure skills.

Children grow in their grasp of concrete maths concepts through play, exploration and everyday routines. Opportunities for learning about numbers, shapes, patterns and measurement are around us all the time – whether out shopping (and counting the change), measuring ingredients when cooking, sorting clothes items for the washing machine, setting the table, measuring a child's height and so on. You can use these day-to-day activities, together with the exercises below, to help develop your child's awareness of number.

Counting

There are five concepts that children need to grasp before they can be said to be counting. These are:

1 The *one-to-one principle*. This means that children match the counting words they're saying to the items they're counting. To understand this principle, children have first to be able to recite the counting words in order, 1, 2, 3, 4 and so on; children as young as three can recite the first few numbers though they do not relate these to the number of objects. Second, they need to touch and count each item only once; you may have noticed that when your child was first learning to count objects, he often touched an object more than once, effectively counting it again. Finally, the child needs to count the number (best out loud to start with) at the same time as touching the object.

2 The *stable order principle*. This refers to the child's realisation that the order of counting words is always the same: we count 1, 2, 3, never 2, 1, 3.

3 The *cardinal principle*. The final number in any count represents how many are in the set or group. The child must therefore be able to stop on the last number of the count and

recognise that number as how many there are altogether. If he counts three blocks, he says, '1, 2, 3,' and can then say, 'There are three blocks.'

4 The *abstraction principle*. This states that the how-to-count procedure can be applied to any situation and any set of objects, whether they are all the same (such as four blue blocks) or different objects (such as a block, a doll, a toy car, a hairbrush). Research has shown that most children aged three and four can only count things that are identical to one another (such as the four blocks). It is not until they are near five years or above that they are able to appreciate that they can count dissimilar objects (like the mix of items above).

5 The *order irrelevance principle*. This refers to children's understanding that the order in which items are counted does not affect the cardinal number of the set. For instance, in a set consisting of a block, a doll, a toy car and a hairbrush, it is perfectly all right to call the block 'one' the first time he counts it and the doll 'one' on the second time he counts them out.

To become successful at counting, your child needs opportunities to:

- Use language of quantity to make comparisons between objects; in particular, he needs to learn words like **more, less, the same,** and so on.
- Recite the number names so he becomes consistent in this.
- Count out a given quantity of items; for instance, give your child 10 blocks and ask him to count out 6 of them.
- Count items in a set (*see below*).

Exercises to Develop Counting Skills
Use Language of Quantity to Make Comparisons
This is all about learning the language of equivalence (the **same**) or non-equivalence (**more, less**). Use common objects,

dolls' house furniture, small toys and pictures to develop your child's understanding of the language of comparisons. You can put out toy animals in a field and then ask your child questions like:

- 'Can you put **all** the cows in the field?'
- 'Can you put just a **few** pigs in the field?'
- 'Are there **more** pigs or **more** cows in the field?'
- 'Count out some pigs and some cows – can you make sure there are **fewer** pigs than cows?'
- 'Let's take some pigs out of the field – can you take the **same** number of cows out of the field?'

Practise Reciting Numbers in the Right Order

There are lots of opportunities for this, whether you are reciting number songs and rhymes, counting children at a party, counting candles on a birthday cake and so on. These activities enable your child to hear the counting names in order and to begin to recognise that the order of numbers is always the same.

Count out a Given Quantity

Ask your child to put four spoons on the table for tea, put six toy cows in the field, give you four of the coins he's holding, put two spoons of sugar in mummy's teacup.

Count Items in a Set

Lots of materials can be used for counting, including blocks, toy cars, shells and pebbles, coins, beads, objects within a picture. Give your child the opportunity to:

- Count objects that can be moved – that is, get him to move the objects to one side as he counts them.
- Count the same set of objects again, with the items in a

different order (they could be in a straight line, which is easiest, or even in a circle, which is harder).

- Count objects that can be touched but not moved, such as objects shown within a picture.
- Count objects that can be seen but not touched or moved, such as teddy bears in a toy shop window.
- Count sounds such as tapping on a table, musical sounds made by a drum or trumpet, words in a little sentence you say to him.
- Count physical movements like claps, hops and steps.

Make a Number Frieze

Notice that many of the activities that give children opportunities to learn how to count can be seen as part of everyday life – centred around cooking, laundry, going to the shops, planting seedlings. There are, however, other activities you may want to plan as actual number exercises; for instance, playing with the toy animals in the field, counting musical sounds and, importantly, putting up a **number frieze**. You might put this in your child's bedroom or on the fridge door.

The frieze will show the link between the numeral (in its written form) and its cardinal value, for example:

the number **3** and three 'smiley faces' ☺ ☺ ☺

You can buy number friezes in children's toy shops, or you and your child can make your own together, which might be more fun. You can draw the numbers (make them nice and big) with black or coloured pens – or even use glue and stick glitter to them. Your child can then trace the glitter number with his finger, which gives him a 'multi-sensory' experience of the number – seeing it, saying it and feeling it. This will help him more easily learn the number symbol so that he will soon be able to write it for himself. You can also use number books to help your child to connect numbers (as quantities) with the numerals they represent.

Number Concepts

When children become familiar with a number frieze or have spent time looking at number books, they begin to learn to recognise numerals: for example, when they see the number **3**, they say 'three'. Many children on starting school will be able to recognise and name numerals from 1 to 9, but don't be too concerned if your child has learned just a few of them before starting school – he will soon learn the rest of them by the end of the first term.

Children first develop an *ordinal* sense of number. This means that they use numbers as adjectives (one finger, two fingers, three fingers and so on as they count along). Later on they develop a *cardinal* sense of number, which means they use a number like a noun. As mentioned earlier, the cardinal number is the last number in the count which tells the child how many there are – for instance, 'Here is a set of six blocks.' When children develop a cardinal sense of number, they realise that the same cardinal number can be arrived at with various different number combinations; for instance, 1 + 6 or 2 + 5 both arrive at the same cardinal number 7.

It has been shown that counting on fingers is very important in children's understanding of both ordinal and cardinal numbers. They count on their fingers and come to see that the more they 'count up', the higher the cardinal number. They recognise, too, that two is one more than one, three is one more than two and so on. This realisation is critical to the child beginning to understand what addition and subtraction mean. At the next stage, children come to use 'counting on' from a given number (usually on their fingers) to add small numbers. Similarly, 'counting back' from a number is used to subtract.

You can encourage your child to learn about addition and subtraction of small numbers (say up to 10) by playing 'one more/one less' games, either using objects he can count like blocks, or through counting on his fingers. For example:

- 'Show me two fingers – put up one more, now there are ...?' (answer: 3)
- 'Show me four fingers – put one finger down – how many are there now?' (answer: 3)
- 'Put four biscuits on the plate – now put another biscuit on the plate – how many are there altogether?' (answer: 5)
- 'Put four biscuits on the plate – why don't you eat one biscuit? – how many are there now?' (answer: 3)
- 'Here are six blocks – let's take one away – how many are left?' (answer: 5)

Note that, in talking about numbers, you are introducing your child to the *language* of addition and subtraction. You are helping him realise that 'more', 'put your finger up', 'another' and 'altogether' are words or phrases that mean he has to move *up* the ordinal scale of numbers, that is, he has to add. Conversely, words and phrases like 'take away', 'eat', 'are left' and 'put down your finger' mean he has to move *down* the ordinal scale of numbers, that is, he has to subtract.

Once your child has got the idea of adding *one more* or *one less* of a number from one to ten, you can try getting him to add or subtract slightly bigger numbers. Make sure, though, that when objects or fingers are added together they do not exceed 10. Leave counting into the teens until after he has started school. Don't be tempted to touch on multiplication and division – these concepts are too difficult for pre-schoolers.

Patterns

Some of the earliest research on children's understanding of patterns was carried out by the great Swiss psychologist, Jean Piaget. He studied the number development of his own three children. He and his colleagues found that children begin to get the idea of *copying* (or, as we sometimes say, *matching*) objects from about the age of three years. For instance, at this age, most children can match colours; they can put the blue counters in the blue box, the red counters in the red box, the yellow counters in the yellow box and so on. By the time they are four, they can *copy the order of a sequence or pattern*, provided they keep their attention fixed on it. For instance, they can copy a set of shapes that you put out for them from their own set of shapes. You could also use beads, coloured pegboards or toy cars of different colours to make the sequence. Talk it through with your child. For instance, if you're using different coloured beads, you might say: 'Let's make a bead pattern with different colours – shall we put the red bead first, then the yellow bead and last of all the blue bead? Now can you copy it to make the same colour pattern?' An everyday situation that could be used to copy a pattern is in setting the table for dinner. You do the first place setting with knife, fork and spoon and ask your child to copy it to make a second place setting.

As soon as your child has got the idea of copying a sequence once, see if he can *repeat* it over and over so that he is continuing the pattern. You can do this easily with shapes, pegboards and with bead patterns. With the example of setting the table, see if he can set out a third and then a fourth place setting.

Children have the *experience of order* at a very young age in all sorts of play situations. They love lining up objects like toy cars, dolls or blocks in a row, even when they are only two. As they get older, they begin to order their toys to form patterns. They might string beads together in alternating colours (red-blue-red-blue), line up bricks in alternating sizes (big-little-big-little), or sequence shapes like circle-square-triangle, circle-square-triangle. Asking your child questions like 'what comes first?', 'what comes next?', 'tell me about the pattern you've made' draws his attention to the order of the objects and makes him aware that he has created a sequence.

Once your child is happily copying and repeating patterns you set for him, see if he can *create a pattern of his own* using some of the materials described above. This is important not just to demon-strate that he too can make a sequence, but it helps develop his creativity as well (*see Chapter 6 for more ideas about this*). After he's made his sequence, get him to tell you what it is about, so you can see he has understood that he is generating patterns that relate to size, colour or shape. Then see if he can repeat or continue his own pattern. You could see if he can create patterns in everyday situa-tions too, like making a pattern or sequence with differently filled sandwiches (egg, then cheese, then ham), or vegetables on his plate (two carrots, then one pea, then two chips).

Another way to help children understand patterns and sequences is to make *line drawings*. You can use paints, crayons, coloured pencils, glue and glitter for this. See if your child can copy, continue and even come up with his own line patterns such as:

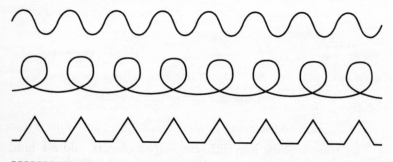

Shape and Space

One of the first and most important ways children come to understand shapes is through using language to describe the *properties* of each shape. They explore objects and shapes at home and at nursery school. They actively play with natural objects around them that differ in colour, size and shape. For instance, they describe the leaves on trees as 'the big, green leaf' or 'the small, brown leaf'. They talk about the path they walk to school as being 'straight' or 'curvy', 'thin' or 'wide'. The house they live in may be 'tall and thin', or 'short and wide', with 'big' or 'small' windows. Pre-school children come to describe, and to classify or sort, objects in terms of their:

- *Texture* – using descriptive words like **rough, smooth, hard, soft, fluffy, sharp.** There are many textured objects around your home that you can explore and label together with your child, like rough brick walls, fluffy rugs, smooth table tops, soft cushions, hard glass vases. You could ask your child to point to all the **hard** objects in your living room, then to all the **soft** objects, and so on.

- *Colour* – pre-schoolers should begin to use the proper labels to describe the colour of an object or to sort objects by colour groups. For example, putting all the **white** clothes together and separating them from the **dark** and **coloured** clothes for putting in the washing machine; sorting all the **red** blocks into one pile and all the **blue** blocks into another.

- *Shapes* – your child might sort kitchen objects into things that are **round** and **curvy** like jars, pans, bowls and plates, and things that are **straight** like knives and forks. Ask him if he can find objects in the living room that are square and objects that are round. Show him different-shaped objects, and ask him, 'What shape is this?'

- *Types of lines* – your child might describe lines he sees or has drawn as **straight** or **curvy**, **long** or **short**, **thick** or **thin**.
- *Size* – your child might describe objects as **big**, **small**, **fat**, **thin** and sort them into groups of big or small, fat or thin objects.

Children have lots of opportunities at playgroup and nursery to explore space and shape by *taking things apart* and *putting things together*. There are lots of putting-together play materials like rings on a post, nests of different-sized beakers, Lego, inset boards, block building kits and jigsaw puzzles. Children learn a lot about size, shape, orientation, fitting things together and constructing objects from working with these.

Make sure you start with simple puzzles before moving on to harder ones that involve putting more objects together. Inset boards are easier than jigsaw puzzles, and you should work on two- to four-piece jigsaws before moving on to ones that have six or seven pieces. Talk to your child to help him develop strategies for construction, saying things like 'Where will this piece fit?', 'Do you think you might need to turn that piece round to fit it in?', 'Which is the biggest block we should start with for our tower; now which is the next biggest?' Once you and your child have made a puzzle or object together, see if he can take it apart and then put it back together again independently. Some shapes can be put together to make different objects – for instance, blocks of different shapes can be put together to make a house, but in a different combination might be put together to make a car.

2-D and 3-D Shapes

Pre-schoolers should have experience of shapes in both two (flat) and three dimensions. Examples of 3-D shapes that can be used to construct models include cubes, cylinders, cones and pyramids. Examples of 2-D shapes that can be used to make patterns, or even drawn, include lines, circles, squares and triangles (it is unlikely that your child will move on to more complicated 2-D shapes like diamonds). You can do lots of activities with 2-D shapes, including:

- Sorting different-size shapes into groups of triangles, squares and circles:

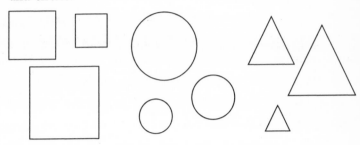

- Copy drawing the shapes you, the parent, draw:

Mummy's turn

Child's turn

- Learning the names of the shapes:

Square   **Circle**   **Triangle**

- Combining 2-D shapes to make patterns or objects like houses, faces, people and cars:

Measurement

Measurement is a very important life skill, one that we use every day, whether we're choosing the right size clothes to buy, measuring for new shelves in our homes or estimating how long a journey will take. Pre-schoolers also make measurement decisions – who has the biggest teddy, who got the smaller piece of cake (they can be very good at this one!), how tall they are in relation to their nursery classmates. There are many different aspects of measurement, though only some of these will be of relevance to your pre-school child. Children begin to use the *language of measurement* and to make comparisons of length, weight, area and volume even before they start school.

A lot of early learning about measurement is to do with learning the language of measurement, in particular using language of comparison to make decisions about which is the longest, which is the heaviest, which is most full and so on. Children need first to develop a vocabulary that describes **length, weight, capacity** and **volume**. Here are some relevant words to use with your pre-schooler when you play measurement games together:

- *Length* – talk about **long, tall, short, little**. Gather together objects (toys or just household materials) that differ in these 'size' properties and use these words to describe them.
- *Weight* – words used to describe weight are **heavy** and **light**. Also, use the verb **weigh** to describe what you are doing when you're deciding whether something is heavy or light; for instance, 'Shall we **weigh** this box on our kitchen scales and see how **heavy** it is?'
- *Capacity* – talk about containers that are filled with liquid, sand, coloured balls, etc. The words used to describe capacity are **full** and **empty**.

- *Volume* – describe the space occupied by objects with words such as **big, little, small, thick, wide, thin**.

In order for children to make sense of the language of measurement, they need to be encouraged to make comparisons and to develop the vocabulary of comparison. This includes words like **bigger, shorter, heavier, highest, thinner, less, more.** There are lots of everyday activities and play situations that involve making comparisons; you can use these to introduce your child to the language of comparison. Here are some suggestions:

- Use two ribbons of different lengths and ask, 'Which ribbon is **longer**?' Use line markings on a wall to decide 'Who is the **tallest** in the family; who is the **shortest**?' Build towers of blocks of different heights – 'Which is the **tallest** (or **highest**); which is the **shortest** (or **lowest**)?'
- Use the kitchen scales to **weigh** the ingredients to make a cake and to compare whether the flour needed is **heavier** or **lighter** than the butter; get your child to hold two objects of different weight and ask him to decide which is the **heavier**.
- Again using the kitchen example, fill cups or mugs with juice for snack time; ask your child to 'Fill the red mug so that it is **full**; put only a little juice in the blue mug – see, it is **nearly empty**. Which mug has **more** juice? Which mug has **less**?'
- Use different-size boxes to compare volumes; talk about **bigger, smaller,** which one will **fit into the other,** which is **too small** to fit, which is **too big** to fit.

One good way to help children understand measurement and to make comparisons is to get them to make *ordered arrangements*:

- Ask your child to order lines, toys or kitchen objects and so on from:
  - Shortest line through to longest line

- Heaviest block through to lightest block
- Most full cup through to least full cup
- Biggest box through to smallest box
- Smallest child through to tallest child

Start with just three objects so as not to confuse or over-whelm your child. Wait until he has really understood the concept before you move on to groups of four, five or more objects.

● See if your child can match the length of an object (say a cylindrical block like this one) by drawing a line of the same length under it.

Understanding the Concept of Time

Another aspect of measurement to consider relates to the child's *understanding of time* and the passage of time. Very young children operate in the 'here and now', and it is only when they get to school age that they begin to understand the concepts of past and future. Telling the time is a skill few children will develop before the age of eight years. However, children's awareness of the sequencing of regular events, and their ability to describe past events and to anticipate future ones, begins to grow during their pre-school years.

Children become aware of sequences of regular events when they experience *routines*. Your child will understand that he gets up, has breakfast, goes to nursery, comes home for lunch and so on, until the end of the day when he finally goes to bed. You can use these daily routines to introduce your child to the *language of time*, using words like **morning, afternoon, bedtime, before, after, then, now, next** and so on. Pre-schoolers relate time to particular events in the day like 'story-time' at nursery or 'bedtime' at home, not to clock times like 10 o'clock or 6 o'clock. However, it can be helpful at this stage to begin to connect specific events to clock times, for instance: 'It's 7 o'clock so it's bedtime'; 'You finish nursery to come home at 12.30 for lunch.' Also, children at this age can be introduced to timers to indicate when something is completed – for instance, the kitchen timer rings when the cake is done and ready to come out of the oven.

Once your child has begun to understand that his daily life operates in a regular time sequence, you and your child can begin to talk about *past events* – what he did **that morning** at nursery; where he went **last weekend**; what mummy bought at the shops **yesterday**. Sometimes, it can be helpful to make what has happened more concrete by using photographs (or video film) or drawing a picture (for instance, showing the birthday party he went to last week).

Finally, your child can begin to talk about or to anticipate *future events*, like his forthcoming birthday, a special outing or holiday or a festival (such as Christmas). Describing to your child what will happen at his birthday party – who will come, what food there will be, what games will be played – is helpful in introducing the vocabulary of future events. Use words like **tomorrow, soon, next week, next month.** Sometimes it helps to do a countdown to a special event; use a simple calendar with stickers and marks to indicate how many days there are to go before the event.

Understanding the Concept of Speed

One last measurement concept you can introduce your child to at the pre-school stage is that of understanding *rates of speed*. This involves talking to the child about how long an activity or event takes. The vocabulary relevant to speed includes words like **slowly, quickly, fast, start, stop.** Again, it is useful to make comparisons so that your child can more easily learn these descriptive words.

Ask your child to:

- Walk **slowly.**
- Now **speed up** and walk **quickly.**
- Now run so you move **faster.**
- Now **stop.**
- Now **start** (again) and run as **fast as you can.**

Once you have worked through these activities, try the checklist again and see how far your child has come. Is your child ready for school maths, or do you need to revise and practise some of the suggested games for a little longer?

Could My Child Be 'Dyscalculic'?

There has recently been a surge of interest in a particular group of children who may have specific difficulties in learning about numbers. These children are said to be 'dyscalculic'. This makes it very hard for them to deal with abstract maths once they start school. Clearly, problems with numbers and with maths concern many teachers.

A tremendous amount is known about the difficulties that dyslexic children experience, but in contrast we know very little about dyscalculia – how common it is, what the underlying learning problems are, whether it 'co-occurs' with other learning difficulties and so on. We are nonetheless becoming aware that problems with maths may be quite common. A recent study of over 11,000 children in Cuba found that nearly 7 per cent of them recorded very low scores on a dyscalculia screening test. It's not clear what proportion of this 7 per cent had *specific* number problems (they had difficulty with numbers but were fine at everything else), or whether they had number problems *in addition to* other learning and educational problems. For instance, quite a lot of children with dyslexia have weaknesses in maths as well as in reading and/or writing. Certainly, this high figure of 7 per cent means that many children struggle with numbers, whether this is in isolation or alongside other learning difficulties.

There are a number of reasons why a child might find maths difficult. Some children have problems with spatial concepts. As a result, they misalign numbers in columns when they are doing pencil and paper maths; and they find it hard as they go through school to deal with visual concepts in maths like geometry, fractions, place values (hundreds, tens and units) and deciding where to put decimal points. Other children have problems with 'verbal working memory'. This means that they find it hard to 'hold on to' numbers in their verbal memory store while they are carrying out a mental operation, so dyscalculic children easily 'forget' numbers when they are doing mental arithmetic. This may well be the particular difficulty for those dyslexic children who have number, as well as reading, problems.

There is some evidence that certain number skills evident in pre-schoolers may allow us to predict how easily they will learn maths when they start school:

- Counting objects accurately – can your child count up to 10 objects in a row without making a mistake?
- The ability to compare two numbers and say which is the bigger and which is the smaller – can your child do this accurately and (perhaps even more importantly) *quickly*? Go back

to the checklist on page 268 and try the number comparison items with your child, using both *spoken* and *written* numbers.

● The ability to *subitise* – can your child look at between two and four objects (usually dots) on a page and say how many there are without actually counting them?

Try your child on a subitising task. Show him three big dots on a page (*see below*) and ask how many there are. If he says 'three' right away, you know he's subitising. If he pauses for a second or so, he's a slow subitiser. If he takes several seconds and appears to be counting the dots, he's a non-subitiser.

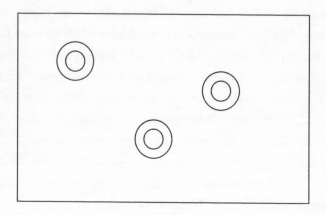

Stick with three dots if your child is three or four years old. Try this with four dots too, if he's a five-year-old. Children of five should be able to subitise four dots readily.

If your child finds it hard to count accurately and to compare numbers – and has trouble subitising by the age of five – he may be 'at risk' for later maths problems. However, don't be alarmed. Again, as with children who are at risk of becoming poor readers, there are two things you should do. First, keep on practising the number activities described in this chapter. Second, once your child has started school, alert his teacher to your concerns and, together, keep an eye on his progress over his first year at school. If he does need extra help, you and his teacher will have detected the problem at such an early stage that he shouldn't have too much 'lost ground' to make up – and, very importantly, he won't have lost confidence in his mathematical ability.

And Finally ...

Of all the educational skills, maths is perhaps the one that lends itself best to learning through everyday activities and routines, and through informal play. You can use all manner of day-to-day events and home-based materials to help foster your child's development of number concepts. Just use whatever you do every day and turn it into a 'number experience' – whether you're having a meal, out shopping, cooking or planting in the garden. All you have to do is be aware that so many of our seemingly mundane activities provide excellent opportunities for your child to develop a concept of number and the vocabulary of maths. And that, combined with encouraging exploratory play, is really all that's needed to prepare him for the abstract maths he'll do once he starts school. Maybe even more importantly, you will have helped your child realise that maths isn't something you do just at school. He will have seen for himself the fascinating mathematical world we live in that goes way beyond the walls of the classroom.

11
Writing

While you're teaching your child about letters, sounds and reading, it will feel entirely natural for you to work on writing letters too. In the UK, most children will start their Reception year being able to write their first name and a few letters of the alphabet. During the Reception year, they will be expected to learn how to write all the letters of the alphabet in both lower and upper case. In this chapter, some of the questions that parents often ask will be addressed, such as:

- How should my child hold the pencil?
- Do I introduce upper or lower case letters first?
- Should she learn to write letters in a particular order?
- Does my child learn to print first (write letters singly) and then use cursive (joined-up) writing later – or go straight to cursive?
- What do I do if my child hasn't decided which hand to use for writing?
- What do I do if my child is a left-hander?
- My child is very clumsy – will she find learning to write difficult, and could she be dyspraxic?

Right- and Left-handedness

We all know that being right-handed is much more common than being left-handed. In general, 90 per cent of people use their right hand for writing. Left-handedness, while clearly less common, is nonetheless an issue for many people, not just young children. Our writing system tends to favour right-handers; left-handers sometimes look awkward when they write; and they can end up smudging or obscuring their writing as they work from left to right.

Handedness is most probably inherited. A widely recognised theory of handedness, developed by neuropsychologist Marian Annett, proposes that there is a special gene for right-handedness but not left-handedness. Therefore, if a child inherits a right-handed gene, then she will be right-handed. However, if neither parent passes on a right-handed gene, then which hand the child eventually uses for writing is left to chance. If there are a lot of left-handers in your family, then there is an increased likelihood that your child will be a left hander.

Hand preference develops quite early on. Ten per cent of one-year-olds show a definite preference for one hand over the other. This strengthens during early childhood. By the age of five, 90 per cent of children will clearly prefer to use either the right or left hand for most hand actions. However, it is not unusual for a child who writes with her right hand to show a preference for unscrewing a jar with her left hand or kicking a ball with her left foot. This is known as 'crossed laterality'. There is no evidence that crossed laterality leads to learning difficulties. Some children appear to be 'ambidextrous' – they may seem to be equally good at using either hand. This isn't anything to worry about – let your child decide which hand to use.

If, however, your child shows no preference for drawing or writing with one hand or the other by around four-and-a-half, this may be a warning sign of problems to come. There is some evidence that children who are late to establish their preferred hand for writing are more likely to have reading, writing and spelling problems after they start school. Do give your child lots of opportunities for drawing and painting, but let her decide in which hand she holds the paintbrush, crayon or pencil. Also, alert your child's teacher to your concerns about her failure to establish clear handedness so that you can work together and watch over her progress in reading and writing.

Apart from determining which hand is used for writing and fine motor actions (like using scissors and cutlery, unscrewing jars and so on), hand preference is related to which side of the brain is dominant for language. For most right-handers, language abilities are centred in the left side of the brain. However, in left-handers there is much more 'sharing of language' between the left and right sides. It is largely for this reason that parents and teachers are discouraged from attempting to influence children's hand preference. While it is true that left-handers can find writing rather more difficult than do right-handers, that doesn't mean the parents of a left-hander should try to change their child to being a right-hander. Let your child work out for herself which hand she prefers to use, and then support her in her choice. There is very little evidence that left-handers are more likely to have learning problems than right-handers, though they might find learning to write letters a little harder than their right-handed friends. In fact, there can even be some advantages to being left-handed; there is some evidence that left-handers are more likely to be mathematically talented, and they often show an advantage in sport (particularly ball games like tennis).

Before your child starts to learn how to write letters, she should have established which hand to use for writing. She should also be able to hold the pencil correctly, and be able to draw, to paint and to copy some shapes. Work through the following checklist to see whether your child is ready to learn to write some letters.

Letter Writing Checklist

	Yes	No
Has your child decided which hand to use for writing?	☐	☐
Does your child hold the pencil correctly most of the time? (*see below*)	☐	☐
Does your child enjoy painting pictures with colours and a paintbrush?	☐	☐
Can your child colour in large shapes with different-coloured crayons and (mostly) stay within the lines?	☐	☐
Does your child draw pictures of people, houses, animals, etc., that are recognisable?	☐	☐
Can your child use stencils for making shapes and pictures (with maybe a little help from you to hold the stencil)?	☐	☐
Can your child copy-draw the following shapes (*see below*)?	☐	☐

Shapes   **Child's Turn**

If you answered 'yes' to the above questions, your child is ready to start to learn to write.

If you have answered 'no' to quite a few of the questions, it would be a good idea to hold off teaching your child how to write letters for the moment while you concentrate on some of the basic skills covered in the checklist.

Working on Prewriting Skills

Holding the Pencil Correctly

During the early pre-school years, children hold the pencil in what is usually called a *tripod* grip – they use more than one finger on top of the pencil in what seems a rather 'fisted' grip. Between the ages of three and five years, children move on to using a correct pencil grip that involves just one finger on the top of the pencil – so the pencil is held between the thumb and the index finger. A correct pencil grip also involves the child not holding the pencil too close to the tip; if she does, it will make it hard for her to control the pencil and she will not be able to see easily what she is writing. Your child should hold the pencil on the coloured part, not too low down on the wood or pointed part. The diagram below shows what the correct grip should be for both right- and left-handers.

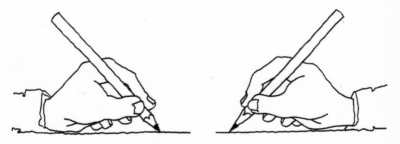

Correct pencil grip

This change from the tripod to the correct grip should happen quite naturally – indeed, it does for most children. However, if your child is not gripping the pencil correctly by around the age of five, it would be a good idea to work on this. It is very hard to change an incorrect pencil grip after the age of six or seven years, so five is a good age to get it right. Probably the easiest way to encourage your child to hold the pencil correctly is to use one of the triangular-shaped rubber pencil grips you can buy through educational suppliers or at educational bookshops. The only way the child can hold the pencil using the triangular gripper is in the correct position. Once you've decided on using the gripper, you need to make sure it's used *all the time*, for all activities that require use of a pencil or pen, not just writing letters but drawing too. It's a good idea to buy a packet of grippers as they so easily get lost or left at playgroup/nursery school!

Some Prewriting Activities and Games

These prewriting activities will help your child develop the pencil control and 'shape awareness' that will be needed when she begins to write letters:

- *Painting with a brush and easel* helps to develop gross motor (large movement) skills that are important for developing the 'postural stability' needed for writing.
- *Colouring in* helps the child practise her pencil grip and the fine up-and-down and side-by-side motor movements needed for printing and cursive (joined-up) writing.
- *Tracing* over pre-drawn lines or dotted lines of different kinds (horizontal, vertical, zigzag, curved, circular) helps your child practise the kind of fine hand movements and shapes she will need to use when writing letters.
- *Fine motor games* – like pencil and paper 'dot-to-dot' picture

puzzles, drawing your way out of mazes, pegboard pattern games, stringing beads, lacing and sewing cards – all help to develop fine motor skills that are important for good pencil control.

- *Other activities that build up the child's motor skills and spatial awareness* include doing jigsaw puzzles, constructing with Lego, stacking blocks and making block patterns, matching shapes and pictures, making objects and shapes with play dough, cutting out shapes with scissors and sticking them on paper to make patterns and pictures – and you can probably think of many others yourself or get some further ideas from your child's nursery or playgroup.

- *Drawing pictures* of favourite objects and scenes will not only help your child develop motor skills and pencil control, it will also enable her to relate pencil and paper activities to creative ideas. This link is important for when your child comes to write little stories at school. Once she's happy doing a single picture to describe what she's seen or done, see if she can draw a series of pictures that tell a little story, working from left to right.

- *Drawing repeated patterns* is really just one step short of writing letters in sequence – see if your child can copy-draw and then 'keep going' the following sequences:

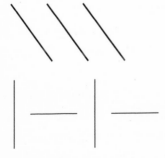

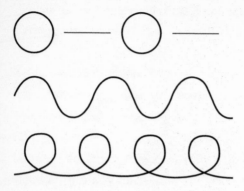

Sequencing patterns like these can be done with materials as well as with pencil and paper – get your child to make the pattern with her index finger in sand, flour or glitter.

Beginning to Write Letters

Once your child is comfortable with the prewriting activities described above, she should be ready to learn how to write some letters. However, before you start teaching your child to write letters, there are three important points you need to get right.

1 *Get the posture right* – it's best for your child to write while seated at a proper table, not while lying on the floor or at a coffee table. Use a straight-backed chair, make sure her feet are comfortably on the ground and that the table is a suitable height.

2 *Get the paper in the right position* – the position of the paper in relation to the pencil is important, particularly for left-handers. If your child is left-handed, the paper should be angled to the left so your child can easily see what she's writing. Also, this placing of the paper means she can write with her hand and fingers pointing upwards, not in a curved 'hook' position. This will make her less likely to smudge her work.

Paper placed in the correct position for left-handers

3 *Get the language right* – practise using words that describe letters and their position on the page. Does your child know what the letter *before*, the letter *after* and the letter *next to* mean? Show her a sequence of letters (or even shapes if you like) and ask her which comes *before*, which comes *after* and which letters are *next to* a given letter.

For example, in the letter sequence:

f t a g m

ask your child, 'Which letter is *before* /a/?' (she should respond /t/); 'Which letter is *after* /a/?' (she should respond /g/); 'Which letters are *next to* /a/?' (she should respond /t/ and /g/).

'Big' or 'Little' Letters?

In general, children tend to learn lower case letters before upper case. In the year or two before your child starts school, concentrate on lower case – maybe leave the upper case letters for her to learn after she's started school. Don't feel under pressure to teach *all* 26 letters during the pre-school years. It's a good idea, though, for children to learn how to write their first name and maybe a few more letters besides (especially if they have a three- or four-letter name like Ben or Lucy). Some children are keen to learn how to write favourite words like 'mum', 'dad', 'dog', 'cat', their best friend's or pet's name, or the word for their favourite food. This makes the idea of writing relevant to your child's life and experiences. There is no harm in doing this, but it's best to get to grips with writing her name first, together with some key letters. You can then bring in additional letters and words little by little. The first letters to teach your child are those that appear in her name. To begin, select a letter from her name that's the simplest to write – letters with straight lines are the easiest, such as 'l, t, k, v' and so on.

Some schools are now beginning to teach cursive (joined-up) writing from the very beginning, but this is unusual. Most schools begin by teaching printing in Reception and in Year One, and then introduce cursive the following year. It's therefore safest for you to start with printing only.

Activities for the Early Stages of Writing Letters

- Start with *matching games*. Make up two sets of the letters in your child's name on individual flashcards, with one letter per card. Put the letters in her name on the table in front of her (not necessarily in the right order). Now give her the second set of cards and see if she can match the letters. Matching games can also be done with sets of plastic and wooden letters.

- Help your child understand how the letters you're working on relate to lines on a page by first drawing a thick line on a blank sheet of paper. Now see if your child can place wooden or plastic alphabet letters in relation to the line so they are correctly positioned. Below is how they should be positioned for all the letters of the alphabet:

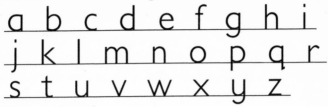

- *Write the letters in the air* using big arm movements, while saying the sound (or name) of the letter as you're writing it. Make sure you start the letter in the right place (*see below*). Also ensure you are saying the sound correctly. How to pronounce sounds is covered in Chapter 9, so go back over this if you need to. You may need to guide your child's hand to begin with until she gets the idea of copying you, and before she can do it independently.

- *Write large letters with a thick marker pen* on pieces of coloured cardboard, squeeze glue over the outline of the letters, and then sprinkle on salt, glitter or sand and let it dry. Mark the starting position of the letter with a coloured dot.

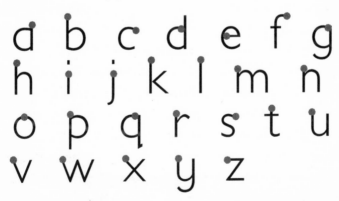

- Starting at the dot, get your child to *trace over the letter* with her index finger while saying its name or sound out loud. Again, you may need to guide her hand to begin with, before she can manage the tracing independently. This is called *multi-sensory learning* because your child is using three senses to learn the letter – the visual sense by looking at the letter; the auditory sense through hearing it as she says its name or sound; and the kinaesthetic ('feeling' and movement) senses through tracing the textured letter with her finger. This multi-sensory learning activity can also be done using finger paint, writing letters in a sandbox or gluing dried pasta or sequins on letters – be imaginative. Having your child 'write' letters on her hand with her finger is another example of multi-sensory learning; she can watch and feel the movement pattern of each letter as she traces it.

- Get some *stencils* of letters (and maybe numbers too) and have your child draw within the boundaries.

Writing Letters Using Lined Paper

Beginning with the letters in your child's first name, ask her to **copy** the letters on the lined paper. Some children can copy straight from the presented letters; others need to start by copying letters shown on the line with dots that indicate the starting position for writing. Encourage her to say the sound (or name) of the letter she is writing out loud so she has the *multi-sensory learning experience* discussed earlier.

Once your child is confident about copying the letters in her name, see if she can do it to **dictation**: ask her to write her name from memory without having the letters in front of her to copy.

Once your child is able to write her name correctly, you can introduce some other letters and maybe the occasional favourite word. Be led by your child in terms of word writing – if she's keen to write some words herself, go with it. If she'd rather stick to just letters – that's fine too! There's plenty of time for her to write words after she starts school.

Is There a Proper Order for Teaching Letters?

After you've worked on your child's name, there is no strictly correct or incorrect order for teaching letters. However, it does seem to be easier for children to learn letters if they are taught in 'families', where the movement pattern is similar for each letter.

In *Handwriting – A Teacher's Guide* (2001), Jane Taylor divides letters into the following groups:

Straight Line Letters	i f t l
Oval Letters	c a d g e s
Humpy Letters	r n m p h b
Cup-shaped Letters	u y j
Zigzag Letters	k v w x z

Exception Letters

There are two letters that are usually taught separately – O (because, unlike any other letter, it starts the curve in the '12 o'clock' position), and q (because it is always followed by 'u').

The easiest letters to write are those with straight lines – so begin with these. Only introduce two to three new letters at a time so as not to overload your child. Remember to begin by having your child copy the new letters, using a dot to show the starting point and a line beneath if you need to. Once she's confident in doing this, get her to write the letters she's learned from memory (with you telling her which letter to write).

If by the time your child starts school she has learned how to:

● Hold a pencil correctly

- Write her first name from memory
- Write around half the letters of the alphabet from memory
- Write a few commonplace and favourite words
- Produce most of the letters legibly and fairly evenly

she will be very well prepared for the more formal writing demands of school. But what if your child is encountering some problems?

My child is clumsy and finds drawing and writing difficult
Some children take to drawing and writing very easily and naturally. Others seem to find it much more difficult.

Have you noticed that your child:	Yes	No
seems to be quite clumsy and unco-ordinated?	☐	☐
is late in deciding which hand to use for writing (over four years and six months)?	☐	☐
is finding it hard to develop the correct pencil grip?	☐	☐
produces drawings that are little more than scribble even though she is four?	☐	☐
is finding it hard to copy letters?	☐	☐
is reluctant to pick up a pencil because it is 'too hard'?	☐	☐

If you have answered 'yes' to most of these questions, you might ask yourself, 'Could my child be *dyspraxic*?' Dyspraxia has already been discussed in Chapters 6 and 9. Unfortunately, we know far less about dyspraxia than about dyslexia. For instance, we don't know how common it is; we are unsure about the causes; and there is a lot of controversy about how we should define, assess and manage dyspraxia. Sometimes dyspraxia is used to describe a child who is poorly co-ordinated and has great difficulty with any 'non-verbal' activity; so the child may not only have poor motor control, but also perceptual, spatial and other visually based learning difficulties. She may, for instance, be poor at discriminating or 'picking out' fine visual details or have a lot of problems with constructional games like Lego, jigsaws and pencil-and-paper mazes.

However, some professionals strongly believe that the term 'dyspraxia' should be reserved to describe a particular group of children who have a very specific difficulty of 'motor planning and sequencing' as part of their co-ordination difficulties. The dyspraxic child defined in this way will typically have problems in planning and drawing her way through a pencil-and-paper maze. She may find it hard to put together, or even copy, a little sequence of two to three movements, like 'Walk towards me, point to your nose and then do a "twirl".' She may also find it hard to jump with both feet together over a low 'high jump'. Sometimes dyspraxia can affect the child's speech: 'developmental verbal dyspraxia' is evident as unclear, and even unintelligible, speech. Dyspraxia is also known as developmental co-ordination disorder (DCD) or non-verbal learning difficulty.

What should I do if I think my child might have a dyspraxic problem?

First, keep up the exercises described in this chapter. Do drawing, painting, colouring in, tracing and stencilling, jigsaw puzzles, mazes, Lego, matching games and so on. These can help your child become more visually and spatially aware, and generally improve her fine motor control. As with addressing any type of learning difficulty, start off with simple exercises and games. Make sure your child is happy and confident in working with these before you move on to harder exercises. Don't start teaching letters until you've worked through the suggested prewriting exercises and you're sure your child is comfortable with these. Also, make the exercises fun – mix up different games and materials, use glitter, colour and lots of pictures. And take it slowly and steadily. Keep the exercise sessions short – make sure that the time you're working together is well within your child's attention span (*see Chapter 7*).

If you're still worried about your child's co-ordination, drawing or early writing skills as her first day at school gets closer, let her teacher know. Together you can keep a close eye on how these skills develop during the first term. It may be that your child is a little slower at non-verbal skills (including drawing and writing) than other skills like talking or reading – your child may 'take off' after a slow start, so be patient and give her time to make her own way. If she is still having problems after her first term, and is beginning to show signs of being reluctant to put pencil to paper, it may be time to involve the school's special needs teacher. Sometimes, if children seem to have particularly marked or persisting co-ordination problems, they may need to be assessed by a physiotherapist or occupational therapist. He or she can then advise on whether or not your child has a very real difficulty that justifies describing her as dyspraxic and also suggest specific exercises to help her.

And Finally ...

Remember that learning to write begins with tracing, drawing, painting and other 'arty' activities. There are lots of fun things you and your child can do together in the pre-school years to prepare her for learning to write letters. Many pre-school children love playing the little artist, so use this as a natural lead-in to teaching her the skills she will eventually use for writing. And, of course, bear in mind the first word you will teach her to write is her name – so now she can autograph her own artwork.

Afterword

Soon the day will come when your child is actually off to school for the first time, or perhaps that time has come already. As you've worked through this book you've been getting your child ready for that first day at school and, in many ways, ready for life. You and your child should now feel more confident, relaxed and eager about starting school.

It may be that, despite all the work you've put in with your child, there are still a few small gaps. This is probably nothing to worry about; you will know what these gaps are and, together with your child's teacher, you can work on them during the first year at school. Of course, the earlier any difficulties are recognised the better. You can then start to deal with the problems more effectively.

It is crucially important to take a sensible and balanced approach to your child's progress. Keep your long-term goals in mind – your child's happiness and ability to cope socially and emotionally are more important than overdoing the intensity of activities; your child's readiness to read when starting school is more important than teaching him to 'remember' whole books in the belief that he can read.

This book is not about demanding that you find huge amounts of time you haven't got in order to be the perfect parent. Nor is it about urging you to spend large sums of money on equipment or activities. What we are suggesting is that you use the time you spend with your child in ways that will develop his – and your – skills. For example, ordinary conversation over the breakfast table provides a great opportunity for language development, for working on self-care and for improving social skills (turn-taking and learning to wait and share). A shopping trip can be brilliant for developing pre-literacy skills (learning new vocabulary, looking at printed signs in shop windows and on the streets), learning about numbers (counting money or shopping items) and regulating behaviour (keeping 'chocolate snatching' and temper tantrums at bay). Making tea dates for your child helps with friendships and play – you can even bring in opportunities for a little drawing and writing too. A story at bedtime gives the ideal opportunity to promote language development and concentration. It is also a special time for you and your child to bond and be emotionally close.

We hope this book helps you set good, useful, productive patterns (and routines) for your child and for all who care for him. To want a happy, fulfilled life for your child is not a controversial aim. We recognise that the kind of happiness either desired or achieved will vary enormously depending on the individual and his circumstances. However, we are convinced that patterns are set early on. The basic ways of thinking, learning, behaving and feeling that are formed during the pre-school years, and reinforced by the first experience of school, tend to last a lifetime.

You can influence the formation of these patterns. This is not to say your child is wholly the product of parental input. Life is much too complex, diverse and unpredictable to make any such claim. Besides, the child's freedom to develop his own potential is a vital ingredient of his well-being. The unprepared child, however, may have a lot of ground to make up when he gets to school. There is a danger that his self-esteem and self-confidence can become battered if he feels all at sea or overwhelmed by what he has to do. The prepared child, on the other hand, will be able to fit well into the wider world when he leaves the security of his own family environment.

Remember, 'good enough' is good enough. The fact that you have been reading this book means you are clearly an involved and active parent. You know that your child will be as ready for school as he possibly can be. You have given him a flying start!

Further Reading

Chapter 2

Toddler Troubles – Coping With Your Under-5s, by Jo Douglas, published by John Wiley and Sons, 2003. This useful book, written by a psychologist, covers a broad range of pre-school children's problems and issues. There are relevant chapters on eating, toileting and sleeping. Jo Douglas also co-authored a book with Naomi Richman entitled *My Child Won't Sleep,* published by Penguin Books, 1984.

Chapter 3

New Toddler Taming – a Parents' Guide to the First Four Years, by Dr Christopher Green, published by Vermilion, 2001. Written by a paediatrician, this popular book offers lots of useful information and guidance to parents about behaviour problems and their management.

The Incredible Years – a Trouble-Shooting Guide for Parents of Children Aged 3–8, by Carolyn Webster-Stratton PhD, published in America by Umbrella Press, 2004. Written by a psychologist and therapist, this excellent book deals with behaviour problems of a slightly wider age group, from the pre-school to the junior years.

Chapter 4

Children's Friendships – the Beginnings of Intimacy, by Judy Dunn, published by Blackwell Publishing, 2004. This book draws together lots of fascinating research about children's friendships from the earliest years onwards. Recommended for both professionals and parents, it is a great read for those who might want to understand in more depth the nature and importance of peer relationships.

How to Promote Children's Social and Emotional Competence, by Carolyn Webster-Stratton, published by Paul Chapman Publishing Ltd (Sage), 2004. Written for teachers to help school children from 4–8, it gives advice for involving parents too.

Asperger's Syndrome – a guide for parents and professionals, by Tony Attwood, published by Jessica Kingsley Publishers, 2001. Offers very helpful and comprehensive advice.

Fighting, Teasing and Bullying – Simple and effective ways to help your child, by Dr John Pearce, published by Thorsons, 1989. The title explains all about this clearly written book.

Chapter 5

Emotional Development in Young Children: The Guilford Series on Social and Emotional Development, by Susanne A. Denham, published by The Guilford Press: New York and London, 1998. Although not aimed primarily at parents, this clearly written book provides a further understanding of the issues, and lots of everyday examples.

From One Child To Two – What to expect, how to cope, and how to enjoy your growing family, by Judy Dunn, published by Ballantine Books (Fawcett), 2002. A lovely, readable book, full of good suggestions to help parents prepare themselves and their first-born for the arrival of a second child. Sibling rivalry and conflict as the children get older are also discussed.

Teaching Children with Autism to Mind-Read – a Practical Guide, by Patricia Howlin, Simon Baron-Cohen and Julie Hadwin, published by John Wiley and Sons, 1999. Also useful in a wider context for understanding about emotions.

Chapter 6

Planning Play and the Early Years, by Penny Tassoni and Karen Hucker, published by Heinemann Child Care, 2000.

Understanding Children's Play, by Jennie Lindon, published by Nelson Thornes, 2001.

These two books are primarily for students and practitioners such as teachers or carers setting up nursery facilities, but also contain lots of information of interest and use to parents.

Chapter 7

Understanding Your Hyperactive Child, by Professor Eric Taylor, published by Vermilion, London, 1985/1997.

Taking Charge of ADHD, by Russell A. Barkley, published by The Guilford Press, New York, 1995.

These are excellent parent-friendly books written by two of the world's leading authorities on ADHD, Professor Taylor from the UK and Professor Barkley from the USA.

Chapter 8

Babytalk, by Dr Sally Ward, published by Arrow Books, 1988. This very readable book for parents whose children have speech and language difficulties covers the pre-school period up to and including age four.

Chapter 9

Early Reading Development and Dyslexia, by Valerie Muter, published by Whurr, 2003. This book was written for professionals, but also discusses management of the dyslexic child in the four- to seven-year age group, which can be a useful guide for parents.

Chapter 10

Mathematics in Nursery Education, by Ann Montague-Smith, published by David Fulton Publishers, 2002 (www.fulton publishers.co.uk). This book is really designed with nursery school teachers in mind, but it also describes lots of number activities you could easily carry out at home.

Chapter 11

Handwriting – A Teacher's Guide, by Jane Taylor, published by D. Fulton Publishers, 2002. An excellent reference book for the systematic teaching of handwriting skills. As the title suggests, this book is mainly directed towards advising teachers, but if you and your child's reception class teacher are worried about your child's handwriting development, it can be a good source of guidance for both you and the teacher.

Organisations and Resources

Attention Difficulties

ADDISS (Attention Deficit Disorder Information and Support Service)
PO Box 340, Edgware, Middlesex HA8 9HL
Tel: 020 8906 9068
Email: info@addiss.co.uk
Website: www.addiss.co.uk

ADHD UK Alliance
c/o Contact a Family, 209–211 City Road,
London EC1V 1JN
Tel: 0808 808 3555 (freephone helpline)
Tel: 020 7608 8760
Email: info@adhdalliance.org.uk
Website: www.adhdalliance.org.uk
The Alliance is a membership organisation for parents, groups and professionals. It aims to raise awareness of ADHD.

Autism

The National Autistic Society,
393 City Road, London EC1V 1NG
Website: www.nas.org.uk

Offers practical help and advice for people with autistic spectrum disorders and their families, carers, partners and the professionals who look after them.

Bullying

Kidscape
2 Grosvenor Gardens, London SW1W 0DH
Tel: 020 7730 3300
Helpline: 08451 205 204

The helpline is for the use of parents, guardians or concerned relatives and friends of bullied children.

Dyscalculia

There are not as yet any specific parent or teacher organisations that give advice and support to dyscalculic children and their families. However, the **British Dyslexia Association** and **The Dyslexia Institute** provide advice to parents and offer special teaching programmes for children with maths difficulties.

Dyslexia

The British Dyslexia Association (BDA)
Helpline: 0118 966 8271
Website: www.bda-dyslexia.org.uk

A charity that aims to increase public awareness of dyslexia. There are local associations throughout the UK that provide advice to parents on how and where to obtain help for their dyslexic child.

The Dyslexia Institute

Tel: 01784 222 300

Website: www.dyslexia-inst.org.uk

A professional organisation with 27 centres throughout the UK. They offer assessments of, and teaching for, dyslexic children as well as teacher training.

Dyspraxia

The Dyspraxia Foundation

8 West Alley, Hitchin, Herts SG5 1EG

Contact the foundation for information about how children with this difficulty can be helped.

Resource Materials

The Learning Development Aids (LDA) catalogue

Tel: 0845 120 4776

Website: www.LDAlearning.com

Has many helpful books, computer software packages and other learning materials, including cards portraying emotions.

Speech Impairment

AFASIC (Association For All Speech Impaired Children)

Helpline: 0845 355 5577

(open Monday to Friday from 10.30am to 2.30pm)

Website: www.afasic.org.uk

A support and advisory charity for families and professionals caring for children with diagnosed speech and language impairment.

References

Annett, M. (1976) 'Handedness and the cerebral representation of speech', *Annals of Human Biology*, 3, 317–328

Baumrind, D. (1971) 'Current patterns of parental authority', *Developmental Psychology Monograph*, 4 (1, Pt. 2)

Berk, Laura E. (2003) *Child Development* (6th edition), Boston: Allyn and Bacon

Bowlby, J. (1969) *Attachment and Loss*, Vol. 1 Attachment, New York: Basic Books

Byrne, B. (1998) *The Foundation of Literacy: The Child's Acquisition of the Alphabetic Principle*, Hove, UK: Psychology Press

Chess, S., Thomas, A. and Birch, H.G. (1968) *Temperament and behaviour disorders in children*, New York University Press

Hay, D., Payne, A. and Chadwick, A. (2004) 'Peer relations in childhood', *Journal of Child Psychology and Psychiatry*, 45: 1 pp. 84–108

Piaget, J. and Inhelder, B. (1967) *The Child's Conception of Space*, London: Routledge & Kegan Paul

Singer, D. and Singer, J. in Zigler, E.F., Singer, D.G., Bishop-Josef, S.J. (2004) *Children's Play: The Roots of Reading*, Washington, DC: Zero to Three Press

Tizard, B. and Hughes, M. (2003) *Young Children Learning*, London: Blackwell

Index